Eight-Step Process to Successful ISO 9000 Implementation

EIGHT-STEP PROCESS TO SUCCESSFUL ISO 9000 IMPLEMENTATION

A Quality Management System Approach

Lawrence A. Wilson

ASQC Quality Press
Milwaukee, Wisconsin

Eight-Step Process to Successful ISO 9000 Implementation:
A Quality Management System Approach
Lawrence A. Wilson

Library of Congress Cataloging-in-Publication Data

Wilson, Lawrence A., 1932–
    Eight-step process to successful ISO 9000 implementation: a
quality management system approach / Lawrence A. Wilson
        p.   cm.
    Includes bibliographical references and index.
    ISBN 0-87389-327-1
    1. ISO 9000 Series Standards.   I. Title.
TS156.6.W545   1996
658.5'62—dc20   95-36252
                                                                 CIP

©1996 by ASQC

10 9 8 7 6 5 4 3 2 1

ISBN 0-87389-327-1

Acquisitions Editor: Susan Westergard
Project Editor: Jeanne W. Bohn

ASQC Mission: To facilitate continuous improvement and increase customer satisfaction by identifying, communicating, and promoting the use of quality principles, concepts, and technologies; and thereby be recognized throughout the world as the leading authority on, and champion for, quality.

Attention: Schools and Corporations
ASQC Quality Press books, audio, video, and software are available at quantity discounts with bulk purchases for business, education, or instructional use. For information, please contact ASQC Quality Press at 800-248-1946, or write to ASQC Quality Press, P.O. Box 3005, Milwaukee, WI 53201-3005.

For a free copy of the ASQC Quality Press Publications Catalog, including ASQC membership information, call 800-248-1946.

Printed in the United States of America

 Printed on acid-free recycled paper

 ASQC
Quality Press
611 East Wisconsin Avenue
Milwaukee, Wisconsin 53202

Contents

Step 3: Determining Shortfalls   107

Step 4: Developing the Implementation Plan   139

Step 5: The Documentation Process   171

Step 6: Other Implementation Activities   209

Preface

My background has been concentrated in the aerospace manufacturing field for over 40 years, most recently as the director of product assurance and safety at Lockheed Aeronautical Systems. In 1989, however, I used my 57th birthday as my excuse to retire from Lockheed and pursue my interest in being a successful quality management consultant. In addition to the experience of managing a large organization (1800) while at Lockheed, I was fortunate in being a chair or an officer in the quality and reliability committees of several major associations. The key associations were the National Security Industrial Association, the Aerospace Industries Association, and the Aviation/Space and Defense Division of ASQC.

It was my previous involvement in the U.S. voluntary standards movement, however, that eventually became the basis for most of my consulting activity. Almost from the beginning of my practice in 1989, my participation as a U.S. delegate and convener (writing group chairman) on the ISO Technical Committee 176 on Quality Management and Quality Assurance, provided the focus for my quality management consulting practice. ISO TC 176 is the technical committee that is the source of the internationally accepted ISO 9000 family of quality system standards.

While assisting companies of all sizes in their pursuit of ISO 9000 implementation, I first noted there was a pattern for success. Using these data as a basis, I instituted an eight-step process for ISO 9000 implementation, which has been universally successful for my clients. This eight-step process is detailed in this book. Acceptance of the concept and commitment to this process as your company's method of ISO 9000 implementation will systematically and cost-effectively guide you through all aspects of ISO 9000 implementation, including the registration process.

The eight-step process, as presented here, is written from the viewpoint of company management and the ISO management representative. The contents of the book questions, addresses, and guides every action that must be considered by the candidate company during ISO 9000 implementation. To augment its guidance approach, background and rationale for each activity are provided. The company or organization that has already started its ISO 9000 implementation process will still benefit from the book's modular approach. It permits the company to intercept the process at the appropriate step, as well as to use it as a check on its prior implementation activities. As with all modular documentation, there is some minimum background redundancy to permit the assignment of each step to separate entities.

I have attempted to limit the background materials to those ISO 9000-related aspects that directly contribute to the implementation of the company's selected quality system directive standard. The details of peripheral or marginal background data, discreet ISO activities in other countries, and similar elements, I leave to the many available reference books on the subject. By concentrating on what you and your company must do to successfully implement the ISO 9000 standards, I hope to focus on the target audience in most need of such information.

You will quickly discover that I am firmly positioned in support of using the implementation of your selected ISO 9000 standard as an excellent means of improving the performance of your company. I must acknowledge, however, that many companies enter into the implementation process with quality system registration as the primary goal. If the eight-step process described in this book is followed correctly, the candidate company will achieve implementation of its selected ISO 9000 quality system standard, with attendant improvement in company management and performance, *and* also derive the benefits of a successful quality system registration.

Note about the companion software

This book has a companion software package that was developed by LearnerFirst and Lawrence A. Wilson. The package is based on the contents of this book and reflects the same eight-step process of ISO 9000 implementation. The software package, *LearnerFirst™ How to Implement ISO 9000*, is also available through ASQC Quality Press. This interactive software is an excellent means of guiding and documenting the implementation of your selected ISO 9000 standard. It allows the candidate company to follow the eight-step process, and permits building company-specific databases in all appropriate topics (document and data control, shortfall analysis, project management implementation plan, corrective actions, audit results, registrars, and so on). It also has the capability to directly print the American version of the five basic ISO 9000 documents, issued in 1994.

Since its release in 1994, the software is the only completely interactive method of tailoring the ISO 9000 implementation approach to the specific user company. Both the software package and this book can be used alone, but each is significantly augmented when used to complement the other.

Note about the standards

This book was written to the 1994 version of the ISO 9000 standards. Because they are cited throughout this publication, they are referred to only within the body of the text. Footnotes or references are not included at the end of each chapter for each quote is taken from the standards themselves. They are referred to by their number in the text, for example, ISO 9001 and ISO 9004-1. The following standards are cited.

- ISO 8402:1994, *Quality management and quality assurance—Vocabulary.* (Geneva, Switzerland: International Organization for Standardization, 1994).
- ISO 9001:1994, *Quality systems—Model for quality assurance in design, development, production, installation, and servicing.* (Geneva, Switzerland: International Organization for Standardization, 1994).
- ISO 9004-1:1994, *Quality management and quality system elements—Guidelines.* (Geneva, Switzerland: International Organization for Standardization, 1994).
- ISO 10013:1994, *Guidelines for developing quality manuals.* (Geneva, Switzerland: International Organization for Standardization, 1994).

Background of the ISO 9000 Quality Movement

0.1 Why ISO quality system standards now?

    0.1.1 Concept of quality improvement

    0.1.2 Arrival of the global economy

    0.1.3 National standards and their application

    0.1.4 Baseline for quality system standards

    0.1.5 Common denominator for voluntary standards

0.2 What is the International Standards Organization?

    0.2.1 ISO voluntary standard mission

    0.2.2 Leadership and support in ISO activities

    0.2.3 Technical committee on quality standards

    0.2.4 U.S. input to ISO standards

    0.2.5 ISO liaison with other standards bodies

0.3 What is the ISO 9000 quality standard family?

    0.3.1 ISO 9000 series of quality standards

    0.3.2 ISO 9000 guideline documents

    0.3.3 ISO document revision mechanism

    0.3.4 Identification of quality standards

    0.3.5 Consensus results in baseline standards

0.4 Chronology for development of a quality standard

    0.4.1 Initial actions on needs for quality standards

    0.4.2 Actions of the assigned subcommittee

    0.4.3 Draft international standard stage

Questions answered in this module

1. What is the ISO 9000 series of quality standards, including source and application?

2. What does ISO represent, and why is it accepted as the source of international standards?

3. What is the membership base of ISO, and how are voluntary standards applied?

4. Who runs ISO, how is it funded, and is quality the only area in which it operates?

5. How do ISO standards get developed, reviewed, and approved?

6. When did the ISO 9000 standards first appear, and why is there so much interest in them?

7. What and who actually requires use of ISO 9000 as the basis of company quality system?

8. Does the United States play a role in determining the need, content, or acceptance of ISO standards?

9. Why are ISO 9000 standards baseline documents without many advanced concepts?

10. How can ISO develop generic standards capable of application to all organizations?

11. How did ISO 9000 become accepted as the U.S. voluntary standard for quality systems?

12. What are the benefits to a company of implementing an ISO 9000 quality system?

13. How can a company contribute to ISO 9000 standards development?

14. What is quality system registration, and where did it start?

15. What requires a company to undergo the registration of its quality system?

16. Who performs the process of registration on a company, and how is it accomplished?

17. If quality system registration is not an ISO 9000 requirement, why is it worldwide?

18. How long will it take to get a company ready for a registration audit?

19. What is the role of quality improvement in the emerging global economy?

20. What criteria are used to determine if a company has a world-class quality system?

Background of the ISO 9000 Quality Movement

The ISO 9000 series of international quality standards were first published in 1987. Five basic quality system documents were released. Since their introduction to a somewhat questioning user base, these standards have become one of the most significant influences on the advance of the global quality movement. Now, it is quite likely most business organizations with international undertakings or intentions are well aware of these standards. Many organizations are currently attempting to learn more about these documents and their application.

The purpose of this book is to provide a sound understanding of the background and application of the ISO quality system standards. This understanding is critical to effective use of the standards. The text will examine the following:

- Interpretation and use of the standards
- Company benefits that can be derived from their use
- Concept of an ISO-defined quality system
- Recommended process for implementing the standards
- Achievement of quality system registration

0.1 Why ISO quality system standards now?

One of the most significant changes in international business is the recent movement toward quality awareness. Although still embryonic, growing international acceptance of the importance of quality is becoming manifested in business operations and performance worldwide. The importance of quality and reliability is becoming recognized as a critical factor for the sale of many products and services. This growth in international quality awareness has resulted in customer and consumer demand for products and services that are entirely suitable for the purposes intended. Furthermore, there is a growing expectation that resultant products will continue to be operational and serviceable for an acceptable period of time.

0.1.1 Concept of quality improvement

Responsible companies have concluded that acceptable quality and reliability can only be achieved if the company's total resources and capabilities are marshalled toward this goal. It is now quite clear that a company's market position, and possibly even its survival, are dependent on the successful implementation of these new quality improvement concepts. An ongoing reputation for quality products and services is the basis for the development and maintenance of any world-class company. In pursuit of a successful role in the global economy, the increasingly accepted means to achieve a world-class quality reputation is the company's basic quality system. Thus, as a company's quality system moves through improvement phases, so does the company's success in the competitive global marketplace improve (Figure 0.1). Additionally, companies are now beginning to acknowledge that all successful quality systems must reflect a standardized and repetitive process. In order to achieve this, the quality system must be focused and measured to some type of generally accepted quality system standard.

0.1.2 Arrival of the global economy

The world's business community is becoming a true global economy. Many companies are now buying and selling products and services throughout the world. Even those companies with current domestic market limitations have some plans for future worldwide competition. With a potential worldwide marketplace, each company must aggressively assert its position by establishing and maintaining a quality-based strategy.

For assurance of market success, such strategies must also involve the company's customers and suppliers throughout the world. This type of outreach will eventually mean that any products or services will be

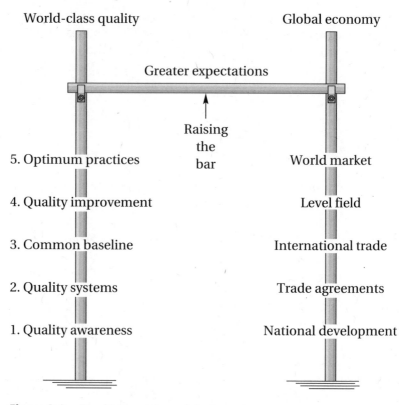

Figure 0.1 Quality matches global economy.

equally capable of supporting the intended quality goals. This will be true no matter what country the affected proactive companies use as trading partners, whether the country is developed or still developing.

0.1.3 National standards and their application

Until recently, virtually every country involved in the global marketplace had developed a system of quality standards. Some quality system requirements were imbedded in product and performance standards, but were used extensively as national standards within certain countries. The concept of the quality system even evolved in countries where system standards had not been developed. It is now generally accepted that a company's quality system tends to be the means of operating the company itself. The following definitions from ISO 8402 are also generally accepted.

Quality system—The organizational structure, responsibilities, procedures, and resources needed to implement quality management.

Quality management—All activities of the overall management function that determine the quality policy, objectives, and responsibilities, and implement them by means such as quality planning, quality control, quality assurance, and quality improvement, within the quality system.

If the quality system is a vehicle for company operation, then every aspect of a company's organization plays a role in achieving quality.

Although their effectiveness varied, over time the resultant quality systems in most countries became well defined. Depending on the specific country being reviewed, the related quality system may have been, (1) generally well developed and acknowledged as being based on an acceptable, documented quality system standard; (2) governed by the best business practices and/or quality standard concepts within the particular country, but essentially an undocumented and informal quality system; or (3) perhaps no real quality system at all, with nonstandard business practices and the complete absence of any governing quality concepts or standards. Of course, within each country, the same diverse range of standards application might also have been found. In addition to variability in the standards, there was also considerable in-country variance in the interpretation and implementation of those same standards, even among the base of national quality professionals.

In this environment of diverse application, the same national standard, even if believed to be fully implemented as intended, could have resulted in a wide variety of results. There was divergence in the in-country interpretations, even using the same business base. Contracting internationally was a gamble. The international customer or supplier was not intentionally producing inferior products and services, but was sincerely trying to adhere to the standards provided (Figure 0.2). Variation to a poorly defined norm was to be expected.

In addition, when these same companies specified quality system standards that they had developed, the same problems were apparent. The variation of independently applied interpretations and best practices by supplier countries and companies resulted in wide quality variations. Clearly, what is considered best business practices in a given country is based on its history. This includes the level of business development;

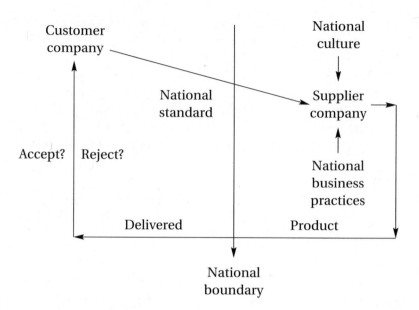

Figure 0.2   Contracting across national boundaries.

commercial understanding; participation in the free international market; and, in some cases, the basic desire to move beyond simple handicraft status.

0.1.4 Baseline for quality system standards

By the early 1980s, it had become quite apparent that a common basis for quality system interpretation and application was needed to assure success in the global marketplace. With a common baseline, it was obvious that the likelihood of achieving attendant commonality of results would be greatly enhanced. The global economy was clearly driving both industries and nations to the point of requiring such a universal quality baseline.

With such a basis, all international interpretations and applications related to quality systems could be systematically derived, defined, and standardized. Such an approach would permit companies to place orders worldwide with a high degree of confidence. The baseline concept would increase the possibility that the end results would be entirely acceptable to the customer's needs and requirements. Certainly it would be far superior to the random success that was being achieved. It would also provide more confidence for the company investing money to assume a proactive role in the global marketplace.

In the mid 1980s, however, the universal baseline approach described would have required worldwide acceptance of international quality system standards. No such standards existed at the time. This concept would also require the acceptance of international standards by all countries, even those with existing advanced quality standards of their own. Some of the affected countries that needed to participate even had reputations for outstanding quality systems. Fortunately, these successful national quality system standards were generally available and were offered for possible use in the international arena.

Obviously, any national standards that could be used as potential sources for the development of an international baseline would require a high level of international recognition and acceptance. This was particularly true since all countries would have to agree to use the resultant international standards in lieu of their national standards. In this situation it appeared quite possible that many countries would exhibit considerable reluctance. Difficulties were anticipated. A generally accepted common denominator or neutral base was needed to permit the development of an international baseline.

0.1.5 Common denominator for voluntary standards

Fortunately, there exists in the world of international standards, just such a universally recognized voluntary standards organization. It has a long-standing reputation for the successful development and promulgation of standards worldwide. Membership in this organization is maintained by countries the world over. Since successful development of internationally acceptable voluntary standards has been part of its long history and reputation, the organizational vehicle for the development of the needed universal quality system standards appeared obvious.

The International Organization for Standardization, also called the International Standards Organization (ISO), was ideally suited to be the focus and channel for mutual and unbiased development of the quality system standards. In the early 1980s, a ballot of the national standards bodies of the ISO member countries confirmed what was already well known. There was a consensus membership position: A set of voluntary quality system standards needed to be developed by the ISO membership for its international interpretation and application.

0.2 What is the International Standards Organization?

ISO is a nongovernmental voluntary standards organization with worldwide membership. Its charter is the development and promulgation of voluntary international standards. The activities take place in many topics and fields. ISO is essentially an organization of organizations, in that no individuals, companies, or countries are typically direct members. Each national membership is generally held by the recognized standards body or agency from the member country (Figure 0.3). With some countries, the national standards body holding ISO membership is a recognized function or quasi function of the government.

With other countries, the membership is held by an accepted nongovernmental body that represents the country. An example of this is the American National Standards Institute (ANSI). ANSI is the designated U.S. voluntary standards body, and it holds the U.S. position within ISO's membership. ISO has approximately 90 member countries. With the

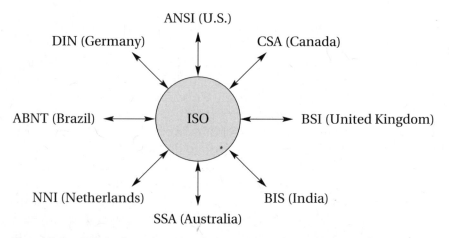

Figure 0.3 ISO is the common denominator for quality system standards.

changing political structure of the world, the exact number of supporting, dues-paying members is somewhat variable.

0.2.1 ISO voluntary standard mission

ISO is based in Geneva, Switzerland. Although it has a limited staff, the primary standards development activities are performed by volunteers from the member countries. The volunteers are usually technical and standards specialists. As noted, ISO's basic mission is the development of voluntary international standards on subjects selected and approved for development by the member countries. ISO is *not* involved in the actual application of the resultant standards to any business or national activity. It is the basic source for international consensus voluntary standards.

The actual application of ISO-developed standards may be achieved in either contractual or noncontractual situations. Usually, the ISO-developed standards are applied by their user organizations. Governments of some member countries have acted to apply the ISO standards directly. Also, the ISO 9000 family of quality system standards has been accepted as the national quality standard by over 60 countries worldwide.

Acceptance as the national quality system standard by a country's standards body does not change the fact that the standards are voluntary in nature. National acceptance does not ordinarily involve invoking the application of the standards. As such, the United States has accepted the ISO 9000 family of standards as its basic national quality system; however, the application of these standards in the United States is only accomplished by voluntary acceptance on the part of affected user companies, or by contractual application as a part of normal customer/supplier relationships.

The ISO thrust is always directed toward accomplishing the systematic development of universally accepted voluntary standards—those having common interpretation within the international user community. The nature, extent, timing, and methods of application are *not* within the ISO charter.

0.2.2 Leadership and support in ISO activities

Leadership within ISO tends to be based on the member country's background in the standards field. As such, western European countries are the most involved in ISO activities and leadership. They are closely followed by Canada, the United States, Australia, and other countries with active standards involvement. This leadership factor is also true in the area of quality system standards. Leadership is based on long-time, extensive experience in the development of quality system standards. Of course, with leadership comes support, so collectively Western Europe has historically provided a large portion of the dues utilized to operate ISO. In recent years, however, with ISO participation now spread around the globe, financial support comes from all areas of the world. In addition to membership dues, ISO and its national member bodies sell the standards worldwide.

The actual day-to-day standards development activities are accomplished by individual standards specialists in various fields. These people perform the work on a voluntarily basis and have been approved for the activity by the standards bodies of their respective nations. They serve on selected ISO technical committees (TC). These are usually comprised of representation from all member countries interested in the specific topic upon which the TC charter was based (for example, quality management and quality assurance). The population of each TC is quite variable, having a direct relationship to the nature and timeliness of its subjects. Of course, with each subject there is also varying levels of individual national interest that is reflected, in part, by the number of national participants available to support the specific standards development activity.

0.2.3 Technical committee on quality standards

ISO has over 200 technical committees that address a variety of subjects. With the approval of the membership, each new TC transforms the charter subject into an appropriate range of applicable international standards. The only ISO technical committee directly involved in the development of quality system standards is ISO TC 176. Its formal title is Quality Management and Quality Assurance. With the increasing interest in quality system standards, most ISO member nations have representatives on ISO TC 176.

ISO TC 176 has three subcommittees, one on quality system terminology, a second on quality systems, and a third on supporting technologies (Figure 0.4). TC 176 is chaired by the standards body from Canada (CSA). Subcommittee 1 is chaired by France's Association Francaise de Normali-

ISO Technical Committee 176,
Quality Management and Quality Assurance,
chaired by CSA (Canada)

Subcommittee 1, Terminology, chaired by AFNOR (France)	Subcommittee 2, Quality Systems, chaired by BSI (U.K.)	Subcommittee 3, Supporting Technologies, chaired by NNI (Netherlands)
Output example ISO 8402	Output examples ISO 9000-1/9004-1 ISO 9001–9003	Output examples ISO 10011-1, 2, and 3 ISO 10012-1 and 2

Figure 0.4 Organizational structure of ISO TC 176.

sation (AFNOR), subcommittee 2 by the United Kingdom's British Standards Institute (BSI), and subcommittee 3 by the Netherlands' Nederlands Normalisatie-instituut (NNI). The organization and structure of these ISO TC 176 subcommittees (SC) has been designed to permit their operation as interrelated units of the same team. Full coordination of the activities of each SC, with those of the other two, assures all resultant standards will be completely compatible for the intended users.

Each SC has a number of working groups (WG) that address various aspects of the assigned standards development activities. On that basis, each WG is normally assigned the development of one specific international standard. Currently, 20–25 WGs operate in the ISO TC 176 development process. As with TC 176, country participation on SCs and WGs varies depending on the level of national interest. Officially, WG membership is comprised of technical experts on the subject assigned, not standards representatives of their mother country.

0.2.4 U.S. input to ISO standards

The U.S. member of ISO is ANSI. In addition to supporting the international development of standards, ANSI is responsible for developing and promulgating U.S. voluntary standards. As with ISO, the majority of ANSI standards development activities are performed by volunteers in the ANSI member community. The ANSI Z-1 Committee is the primary source of quality system activity for ANSI. In addition, other standards writing bodies submit proposals to ANSI for consideration as U.S. national standards.

To support the U.S. role in the ISO TC 176 quality system activities, ANSI formed a technical advisory group (TAG). It is designated the U.S. TAG to ISO TC 176 (Figure 0.5). Its secretariat is the American Society for Quality Control (ASQC). This TAG provides individuals to support the ISO TC 176, including participation on ISO-related SCs and WGs.

The U.S. TAG for ISO TC 176 is also responsible for developing the U.S. position on the development and approval of all ISO TC 176 quality standards. Valid U.S. business input is assured by the presence of many industry and business associations within TAG membership.

0.2.5 ISO liaison with other standards bodies

The ISO TC 176 on quality management and quality assurance maintains liaison with a number of other organizations, both within and outside of ISO. This assures that the quality standards that are being developed or used by each body do not have conflicting requirements, and that there is no omission of any valuable information.

Figure 0.5 How the United States provides input to ISO standards.

Many topics are closely related to the work of the ISO TC 176, such as those within the charter of ISO TC 69, Committee on Statistical Methods. Such relationships may mean the charter and expertise of another standards development or user group may cause it to be a more suitable authority in a given area of common interest. In addition to this type of liaison, the level of interest in the work of TC 176 has caused this committee to be an ISO technical committee with a most significant following. As with other countries, many members of the U.S. TAG to TC 176 are not only supporting the TAG directly, but are also providing information to the many other constituents and organizations they represent. This expanded business community influence helps the TAG develop related consensus positions needed for U.S. ballots.

0.3   What is the ISO 9000 quality standard family?

The ISO 9000 quality system standards are a series of documents that have gained universal acceptance. A universally accepted standard must be embraced by the business communities of each member nation. To assure acceptance by businesses, all standards' requirements are generically written. Each affected business interprets and applies the standard. The generic nature permits a singularly focused company interpretation for all potential users. The ISO 9000 documents are written in this generic format so that they are equally applicable to all fields, industries, businesses, agencies, organizations, enterprises, and entities.

The specific interpretation of the standards' generic requirements must be accomplished by the user. Only the affected organization can fully consider the requirements in relation to the nature of its business. The interpretation and application of how those requirements then relate to its operational activities must be determined by the organization itself. Of course, each organization has a unique frame of reference and tailors application accordingly.

0.3.1 ISO 9000 series of quality standards

When potential standards users speak of the ISO 9000 series, they are usually referring to the original set of five documents issued in 1987, and revised and reissued in 1994 (Figure 0.6). This set of documents is comprised of (1) three basic directive or contractual standards that set forth

ISO 9000-1:1994	*Quality management and quality assurance standards—Part 1: Guidelines for selection and use*
ISO 9001:1994	*Quality systems—Model for quality assurance in design, development, production installation and servicing*
ISO 9002:1994	*Quality systems—Model for quality assurance in production, installation and servicing*
ISO 9003:1994	*Quality systems—Model for quality assurance in final inspection and test*
ISO 9004-1:1994	*Quality management and quality system elements—Part 1: Guidelines*

Figure 0.6   The titles of the 1994 quality system standards.

three levels of coverage for specific quality system requirements; (2) a guideline document that provides extensive direction in the nature of quality systems, as well as the selection and interpretation of the directive documents; and (3) a guideline document that provides a best practices approach to developing and managing a quality system capable of complying with the three directive standards.

The document numbered ISO 9000-1 is basically a user's guide to understand what constitutes a quality system, the basic quality principles involved, and the selection of the most appropriate directive or contractual standard for the candidate business. The documents numbered ISO 9001, ISO 9002, and ISO 9003 are the directive or contractual documents that reflect three different levels of the quality system requirements scope and intensity. ISO 9001 is the most complete set of quality system requirements, then ISO 9002, and finally ISO 9003. The nature of the documents is extensively covered in this text. Briefly, ISO 9001 is for companies that conduct in-house design and/or development activities. ISO 9002 is appropriate for those companies that have production, installation, and services, but no design or development activities. ISO 9003 is only for companies that solely perform final inspection and test. Although revised for the 1994 release, these three documents do not carry a dash one (-1) revision designation.

The fifth document in the series is 9004-1, which is a guideline for the development of a quality management system that will be capable of successfully achieving an acceptable application of the contractual documents. As with the other documents, this text examines this standard in detail.

0.3.2 ISO 9000 guideline documents

After the 1987 release of the original ISO 9000 standards, it was apparent that additional guidelines would be necessary for full and beneficial use of the series. A common interpretation for successful application of the three contractual documents was a primary concern of users. This was particularly true in certain areas of subject matter and specific terminology.

Now, there are a number of ISO TC 176-developed supplemental and/or guideline documents available or in the process of development. These cover many topics. In addition to the basic hardware approach of the original series of standards, guidance is now available to businesses with services, software, and processed materials as their product base. There is also guidance available for the development of quality manuals, quality plans, quality improvement, project management, configuration management, quality auditing, calibration, and similar topics.

Approximately 20 such ISO 9000 guideline or supportive documents have been released or are in a state of near-term availability. See Appendix B for a list of these documents and their current status as of August 1995. Of particular note is ISO 8402, which is the quality system terminology document controlling the interpretation of terms used in all of the other ISO documents. As noted, such a worldwide interpretation is essential to maintain the original goal of having a universally accepted baseline.

0.3.3 ISO document revision mechanism

The five basic ISO 9000 documents were in development for nearly five years before their 1987 release. Unfortunately, achieving international consensus is a slow, deliberate, and sometimes frustrating process. Once released, individual nations accepted the basic series in lieu of their own national quality system standards. Global application of the ISO 9000 series was quickly obtained. Even countries that were not directly involved in their development found the ISO 9000 standards acceptable for application within their country.

There were, however, topics and system elements within the three directive documents that needed further clarification and interpretation.

Some clarification had been achieved through the guidelines and supplements, however, the basic directive documents needed considerable improvement. Fortunately, operational ISO Directives have a built-in corrective measure.

ISO Directives require that each released standard undergo a reevaluation every five years for reaffirmation, revision, or cancellation. Thus, when the ISO 9000 series of standards was reevaluated it was decided that the documents should be retained, revised, and upgraded. The revision process actually started in 1991; however, the acceptance balloting on the proposed revisions extended into late 1993. A final confirmation ballot was not concluded until June 1994. As such, the release of the revised basic documents did not take place until July 1994. Note that although the revised directive documents ISO 9001, ISO 9002, and ISO 9003 retained their original numbering, the associated series guidelines became ISO 9000-1 and ISO 9004-1.

The changes in the ISO 9000:1994 documents were primarily for points of clarification or basic document improvement. The addition of significant new requirements was judged unnecessary. Significant changes would only tend to complicate the widespread, but somewhat embryonic, global implementation activity in process. The advanced quality system concepts, coming into use in developed countries, were held in abeyance for consideration at the next reevaluation cycle. Thus, newer quality system concepts and tools, such as benchmarking, total quality management, and continuous process improvement will be evaluated for inclusion in the 1997 (more likely 1999) revisions. To assure the 1999 revisions gain an early start, the assigned working groups are already collecting, identifying, and evaluating changes that may be appropriate in 1999.

Note that TC 176 has implemented its own customer satisfaction program. To assure the 1997/9 revisions are user-friendly and customer oriented, the assigned WGs are developing document specifications for the upcoming standards. Before the groups start the actual document writing and revision process, they are attempting to determine what presentation and content will best serve users' needs. The groups' intent is to have customer-based document specifications that have been coordinated across all other working groups. The design standards will represent all five of the basic ISO 9000 series of standards, assuring the end result will be an excellent user-friendly product of immediate benefit. It is currently planned that the document specifications will have an ISO member acceptance ballot before the work on the actual standard revision is permitted to officially begin.

0.3.4 Identification of quality standards

Most countries have now accepted the five basic ISO 9000 documents as their national quality system standards. This was accomplished when the nations' standards bodies or their designated support units balloted for national acceptance. Subsequently, many of those same user countries have now applied their nation's own standards numbering system to the ISO documents. With a national number, these ISO standards have been easily incorporated into the national standards catalogs of the affected countries.

In the United States, the five basic ISO 9000 documents were originally identified as the U.S. Q90 series, and so ISO 9000 was numbered Q90, ISO 9001 became Q91, and so on. With the release of the 1994 revisions, the U.S. approach was modified to provide more international recognition. The U.S. has now numbered its national equivalents of the series as Q9000-1, Q9001, Q9002, Q9003, and Q9004-1. A few countries are directly using the ISO 9000 numbering system, having incorporated it as their own. Other countries, such as the United States, have used a numbering system that readily links their national standard back to the related ISO 9000 document.

On the other hand, some countries have simply utilized the next number in their national standards listing as the number for their national equivalent of the ISO 9000 documents. There is no relationship to the ISO 9000 number whatsoever, other than through the title. This diverse approach to numbering the quality system standards sometimes causes difficulty in interpreting which ISO 9000 standard a foreign company is using. It even causes trading partners to wonder whether their counterparts have truly implemented ISO 9000 or are using another approach. Because of this complex situation, there is a movement within the ISO community to simply use the ISO numbers or a direct form of linkage. There is still some debate on the subject, but it appears likely such changes will occur in the future.

0.3.5 Consensus results in baseline standards

The ISO 9000 standards are essentially consensus standards, with acceptance having to be balloted by the total affected ISO membership. Each country has just one vote and will not ordinarily vote acceptance for something that the nation or its businesses simply can not perform. Thus, the ISO documents do not ordinarily involve all of the latest state-of-the-art techniques and concepts.

This situation is true for all ISO standards, including those relating to quality. Potential changes that incorporate requirements for advanced quality system techniques and concepts may only be capable of being achieved by the technically developed and economically strong countries. Implementation may be very difficult or too expensive for many ISO member nations and simply impossible at the present time. As such, the majority of members of the ISO TC 176 committee on quality management and quality assurance are very cautious about voting to accept changes reflecting such advanced requirements in their national standard.

The consensus ballot process brings forth change but at a rate acceptable to the majority. The ISO 9000 standards tend to trail new quality system concepts by three to five years; however, the standards are always written to allow the incorporation of new concepts at any time the user company determines appropriate.

In order to achieve consensus and approval among the entire ISO TC 176 organization, the standards, as released, are simply baseline quality system documents. Additionally, to achieve consensus, all of the concepts included in the standards had to be basic, sound quality system interpretations. Commonly accepted interpretations include such aspects as

- Customer satisfaction
- Multifunctional participation in quality
- Documentation of quality systems
- Structural and functional elements of quality systems

As noted, advanced concepts such as benchmarking, total quality management, continuous process improvement, and use of process metrics, are not included in the 1994 revisions. For the proactive company, however, the possibility of their incorporation is well within the current 1994 wording.

The 1987 ISO 9000 series captured and presented many basic quality system concepts that were generally accepted and incorporated in existing national quality system standards. The advantage to the ISO 9000 standards is these same concepts, as incorporated into the 1987 ISO documents, have now been introduced and accepted worldwide. This has been a giant step in the global promulgation of quality system improvement. The ISO 9000 quality standards may not be considered advanced by many technically competent companies (or countries), but they have tended to bring virtually all countries to a higher quality system baseline (Figure 0.7). This increase is not meant to imply the ISO

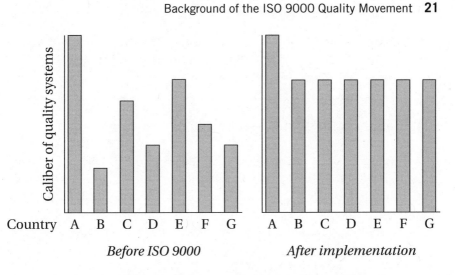

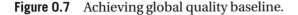

Then improvement after baseline achieved.

Figure 0.7 Achieving global quality baseline.

9000 series is the highest order of quality system standards available— far from it. They are simply a sound baseline quality system approach which has gained universal acceptance. There are many companies that have accepted the ISO 9000 standards as their baseline system, but have utilized other complementary quality or industry standards to go well beyond the basic ISO 9000 requirements.

The temporary withholding of advanced quality system concepts for possible 1997/99 inclusion, should never cause a proactive company to withhold its incorporation of advanced approaches. Company management must apply whatever beneficial quality system complement aids in achieving its business strategies. ISO 9000 can remain the baseline for a proactive company's expanded quality system. The ISO documents permit, and even encourage, exceeding the basic requirements.

0.4 Chronology for development of a quality standard

The actual process of standards initiation, development, approval, and release is well defined and regulated per ISO Directives. These directives are the "standards" for standards development and it is appropriate for an organization such as ISO to use them. These detailed regulations are designed to assure all countries have an opportunity for their input and ballots to be fully considered and quite meaningful.

0.4.1 Initial actions on needs for quality standards

The implementation of the standards development process starts with the determination of a need for a standard or guideline on a given subject. This need may be identified by a specific country, a particular subcommittee, the ISO TC 176 itself, or another activity with which TC 176 has liaison. Once presented for consideration, the question or issue is then determined by means of the TC 176 forwarding a ballot to all member countries. The countries, as represented by their national standards body, establish their view. The ballot results *in total* will indicate whether the membership base has sufficient support and acceptance for such a document.

Note: The ballots also ask about the voting country's interest in participating in the standard's development, if it is accepted by the balloting.

If the need for a new standard is justified by ballot results, a working group (WG) is formed (Figure 0.8). A WG is comprised of international experts in the particular field or subject that is the basis of the proposed standard. Depending on the topic, the WG is assigned to one of the ISO TC 176 subcommittees and chartered to address and develop the proposed document. Before starting, a chairperson or convener is selected to lead the WG through the steps of document development, approval, and release.

Initially, the WG collects all available source documents on the subject of its charter. Frequently, there are some national standards that relate very well. The first development task is to establish a scope for the proposed document and, once it is approved, to develop a WG draft. The WG's goal is to address the subject matter in a fashion which discharges the assignment of its charter. The WG draft or working draft (WD) may require a number of revisions before all the WG members regard it as satisfactory. To this point, satisfaction with the draft standard will have been solely determined by the experts assigned to the WG. No national inputs or comments will have been solicited during the WD stage. When consensus is finally reached among the experts, the draft document is ready for the next step.

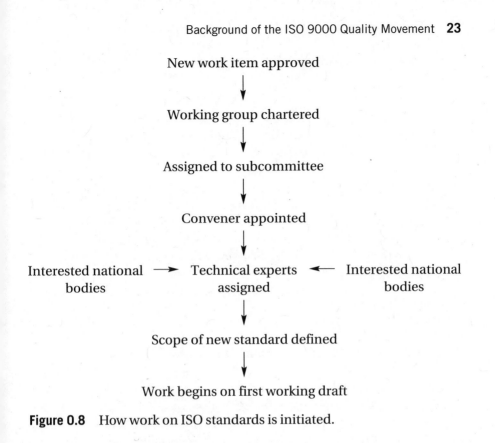

Figure 0.8   How work on ISO standards is initiated.

0.4.2 Actions of the assigned subcommittee

The WD is forwarded to the cognizant subcommittee. Depending upon the WD's degree of maturity, it may be elevated to a committee draft (CD). If judged suitable to be a CD, the document is then distributed to all member countries of the subcommittee. Distribution may be for comments only or for actual subcommittee acceptance balloting. During the CD acceptance vote, member countries provide ballot results in accordance with ISO Directives. The ballots from all of the member countries must indicate the ballot categories of "approval as is," "disapproval," or "approval with comments." All disapproval ballots must include comments as to why the country believed it necessary to reject the CD. Frequently, the process of gaining acceptance of a CD will involve balloting on a series of improving versions, incorporating national comments as appropriate. Subcommittee balloting continues until the acceptance meets ISO Directives.

0.4.3 Draft international standard stage

Once the subcommittee members are satisfied with the CD, it is elevated for consideration as a draft international standard (DIS). All DIS documents are forwarded to the entire membership of national standards bodies in the full ISO TC 176 for balloting and comment. The same ballot categories as in the CD acceptance process are used at the DIS stage, however, the comments are supposed to be limited to those of an editorial nature. If a country elects to provide substantive comments at this point, those that can not be incorporated may be retained for consideration at the next mandatory five-year reevaluation and revision.

Acceptance of a DIS may involve one or more ballots if the positive ballots do not exceed 67 percent of the total returned, or the negative ballots exceed 25 percent of the total returned. Thus, several ballots at the DIS level may be required to achieve acceptance.

0.4.4 Release as an international standard

Once judged acceptable, the document is approved as an international standard and will be forwarded through ISO channels for publication and release. This is done through ISO headquarters in Geneva and, of course, the format, structure, and so on must be in accordance with ISO Directives. One of those requirements is for each standard to have dual language text, traditionally English and French. This is usually accomplished by having each page printed with a two-column split, with each column having its text in one of the languages.

Once published and released, ISO documents are available for purchase through Geneva or member country standards organizations. Availability in the United States is primarily through ANSI, but other Washington D.C. offices for ISO-related activities can provide copies (see Appendix D). One of the benefits of having the standards converted into the member country's numbering system, such as Q9001, is it also permits the sale of the tailored national version. This often reflects a price less than the ISO Geneva issue, usually with a reduced delivery time. National versions in the United States are identical to international versions except that they (1) exclude references to the ISO international standards, (2) use the U.S. numbering equivalent in references, and (3) utilize the American spelling rather than the British equivalent of the same word. Of course, the U.S. version does not have the attendant French translation of text.

0.4.5 Time frame for standards development

The process for developing a generic quality system standard is both slow and deliberate. In fact, even ISO Directives acknowledge it is acceptable for the total process to take five to seven years before the actual release of a finished standard. Observation shows it usually does not take that long, but it often approaches such limits. Experience shows that a standard could be issued in three to four years (Figure 0.9).

ISO Directives stipulate that standards must be reaffirmed, revised, or cancelled every five years. Since it may take five years or more to get a document revised and released, it is quite possible any ISO standard might have ongoing revisional activity in progress throughout its published existence. While this extensive process is frustrating to many participants, it does accomplish the ISO goal of a properly prepared consensus standard that serves its users for the purpose intended.

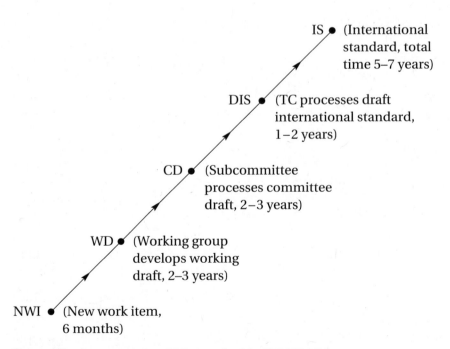

IS ● (International standard, total time 5–7 years)

DIS ● (TC processes draft international standard, 1–2 years)

CD ● (Subcommittee processes committee draft, 2–3 years)

WD ● (Working group develops working draft, 2–3 years)

NWI ● (New work item, 6 months)

Figure 0.9   Progress of an ISO standard in ISO TC 176.

0.5 European Community's international standards role

The activities of the European Community (EC) officially started with the Treaty of Rome in 1957, wherein six countries determined that the European market could benefit from pooling economic approaches and resources. The EC has since developed into a significant economic force, with the country membership in the consortium rising first to 12 and recently indicating it may reach 18. The EC has been fully defined by the Maastricht Agreement, which for economic purposes, has essentially created a "united states" of Europe. The EC has been formalized as the European Union (EU). The continuing intent of the Union is to assure that the economic benefits of pooled resources and markets are available to all participants, while it offers a single economic face to the rest of the world. Final member ratification of EU structure, operation, and interrelationships has not been a completely uncomplicated process. The success of the concept can only be judged with time.

0.5.1 EC's requirement for certification

The current members of the EU are essentially the Western European powers. As such, it is not at all surprising that long-standing European quality initiatives quickly found their way into EC regulations. In fact, the United Kingdom's concept of quality system registration or, as the Europeans say, *certification,* found its way from being essentially a UK concept to its inclusion in the original EC regulations. These regulations affect any company that is involved with the buying or selling of EC designated "regulated products" (essentially environmental, health, and safety related). Only those regulated products produced within a certified quality system will be acceptable to the Union and its marketplace.

0.5.2 Use of ISO 9000 in EC certification

The required EC quality system certification must be based on demonstrated compliance with the ISO 9000 series of standards. Originally, these certification requirements were to have been in effect and enforced by the end of 1992. However, the EC members were not fully prepared by then, and the requirement could not be fully implemented in Europe. Although not cancelled, the requirement has not been rigidly enforced.

Many countries have experienced difficulty with the EU-required process of quality system registration or certification. Some of the countries experiencing difficulty are within the EU itself. The problem stems from the EU requirement which states the process of certification will be conducted by an approved independent auditing body or agency. Further, the independent auditing body must be approved or accredited for the purpose, in accordance with each country's national accreditation body or system (Figure 0.10).

0.5.3 Countries unprepared for certification

The United States, for one, had neither a program of quality system registration (certification), nor the related national accreditation body

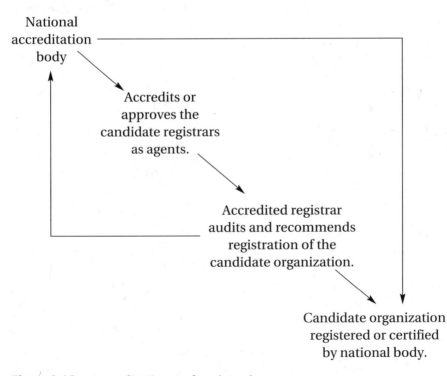

Figure 0.10   Accreditation and registration.

or system. At the time of announcement of the EC quality system registration policy, it appeared to U.S. industry as a not-too-subtle means of implementing a nontariff trade barrier to protect the EC marketplace. It appeared to be an obvious ploy to prevent the United States and other countries from having reasonable access to the European marketplace.

In a panic to meet the 1992 registration target, many companies, in many countries, that were interested in doing business in Europe, suddenly became involved in ISO 9000 quality system implementation. In the United States, businesses encouraged the Department of Commerce to intervene on behalf of U.S. interests and develop some approach which would alleviate the apparent EC trade barrier.

0.5.4 United States deals with accreditation gap

Three approaches were developed that have permitted U.S. businesses to meet EC requirements. The first approach was for U.S. companies to have the opportunity to be audited and registered (or certified) to ISO 9000 by visiting European registrars. These registrars had been accredited by a European accreditation body. Activity has since expanded so a number of the foreign registrars have now located offices in the United States.

The second approach was to encourage foreign registrars to establish a contractual relationship with U.S. companies. The foreign registrars essentially selected some U.S. firms as candidate co-registrars. When approved, and while still in a mentoring arrangement, the candidate U.S. registration firm acted to certify U.S. businesses on behalf of the foreign registrar.

The third approach was to initiate the establishment of some type of national quality system registration/certification process, including an acceptable accreditation board system for the United States. This effort eventually resulted in the formation of the Registrar Accreditation Board (RAB) under the auspices of the American Society for Quality Control (ASQC).

All of these approaches are currently being used in the United States, including the ongoing RAB accreditation of foreign firms and U.S. companies as registrars (see Figure 0.11). Business opportunity for being an accredited quality system registrar is clearly one that has exhibited a

- Foreign-accredited registrars based in the United States
- Foreign-accredited registrars operating from homeland
- U.S. companies working under foreign-accredited registrars
- U.S. registrars accredited by the U.S. RAB
- U.S. registrars accredited by foreign agencies
- Registrars with multinational accreditations

Figure 0.11   Registration schemes in the United States.

great amount of recent growth. The registration process and registrar selection is addressed in this text as Step 8.

0.5.5 Marketplace outpaces EC on registration

Although the EC may have originally promulgated the concept of registration, it has now spread worldwide. The primary reason for the phenomenal geographic growth is due to the pressures of the global marketplace. Global customers have found the concept to their liking. It gives them more assurance that their supplier's performance will be satisfactory. Further, the customers have nothing to lose, since the affected suppliers bear the cost of the entire registration process. Companies experience a significant marketing advantage when they advertise that their ISO 9000-based quality system was approved by an accredited, independent third party.

Note: The cost of ISO implementation varies, depending on how close the company complies with ISO 9000 requirements. Implementation costs are usually substantial but recovery tends to be near term. Full discussion of the implementation process constitutes the major portion of this book.

Although registration is not required by ISO, a company that is independently judged in compliance with its ISO 9000 standard has excellent credentials. With acceptance of the registration concept, its worldwide usage and confidence to all parties involved, the registration process is here to stay.

Conclusion

This background discussion covers the nature and source of the ISO documents, their interpretation and implementation, and the benefits of implementation. The discussion also addresses why and how the ISO 9000 standards have evolved into the only set of quality standards that have gained worldwide recognition and acceptance.

The genesis of the ISO 9000 standards lies in the international efforts to improve the quality of products and services and the increasing awareness of what it takes to operate within a global economy. These two situations demand a common quality baseline upon which to control and judge the acceptability of products and services worldwide. Nations have shelved their own quality system standards in favor of the ISO 9000 family. The ISO documents are now a common denominator for establishing and operating baseline quality systems in the global economy.

The International Standards Organization (ISO) develops and issues international voluntary standards of all types. ISO is accepted as the source of most internationally controlled standards, ranging from product-related specifications to the commonality of quality systems. ISO assigns major subject areas to a technical committee (TC) such as ISO TC 176, the one for quality management and quality assurance. U.S. membership in ISO is held by the American National Standards Institute (ANSI). A technical advisory group (TAG) supports ANSI in its TC 176 membership. The TAG is comprised of representatives from U.S. businesses, and actions taken are reflective of U.S. business/commercial interests.

The chronology of ISO standards development is quite detailed, often resulting in many years before final acceptance and release. Assigned representatives of ISO member countries work as part of a technical committee (TC) to (1) provide technical input to the draft standard; (2) provide review and improvement of the developing standard; and (3) comment/ballot on document acceptance as an international standard.

Registration is the concept of an independent third party approving a given company's implementation of its selected ISO 9000 directive quality system standard. Registration has moved from a European requirement to international acceptance as a global means of assuring quality systems. Such registration or certification of a company's quality system is funded by the affected company. Advantages of registration are not only evident by the increased competitiveness of the affected company, but also by customer acceptance of registration. Customers are assured that supplier companies have implemented the accepted baseline ISO 9000 family quality system.

Implementation actions required by this module

1. Obtain some basic information on the ISO 9000 quality system standards.
2. Determine whether the company works to an accepted quality system standard.
3. Assure that the company has an established objective to improve current quality performance.
4. Decide if ISO 9000, as a basis for quality system improvement, meets the company's strategy.
5. Determine if the company has any plan to pursue any foreign marketing activities.
6. Determine if current/potential customers have an interest in ISO 9000 compliance.
7. Obtain some basic information on the process of quality system registration.
8. Consider joining a local/on-line ISO 9000 and registration networking activity.

Instructions—Please Read Before Proceeding

Guidance for using the eight-step process to ISO 9000 implementation

The eight-step process is the product of the author's extensive experience in assisting companies toward successful ISO 9000 implementation and registration. The process addresses all the requirements necessary for the company to achieve compliance with the ISO 9000 quality system standards.

Setting the stage

1. ISO 9000 implementation is a process. It begins with deciding to use ISO 9000 as the basis for the company's quality system and ends with the verification and validation of the installed quality system. *From experience, the eight-step process described in this text is the best way to undergo the implementation process.* Only executive management can make the decision for use of this approach, because it involves company-level commitments and changes.

2. The eight-step implementation process is suitable for applying the selected ISO quality system standard whether required by the customer or by proactive company management. As decided by management, the objective may be acceptance of the company's ISO 9000 compliance by the customer directly or through the registration process.

3. Management needs to assign individuals to coordinate the company's use of the eight-step process, but the responsibility for a successful effort is still that of management itself.

How to get the best use of modules

1. The process of ISO 9000 implementation involves a series of eight well-defined steps that are clearly subprocesses of the overall activity. The eight steps are essentially sequential.

2. Since many companies approach these steps with different personnel, they are written as related, but somewhat independent modules. Each module stands alone. When the modules are linked, the total process implements the selected standard.

3. On that basis, there is always some brief introductory redundancy to assure that readers have a satisfactory baseline for pursuing the topics in the new module. Any redundancy is building toward establishing a different point.

4. The contents of the eight modules attempt to address all possible situations in which the company might find itself during implementation of the quality standard. Not all situations will apply to each company, so readers will have to determine whether the particular discussion applies to their organizations. The situations are clearly separate, and the distinction is not difficult.

What are the eight steps or modules?

1. The eight-step process begins with Step 1, the module which addresses all of the considerations that the prudent company must investigate *before* having enough information to assure ISO 9000 implementation is actually going to be beneficial.

2. The Step 2 module assumes a go-ahead decision on ISO 9000 implementation. It guides the company through the identification and accomplishment of those pertinent activities associated with preparing for the compliance shortfall analysis. One of the critical actions in Step 2 is the selection of the ISO 9000 directive quality system standard that is the most suitable for focusing the company's implementation activity.

3. Step 3 is the module where the shortfall analysis and its associated activities are accomplished. The analysis permits the company to determine its actual variation from acceptable ISO

9000 compliance. The module concludes with the company organizing the resultant shortfalls into potential remedial actions for inclusion in the detailed implementation plan.

4. The ISO 9000 implementation plan is developed in the module for Step 4. This project management-type plan must include every activity that is required for successful implementation. Each task must be identified, scheduled, assigned, and provided with resources. *The full compliance task is now defined.* The plan is implemented in the next two modules. These next two steps can be essentially worked in parallel.

5. Step 5 is the module that resolves all compliance variances with those elements of the standard that are associated with the company's documented quality system. The module develops and achieves complete documentation of the newly revised system. It uses as much existing company documentation as possible. The module addresses system documentation writing, review, coordination, and release processes.

6. The module for Step 6 covers all of the remaining ISO 9000 implementation activities, including related orientation, training, management approaches, employee interfaces, and system-related transitional concerns. This module is unique in that the content is usually implemented across all other modules, as appropriate. The company may elect to accomplish some aspects of its content in modules prior to fully defining the implementation plan.

7. The Step 7 module provides guidance for the company to assure it has satisfactorily implemented its selected standard. Through a series of reviews and audits, the company will undergo its own quality system verification and validation activities. This review is performed in preparation for the independent compliance acceptance audit from the customer or a registrar.

8. Step 8 is the final module wherein the company is visited by the selected acceptance agency. The on-site compliance acceptance audit may be performed by the customer or registrar, as decided by the candidate company. The module takes the company through the entire compliance audit process, giving advice as to what is expected and how the company can increase its chances of being successful.

General background

1. For convenience, the term *company* is used throughout the text as the single most appropriate word for relating to readers. The term also applies to any entity that is interested in ISO 9000 implementation, including businesses, agencies, academe, and all other organizations (commercial and military, profit and non-profit).

2. Not every aspect of each quality system element for every company is interpreted. There are suitable ISO 9000 family guidelines (for example, ISO 9000-2) and reference books available for that purpose. Since company personnel are the only ones who have the knowledge required for interpreting ISO 9000 application to their company, the author has concentrated on facilitating the implementation process itself. In addition to discussing the steps in the process and subprocesses, examples from the standards are used to demonstrate how specified requirements may be achieved.

3. The recommended approaches and methods in the text are not necessarily the minimum to meet the standard. Several techniques that have been found to enhance a company's benefits derived from implementing the standards are included. Any such recommendations are considered in the best interest of the company and will facilitate the implementation process. Although approval of compliance is important, the primary gain to the company is cost-effective, repetitive processes which can increase company performance.

4. Most companies are inclined to overdocument their processes when implementing ISO 9000. The tendency seems to be that companies write *about* the processes rather than assure the causative documentation is clear, direct, factual, and brief. Documentation should be written for the benefit of users, not for management, the auditors, or the writers' credentials.

5. Although the implementation task is clearly the responsibility of the candidate company, readers must assure the interpretations used in the company's implementation process match those in the text. In those subject areas where more information to assure proper interpretation may be required (that is, quality manual,

internal quality audit, and registration), expanded detailed guidance has been provided.

6. Discussion of ISO 9000 implementation may cause some to assume the process is very complicated and detailed. Although most companies will have no trouble applying this eight-step guide to their activities, small organizations may have difficulty interpreting the requirements to their scale. On that basis, a discussion on using the eight-step implementation process for small companies is provided in Appendix C.

7. There is an interactive software package available as a companion for this book. The book and the software are designed to be entirely capable of independent use, but the software makes an excellent tool for assisting in the application of the eight-step approach. The software provides for company-specific databases on document and data control, shortfall analysis results, project management implementation plan, corrective actions, registrars, training, and audit results.

Step 1: The Decision to Proceed

1.1 Driver for company implementation of ISO 9000

1.1.1 Implementation must be planned

1.1.2 A tentative plan to scope activities and resources

1.1.3 Gaining some background

1.1.4 Why ISO 9000 implementation?

1.1.5 Early EC influence

1.2 Background for tentative implementation plan

1.2.1 ISO 9000 implementation and company strategy

1.2.2 Basic quality-related planning documents

1.2.3 Guidance from senior management

1.2.4 Supplying information to senior management

1.2.5 Enlisting workforce support

1.3 Developing the tentative plan for ISO 9000 implementation

1.3.1 Tentative date for completion of implementation

1.3.2 Developing an approximate cost of implementation

1.3.3 Functional involvement in the tentative plan development

1.3.4 Details of the tentative implementation plan

1.3.5 Typical time frame for implementation

1.4 Management of the ISO implementation process

1.4.1 Plans to have management monitor process

1.4.2 Planned functional and multifunctional activities

1.4.3 Keeping the workforce involved and aware

1.4.4 ISO 9000 management representative

1.4.5 Management representative qualifications

1.5 Barriers to successful ISO implementation

    1.5.1 Insufficient management involvement

    1.5.2 Inadequate resources to perform the task

    1.5.3 Inappropriate assignment of personnel

    1.5.4 Unreasonable plan and/or schedule

    1.5.5 Inadequate acceptance by the workforce

Conclusion

Questions answered in this module

1. How does a company make the decision whether to implement ISO 9000?

2. Why isn't the decision to proceed with implementation a simple yes or no?

3. What are some things that should be examined before the ISO 9000 decision is made?

4. How should information required to make a sound decision be obtained?

5. What are typical drivers for companies considering ISO 9000 implementation?

6. Should a company consider registration or just ISO 9000 implementation?

7. What should be the company's quality objectives and goals for ISO 9000?

8. Why is it necessary to include ISO 9000 implementation in the strategic plan?

9. What type and level of policy documentation is required to get started?

10. Why is there a need for a tentative implementation plan and what should be in it?

11. How is management expected to be involved in the implementation process?

12. What is an ISO 9000 management representative, and on what basis is one selected?

13. What can be done to achieve workforce commitment to ISO 9000 implementation?

14. Are ISO 9000 implementation activities better performed by individuals or teams?

15. What are the typical barriers to successful ISO 9000 implementation?

16. How can a company assure the ISO 9000 implementation process goes well?

Step 1

The Decision to Proceed

Should a company implement the ISO 9000 series? Should management move the company toward compliance with these international quality system standards? At first look, it would appear this decision is simply a matter of yes or no; but such a casual approach will not be the case for the prudent company. This module discusses the many influencing factors that must be considered by the company senior management during the decision process. In this case, the term *process* is appropriately used.

1.1 Driver for company implementation of ISO 9000

The exact impetus for a company's implementation of the ISO quality standards becomes the primary driver for deciding the specific approach the company should take. The reasons for implementation may be quite varied but usually fall into one of two categories: customers may have expressed an anticipated requirement for ISO 9000 compliance by their suppliers, or company management has determined a marketing/cost advantage that can be derived by ISO implementation. Whatever the driver, company management must evaluate the most suitable approach for its ISO 9000 implementation. To do this, leadership must have a reasonably sound idea of the extent of resources that it will have to direct toward the implementation process. Prudent plans and schedules must always be developed in light of the company's ability to identify, commit, and release those resources to the process.

1.1.1 Implementation must be planned

Launching into a vague, unplanned activity is not prudent management. Management commitment to the ISO 9000 implementation process must be based on specific knowledge. Thus, management must

- Review the rationale for implementation
- Examine the resources that are currently anticipated
- Develop a likely implementation schedule
- Determine personnel loading for the achievement of these tentative schedules/actions
- Review the level of senior involvement and management leadership

To lend validity to these actions, management must examine each of the stated actions in some detail. A tentative implementation plan or schedule should also be outlined so that company leadership can base its projected resources/funding requirements, as well as the actual go-ahead decision, on it.

1.1.2 A tentative plan to scope activities and resources

Such an initial plan will be incomplete, since it is based on the company's existing level of understanding of the ISO 9000 implementation process. It will be further compounded by the absence of any precise knowledge of just what the company will actually have to do to comply with the standards. This is also known as the company's *shortfall* to the requirements. Even in the absence of definitive data, some type of initial plan will provide the basis for a reasonably *considered* decision by management. It is not a one-step, point-in-time action. The decision must be made with as much information as possible.

1.1.3 Gaining some background

To facilitate the preliminary planning process, most companies send key personnel to one or more ISO 9000 implementation seminars or classes. The training companies providing the instruction are based in every major business center in the world, and service virtually all other centers.

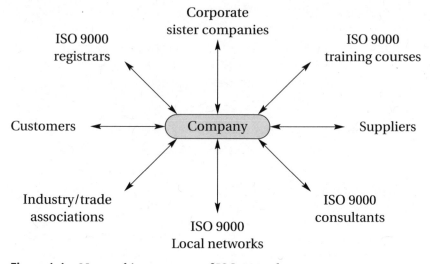

Figure 1.1 Networking sources of ISO 9000 data.

In addition, most companies begin some type of informational networking. This is normally conducted with other companies that are planning or undergoing the ISO 9000 implementation process (Figure 1.1). The information gathered during these networking activities can be used to develop or refine the company's implementation plan. Management must know the plan has enough validity built into it to actually begin the implementation process. For some period of time, the company will be learning as it goes.

Note: The average company can not fully evaluate the extent of its total implementation task until the true variance or shortfall between the specified ISO 9000 requirements and the company's current practices are thoroughly examined. Determining the shortfall is covered in Step 3.

1.1.4 Why ISO 9000 implementation?

Company management cannot overlook its primary duty and obligation as it considers implementing the ISO quality standards. Whatever the reason for deciding on ISO 9000 implementation, management must always be completely assured the end result will benefit the basic operation of the company (Figure 1.2). To achieve such a result, prudent managers must ask

- What objectives and goals must be achieved?
- What real benefits are expected?
- Does ISO 9000 implementation have immediate benefits or is it really a long-term strategy?
- Is the company being driven to ISO compliance unwillingly or is it clearly in its best interest?

Most companies consider implementation for one of the following reasons, each of which acknowledges some type of benefit to the company.

- Pressure from customers
- Marketing pressure, real or perceived
- Directive from corporate or parent company management
- Vehicle for company improvement
- All of the above

Pressure from customers. Many companies are notified by their major existing customers that ISO 9000 implementation is expected in the near term. Frequently this is a condition of doing future business. Some customers, themselves, are under pressure to comply with the ISO 9000 documents and are simply passing the requirement to their suppliers.

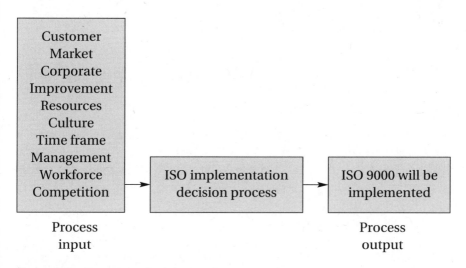

Figure 1.2 Inputs to decision process.

This flow down may reflect either a requirement of an ultimate customer (or market), or simply one stemming from the needs of the company's immediate customer. It should be noted that seldom is any customer interested in paying the cost of supplier ISO 9000 implementation and certainly not the costs associated with the registration process.

Marketing pressure, real or perceived. This reason for ISO 9000 implementation is often the result of a company becoming aware of its competitors moving toward ISO compliance. The interest by competitors may be due to acceptance of the ISO quality standards by an overall industry, a specific business base, a local initiative, or simply because the competitors are attempting to gain a marketing advantage. There are enormous benefits to any company that is able to declare its compliance to quality system standards which have worldwide recognition and acceptance. Such a position will be of tremendous importance in the global marketplace.

Since ISO 9000 implementation is not an overnight action, the prudent company must always try to be ahead, or at least in step with, the competition. On that basis alone, management must consider ISO implementation as a possible company strategy, the timing of which should be keyed to the company's interest in protecting or expanding its market position.

Directive from corporate or parent company management. Proactive corporations always note industry trends. Although perhaps not under immediate pressure from the marketplace, such corporations may decide to gain an advantage by initiating implementation actions ahead of their competition. This is clearly for ultimate marketing gain. If not leading the industry in total, it will at least lead the target niche for the corporation's products or services.

The primary advantage of having a corporate base make the go-ahead decision is, with it comes the authorization to expend the necessary resources for a successful implementation process. Another benefit of the corporate directive is that quite likely one unit of the corporation will be selected to play the lead role in moving through the implementation process (and maybe registration). Such an action provides the rest of the corporate units with an implementation model or "lessons learned" base. It will also provide an assistance reservoir from which to draw. This type of cooperative approach has served a number of corporations in successfully implementing the ISO 9000 series across their entire structure of subordinate units.

Vehicle for company improvement. Prudent companies are always looking for ways to improve their overall operation. Many have determined that ISO 9000 compliance will result in just such a benefit. The structured discipline and process improvement potential offered by a sound, fully implemented ISO 9000 quality system has been repeatedly demonstrated as a suitable means for achieving improvement goals and optimizing systems. This is done by systematically determining the best way to approach each requirement of the ISO 9000 standard. Part of the quality system's recognition is based upon its capability to act as the focal point for operational improvement.

ISO 9000 implementation is not only associated with companies attempting to establish a basic quality system but also with companies that already have a system. It is not unusual for companies with existing quality systems to modify their activities so as to comply with the ISO standards. These actions are usually market driven. Whatever the driver, such a move is often implemented even when the existing operations have appeared to be stable and satisfactory. Thus, ISO quality systems provide for a comprehensive and efficient way to operate the company, while achieving the company's identified quality goals.

A surprisingly large number of companies are not waiting for customer direction but are electing to proactively move toward ISO 9000 compliance. This self-instigated effort allows the company to pace its implementation rate to its available resources. This approach also places the company in a responsive position to any of its customers that might have a future ISO 9000 system requirement.

All of the above. ISO itself does not require registration as a prerequisite or even a follow-on to successful implementation of the ISO 9000 series; however, most companies interested in the implementation process are likely planning to undergo quality system registration as a final step. These companies are fully aware of the marketing benefits derived from having an independent third party registration agency evaluating and acknowledging the company's ISO 9000 compliance. Thus, it is not surprising that the vast majority of companies measure the success of their implementation activities by having satisfactorily completed the requirements of the registration process.

Although quality system registration may be selected as the culmination of the ISO 9000 implementation process, it is *not* the primary benefit. Those companies that have been through the entire process, including registration, have generally stated the primary benefits are derived from the quality system improvements within the company's operations.

Although the reasons for ISO 9000 implementation are varied, it should be emphasized that before starting the process, the company must clearly understand exactly why it is pursuing ISO compliance. This focuses the company's business and quality strategies. It also helps in developing the detailed implementation plan, which is covered in Step 4.

To focus the effort, the company must know precisely what it is trying to achieve with ISO 9000 implementation. For example, customer or marketing pressures require strong guidance from the company's marketing activity, while corporate directives involve close liaison with the parent company. Using ISO implementation as a vehicle for company improvement invokes an internal task force concept. In the final analysis, the company management must assure that the basic reasons for ISO implementation are not lost in the details of the process itself. There is no reason to attempt ISO 9000 implementation in a company environment that does not accept or understand the need for it. Management must create a receptive environment before any implementation has a chance of success. Only management can create such an environment.

1.1.5 Early EC influence

As discussed in the background module, during the late 1980s and early 1990s many companies were influenced to begin implementation activities by the European Community (EC) requirement for ISO 9000 compliance. This requirement stated that an accredited registrar had to validate implementation of an ISO 9000-based quality system for any potential trading partner. The approval was a prerequisite for permitting the company to sell regulated products (health, safety, and environment related) in the EC marketplace. In setting the requirement, the EC became one of the main vehicles for furthering the use of the ISO 9000 quality standards. With the rush to implement the standards, came recognition of the use and benefits of the ISO 9000 system. The EC's influence as a catalyst for the promulgation of the ISO 9000 standards, and therefore the quality system concept, cannot be underestimated.

The original registration requirement has now escaped the EC confines and has become an accepted market-driven activity around the world. The level of acceptance of the ISO quality systems, coupled with the concept of an independent third party verification and registration process (which is paid for by the affected supplier) has caught the attention of customers worldwide (Figure 1.3). It would be an unusual customer, indeed, that did not regard the benefits of registration to be in its best interest. Registration is now being used to assure supplier compliance and control by some major world-class corporations. The registration process is addressed in Step 8.

1.2 Background for tentative implementation plan

Company management must be able to make an informed decision about ISO 9000 implementation. To facilitate this decision, an understanding of the nature and magnitude of the implementation process is needed. Developing some type of basic overall or tentative planning tool, such as a tentative implementation plan can provide this understanding. The tentative implementation plan permits company management to determine what resources will be needed over a set time period. This knowledge will help management balance needs, resources, and schedules. The following activities should be considered as background and guidance for the development of a tentative plan. Remember, prudent management must create the environment and basis in which ISO 9000 implementation can be achieved. If these background requirements do not exist, then management needs to either cease or delay implementation plans, or identify and initiate the actions needed to meet the environmental and background requirements. The latter can be accomplished either prior to starting ISO 9000 implementation or as an early action within the implementation process.

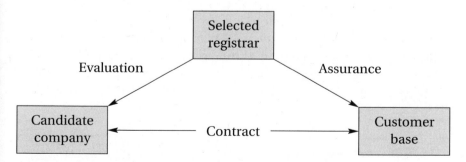

Figure 1.3   Registration is an independent judgment.

1.2.1 ISO 9000 implementation and company strategy

How does ISO 9000 implementation fit into the existing company planning activity? Responsible managers of competitive companies customarily have some form of strategic planning to help guide their decision process as it relates to the establishment and pursuit of goals and objectives. In addition, most successful companies address the quality of their products and/or services, as well as the company's customer satisfaction efforts in its strategic plan. If this is not the case, the candidate company should consider including the ISO implementation process directly in its strategic plan. *Quality strategies must always be company-level strategies.*

The company should have three essential quality-related documents in its strategic plan. If a company does not have these documents, their absence must be regarded as a shortfall to the ISO quality concepts and even some of the stated ISO 9000 requirements. It is mandatory that company management take the necessary actions to remedy the situation. Strategic planning is not a frill, it is an absolute necessity to the success of any company interested in the global marketplace.

1.2.2 Basic quality-related planning documents

The company's strategic vision, developed by senior management, is the basis for all subsequent strategies and objectives. The vision normally states where leadership would like to see the company at some future point. The future status of such things as company market scope and position, profitability, ethics and community acceptance, reputation for product or service quality, skill level of its workforce, and so on are usually examined.

The company vision becomes the basis for all aspects of the company's strategic plans. The vision creates the need for a definition of the company's mission. The strategic and operational plans simply become the incremental means of achieving the vision. Individual quality objectives and goals may also include the development of a quality policy that addresses aspects of the company's quality system (Figure 1.4).

Some companies may even have a separate quality vision to guide its decision process, particularly if the company is attempting to pursue a world-class quality reputation. An example follows:

> *By 1999, the XYZ Company will achieve 100 percent customer satisfaction on all products and services; the company will be recognized as a world quality leader in its field; and the company will have been selected as a finalist for a national quality award.*

Company vision

Company mission

Company strategic plan

Company objectives

Quality policy

Quality-related objectives

Implemented quality system

Figure 1.4   Company quality system genesis.

An overall quality strategy should be part of the company's strategic plan. Although not specifically required by ISO standards, all progressive, customer-oriented companies have established a basic quality strategy, which fits well with the ISO 9000 requirements for company quality objectives. The planning attention given to the quality strategy must be equivalent to the interest given to any of the other strategic goals. Achieving company quality objectives must be part of the overall company strategic planning base. Therefore, pursuit of quality strategy implementation must be regarded as one of the company's basic business improvement processes.

Further, achievement of the company's quality strategy must have senior management assignment, involvement, commitment, and responsibility. The strategy must also include capture plans for implementation, identification of required resources, measurements of success, and so on. If ISO 9000 implementation is planned and acknowledged at the company strategic plan level, it is assured the same senior management involvement and attention as other business strategies. If this is not done, the affected company stakeholders will not regard the intent as being sincere.

Some companies integrate their quality strategies with other business strategies. This approach is quite satisfactory since success in quality performance is often the key to achieving many other objectives. This method leans heavily on the concept that states all activities within the company are actually quality system based.

The quality policy is the company's governing quality system document. Certainly all businesses must have a company quality policy, particularly those implementing ISO 9000 standards. Compliance with the standards typically begins with senior management developing a policy.

This quality policy is a management commitment to meet all company quality requirements and objectives. The policy often addresses customer satisfaction, quality of products and services, improvement in company performance, employee involvement, and so on. This quality policy must always be documented. The ISO 9000 definition of a quality policy, as stated in ISO 8402, acknowledges it must come from top management.

> *Quality policy—The overall intentions and direction of an organization with regard to quality, as formally expressed by top management.*

The quality policy is implemented by both positive management action and the application of the requirements in the company's quality system documentation. The ISO 9000 standards require a company to establish, implement, and maintain a quality policy, which is understood and accepted at all levels of the organization. The documented quality policy is a visible manifestation of management's intent and commitment. All employees must know the policy's content and how their assignment supports its achievement. An example follows:

> *It is the policy of the XYZ Company to achieve total customer satisfaction with all products and services delivered, and to strive to continuously improve overall quality performance by the use of premium quality materials and equipment, by a selected well-trained, skilled, and professional workforce in a work environment that promotes proactive management and employee responsibility and ownership of all company processes.*

1.2.3 Guidance from senior management

ISO 9000 compliance requires senior management to take part in a review of basic company quality operations and to guide the quality system (see Figure 1.5).

If a company has not approached quality in this manner, the failing must be corrected in the very early phases of ISO 9000 compliance efforts. The correction should be made a basic part of the company's detailed ISO implementation plan, which is covered in Step 4.

Having seen where quality fits into company operations, the next aspect is to examine the attitude of senior management on ISO implementation. Since ISO requirements are basically a set of activities that management must assure and/or accomplish, it is often said that the standards are documents that may affect management style. As seen in the discussion on quality vision, strategy, and objectives, ISO standards require senior management to lead and direct the implementation process. This is neither unexpected nor should it be a change in management style. As with all company-based activities, senior management is fully responsible for the company's implementation success.

Depending on how the implementation requirement has been invoked, some company leadership may have had little or no input into the decision, especially if it is from corporate direction or customer initiative. Management may not be fully committed to the need for ISO 9000 compliance imposed in such a manner; however, senior-level commitment is essential to the process. This is true even if the process does

• Develop vision.	• Provide policy.
• Establish objectives.	• Convey commitment.
• Pursue strategy.	• Assure resources.
• Embrace ISO 9000.	• Eliminate barriers.
• Monitor implementation.	• Participate.
• Provide leadership.	• Present information.
• Assure success.	• Select representative.

Figure 1.5   Senior management ISO 9000 involvement.

cause some changes in the way management currently operates or how individual managers deal with their areas of responsibility. Successful companies always have the commitment and involvement of the senior management as the basis for successful ISO 9000 compliance.

If there is uncertainty about the degree of senior-level commitment, either as a group or as individuals, some early efforts to gain full enlistment are mandatory. Initial senior management attitudes on ISO 9000 implementation may range from negativism and apathy to participation and involvement. In some cases, senior management actually becomes the focus for accomplishing day-to-day implementation activities. While specific backgrounds and personalities will govern the nature of how individual members may react to any situation, for successful ISO implementation the overall management must rate in categories 5–8 on a scale of interest (see Figure 1.6). If such is not the case, and steps to overcome the situation are not successful, then meaningful implementation is unlikely and the company should seriously consider placing ISO 9000 implementation in abeyance.

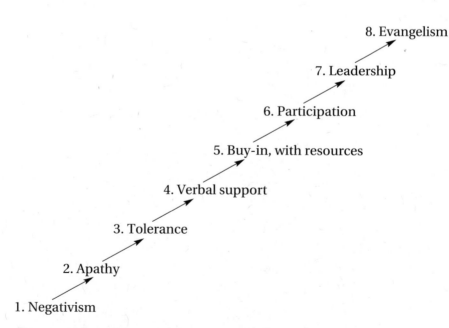

Figure 1.6 Possible management positions on ISO 9000 implementation—eight-point scale of interest.

1.2.4 Supplying information to senior management

Most negative attitudes are due to either a lack of input into the implementation decision process or an absence of information about ISO 9000 implementation and its benefits to the company. In such a situation, the rationale for implementation may still need to be presented and sold to management. The following activities are possible approaches to achieving senior management commitment.

- Basic ISO 9000 informational presentations
- Group discussions with the marketing analysis staff
- Presentations on the benefits from successful ISO-based companies
- Analysis of expected changes
- Benefits to the company, management, and workforce
- Possible use of consultants as a sounding board for answering management questions

Management *will* recognize potential business-based advantages once it hears and understands them.

In almost all companies, some senior managers will be perceptive enough to easily recognize the need for ISO 9000 implementation and the gains associated with its benefits. These people can act as magnets for such a positive position. They essentially become champions for focusing the company's implementation efforts. Many successful companies have used this peer concept.

Within the company there are likely other situations and resources that can be used to gain and assure necessary management acceptance. Some companies have simply utilized executive management-level directives, peer pressure by enlightened members of management, or ISO-based management focus groups. Several progressive companies have even translated both the expected ISO 9000-related marketing gains and/or the absence of being an ISO-based competitor into the effect each position will have on senior management financial packages. The company must use whatever resources are available to gain management's full acceptance. Failure to do so will result in an extremely costly or failed implementation process.

1.2.5 Enlisting workforce support

Successful ISO 9000 implementation is also heavily dependent on the workforce itself. Just as management must see the benefits of ISO standards and be committed to ISO 9000 implementation, so must the workforce. Whereas management creates the company requirements and resources for ISO implementation, the workforce is the ultimate agent for assuring the specific tasks, processes, and requirements are actually achieved. The workers accomplish this by adhering to the requirements, as they have been interpreted and documented in the governing company procedures.

The normal company workforce is frequently skeptical of quality improvement activities, because, in the past, such activities may have frequently been do-better programs. The focus of previous improvement efforts may often have been on the workforce. Such programs normally assume the workforce is the sole source of quality and performance problems. The assumption may have been: If the employees would simply work harder and with more attention to requirements, all of the major company problems would disappear. It is now generally accepted that the majority of company quality and performance problems stem from poor systems, poor designs, poor training, poor equipment, and/or poor management. Very few problems are associated with employee performance.

Virtually all employees want to perform well. They want to know their contributions are meaningful. They would like to believe the company recognizes their performance and is willing to listen to their suggestions. They want to know what they can do to benefit the company and how those gains are going to ultimately benefit them. If the workforce reacts negatively or apathetically to the idea of ISO 9000 implementation, it is probably related to the failure of past quality improvement efforts. The workers might believe ISO 9000 may well be just one more pending failure coming down from an insincere management.

The solution to almost all workforce apathy is clear and straightforward information from management on the following:

- What the ISO 9000 standards really are.
- Their implementation is a new way of operating the company.
- ISO 9000 implementation is unique in that it has direct marketing benefits.

- ISO 9000 has demonstrated that it increases company competitiveness and market share.
- ISO 9000 increases job security of all concerned.

Furthermore, the ISO 9000 implementation process will actually get the workforce involved in the necessary preparatory activities (see Figure 1.7). Even the ISO 9000 quality system standards assume and expect the workforce to be both supportive and contributory to company policies, operational and performance requirements, training requirements, and so on.

To assure employee acceptance and support for ISO 9000 implementation, management must share the rationale for implementation with the workforce. Employees will be receptive, but, because of past experience, may carefully observe the demonstrated level of management commitment and involvement before they fully commit. Keeping workers aware of progress or directly involving them in implementation activities will facilitate the necessary changes. Success will be ensured by the very people who will actually operate the ISO 9000-based quality system.

Simply stated, if the company does not fully deploy the quality policy, the basic quality strategy, and the rationale for implementing ISO to all levels of the workforce, ownership will not be achieved and an outstanding

---

- Having basic information on the background of the ISO 9000 movement
- Understanding why the company is implementing ISO 9000
- Knowing how company improvement activities affect competitive position
- Understanding that employee involvement is crucial to implementation success
- Knowing the nature of the employee's role in the ISO 9000 implementation process
- Knowing a process exists to keep employees current on the company's overall implementation status
- Having assurance that workforce will be directly involved in registration activities

Figure 1.7   General workforce awareness factors.

Workforce ownership comes from

- Understanding need
- Benefit awareness
- Process participation
- Management liaison
- Appropriate training
- Management recognition

- Sharing strategy
- Valid information
- Policy deployment
- Assurance that contributions are accepted
- Gain sharing
- Status reporting

Figure 1.8 ISO 9000 workforce ownership.

source of support for the process will be lost (see Figure 1.8). As a result, success will be unlikely.

1.3 Developing the tentative plan for ISO 9000 implementation

Having determined the following, it is now appropriate to discuss the tentative plan for the ISO 9000 implementation process.

1. The company's reasons and goals for implementation

2. An understanding of how the quality objectives and ISO standards fit within the company's quality policy and strategy

3. Commitment from both management and the workforce

1.3.1 Tentative date for completion of implementation

Individuals assigned to the process owe senior management their best assessment of a tentative schedule for ISO 9000 implementation. This estimate must be based on the most effective use of anticipated labor resources. If a customer has placed the company on notice for ISO 9000 implementation, the plan may already have a required completion date and an established time frame. If the company has no such limitation, a reasonable schedule should be developed and forwarded to management for approval.

Note: A short customer-directed compliance date can usually be modified with a reasonable, company-developed implementation plan. It should be given to the customer along with management's commitment for accomplishment.

1.3.2 Developing an approximate cost of implementation

The cost of ISO 9000 implementation can be estimated by coupling the labor requirements with any other required resources. In addition to a proposed plan, some alternative schedules will need to be developed for consideration and comparison by management.

Since this tentative plan is only a well-considered estimate, management will need to be provided with some degree of possible time and cost error. Although the decision to proceed or not is clearly the responsibility of management, employees responsible for developing the data upon which the decision will be based must provide as much appropriate information as possible.

If not already accomplished, the plan at this level should address resolution of any problems identified in the ISO 9000 review (for example, the absence of any available resources or no company quality policy). The plan should be multifunctional since every part of the overall company quality system will likely require some attention. The scope of this review will involve all functions—from the start of marketing activity through to achievement of customer satisfaction.

1.3.3 Functional involvement in the tentative plan development

Senior management has the initial responsibility for ISO 9000 activity in each area of its functional assignment. Managers must select and designate the appropriate people to implement the ISO 9000 quality system. By choosing suitable people for the task, both in expertise and number, management assures a thorough review and analysis of all the selected ISO requirements. These are then used to evaluate what the company is doing in each of the system element categories. As noted, this process is termed *shortfall analysis.*

1.3.4 Details of the tentative implementation plan

Once a proposed schedule has been determined, then the contents of the tentative plan must be developed. The company will have to attempt to project all of the expected activities that it needs to perform, up to and including a compliance audit. This will result in an outline of what the company will eventually have to do during actual implementation. Aiding in this forecast is the fact that all ISO 9000 candidate companies must accomplish certain major implementation tasks. These tasks can be used to prepare an outline of the tentative plan for management to use to evaluate actions, schedules, and costs for the decision process. It will, however, be the only operational plan available until the company can perform the shortfall analysis in Step 3. The output of the shortfall analysis is needed before the final detailed plan can be developed.

The basic eight step process of ISO 9000 implementation, which is the core of this text, provides a general outline of those tasks (Figure 1.9). The steps are explained as follows:

Step 1 develops data, methods, and background to consider and provide to company management, who decides on ISO 9000 implementation. A major factor in this decision process is the availability of a tentative implementation plan.

Step 2 permits the company to determine the selection and application of an ISO directive standard, and to evaluate the company's position on the extent of its current quality system and its documentation. Step 2 also explains how to organize and train teams and individuals for multifunctional shortfall analysis.

Step 3 addresses the performance of the shortfall analysis as the company interprets ISO 9000 requirements. This step permits the evaluation of company compliance variances and proposed remedial actions, then deals with the organization of the results for the final plan.

Step 4 covers all of the project management activities associated with the development, organization, and scheduling of the detailed implementation plan, including all the factors that will make the plan succeed.

Step 5 examines ISO 9000 documentation activities, including its structure, purpose, usefulness, and how to assure user ownership. The

1. Decision to proceed
   a. Overall plan/quality strategy
   b. Management commitment/resources
   c. Leader/team selection
2. Current position assessment
   a. Collect documentation
   b. Analyze selected standard
   c. Make team assignments
3. Shortfalls determination
   a. Assess procedural adequacy
   b. Identify gaps/omissions
   c. Scope task/resources
4. Implementation plan
   a. Tasks/assignments
   b. Schedule actions
   c. Work discipline
5. Documentation process
   a. Documentation structure
   b. Document control
   c. Writing/review process
6. Implementation activity
   a. Involve users
   b. Conduct awareness training
   c. Assure useability
7. Compliance audit
   a. Document versus performance
   b. Internal quality/self-audits
   c. Preparation for registrar
8. Customer/registrar audit
   a. Company assures quality system
   b. Corrective action closed beforehand
   c. Compliance demonstrated

Figure 1.9   Eight-step procedure to ISO compliance.

factors that contribute to developing satisfactory documentation are identified.

Step 6 addresses the completion of all ISO 9000-related awareness, orientation, and training activities. It also examines how to achieve the new responsibilities and roles expected of both management and the workforce.

Step 7 involves the development, implementation, and documentation of the company compliance verification activities. This involves management and user efforts, as well as creating and operating a formal, internal quality auditing program.

Step 8 provides the method for selecting a registrar, how to deal with the on-site registration audit process, handling actual on-site audit activities, and successfully responding to findings for audit closure and ISO 9000 compliance acceptance.

Steps 2 and 3 usually involve many employees, since all functions and all areas have to be thoroughly reviewed. Frequently, it takes a team from each function to perform the task in a timely manner. Some areas or subjects will even require multifunctional involvement to gather the information and perform the shortfall analysis. It is advantageous to perform Steps 2 and 3 as quickly as possible, so that management is fully aware of the task ahead or in case a reexamination of the tentative plan or the company's commitments to customers is necessary.

The development of the detailed or final implementation plan in Step 4 requires relatively few people to achieve. The plan creation, however, is frequently incremental and ongoing, as shortfall data become available. Sometimes plan development begins to blend with managing the implementation of early inputs.

Most of the actual implementation efforts in Steps 5 and 6 will be the responsibility of functional management. Scheduling the workforce for support of the implementation process may not be difficult. Although many employees will be working on remedial actions throughout the company, the assignments may well be intermittent for a given individual. As such, even with the broad-based activity anticipated, the number of equivalent people for Steps 5 and 6 is usually half the number required for Steps 2 and 3.

The tasks in Step 7, verification and validation, are performed by both functional and multifunctional organizations. The user-based activity is normally accomplished in conjunction with the employees' basic responsibilities, so the number of full-time equivalent people involved is relatively small. Area management can coordinate this type of review; however, required formal internal quality audit activity will likely be intensive until all problems are identified and resolved. As the company begins to achieve the full compliance necessary for Step 8, the few remaining, dedicated implementation personnel are usually associated with facilitating the outside independent compliance audit.

In a relative sense only, but to give a general idea of the number of dedicated personnel for each step, the following can be applied to any size company. Assuming every step is scheduled for the same length of time and using an arbitrary basis of 100 dedicated people for Steps 2 and

3, then Steps 5 and 6 would require 40–50 dedicated people, Step 7 would require 15–20 dedicated employees, and Steps 1, 4, and 8 would require 5–10 dedicated people. This scale should be applied to a company for planning purposes only and the relative number of people is set by the actual number determined by the given company for Steps 2 and 3. This exercise is only for people actually dedicated to the implementation tasks. It does not include those employees involved by way of performing their normal assignments.

Note: In a small company, Steps 2 and 3 may require only 5 or 10 people.

1.3.5 Typical time frame for implementation

To schedule every aspect of the tentative implementation plan, each company will have to estimate time for both the total process and each individual task. This is a fairly wide range (Figure 1.10). The variation is related to the size of the company, is based on the resources committed and on the degree of acceptable documentation within the existing quality system. Personnel and resources from each involved function can be estimated only with this schedule information. Combining these estimates with the anticipated tasks completes the tentative implementation plan. Companies that already comply in full or in part to an existing recognized quality system specification can considerably shorten the anticipated time for implementation.

1.4 Management of the ISO implementation process

As with any activity that has companywide implications, the company's senior management is solely responsible for making the decision as to whether the company should implement the ISO 9000 series. Most successful companies approach this decision much as they would any other company-level project or program, such as bringing a new product online or bringing an acquisition into the company structure. They gather all the available data pertaining to the pros and cons of the activity, evaluate them, and render the decision. Once made, the company will assure the ISO 9000 implementation becomes a well-planned activity—approved

Organize and address issues.	3–4 weeks
Complete awareness training, as required.	2–3 weeks
Assign teams to tasks.	1–2 weeks
Perform shortfall analysis.	4–8 weeks
Determine corrective actions.	4–6 weeks
Plan, scope, and schedule actions.	2–4 weeks
Implement actions.	6–8 weeks
Review implementation.	3–4 weeks
Audit compliance.	3–4 weeks
Prepare for registrar.	3–4 weeks
Registration audit performed.	1 week
Complete follow-up actions.	3–4 weeks
Registration is complete.	2–4 weeks
Total	36–56 weeks

Note: It is only after the shortfall is fully determined and the nature/scope of remedial actions have been established and planned that the company's full and final implementation plan can be developed. (The final implementation plan is covered in Step 4.)

Figure 1.10 Typical time frame for implementation tasks.

and guided by responsible management until it is fully implemented and compliance is validated. Once such a point is reached, ISO 9000 will become a significant factor in the company's way of doing business.

1.4.1 Plans to have management monitor process

To assure ISO 9000 implementation is handled as smoothly and efficiently as possible, senior management must approach the implementation activities as a process (Figure 1.11). Management is responsible for

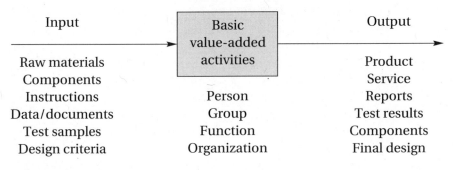

Figure 1.11 Nature of a process.

establishing a way to monitor all of the process input steps and all the value-added activities of each subprocess. If monitoring is accomplished in such a manner, the process output will be successful implementation of the selected ISO 9000 quality system standard.

Some companies develop an oversight activity to specifically concentrate on ISO 9000 implementation. Such teams have been called quality councils, senior ISO 9000 guidance teams, and so on. It is mandatory such groups be formed from within the existing management structure, not unlike special senior-level groups formed for other major projects. As an alternate to a special group for monitoring implementation, it can be handled entirely within the normal management structure and operations. At no time, however, should this basic oversight assignment be delegated to personnel outside the management level. If ISO implementation is important to the company, it should be addressed by senior management as a part of doing business.

1.4.2 Planned functional and multifunctional activities

It is axiomatic that each functional head must be responsible for his or her portion of the ISO 9000 implementation process. As with other business activities, individuals may be assigned to assist management in the process. The most apparent activity for support staff and/or functional teams is shortfall analysis. The identification, implementation, and verification of remedial actions all have heavy functional involvement. By charter, each functional head must assure all implementation tasks are achieved as planned and scheduled. Experience shows only the people within the individual functions are knowledgeable enough of what takes place to successfully perform these internal tasks.

The ISO quality standards are comprised of system elements that are either related to individual company functions or to the overall quality system. The former are termed *functional* elements, while the latter are *structural* elements. Where assignments address those structural quality system elements that bridge multiple functions, or even the specific interfaces between functions, the ISO 9000 implementation teams must also be multifunctional. As such, the teams will be capable of working all facets of the interacting quality processes. An example of such a multi-functional subject might be the company's approach to the requirement for internal quality audit. By ISO definition, audit clearly affects all functions even though the activity may be assigned to a given functional organization. The same is true for corrective and preventive actions, quality data/records, and similar activities.

1.4.3 Keeping the workforce involved and aware

Since senior and functional managers will be actively involved in the ISO implementation process, they will also determine and assure the appropriate level of employee awareness, training, and participation in the process. Employee buy-in is primarily achieved by workforce knowledge of ISO 9000 benefits. Workforce buy-in is also accomplished through employee participation in the company's implementation process. With enough involvement, employees will develop ownership of implementation actions. Employee ownership of the process is essential to the success of ISO 9000 implementation.

1.4.4 The ISO 9000 management representative

Detailed coordination of the overall implementation process usually requires full-time participation of one senior manager. As such, the affected individual may be specially assigned to the task of acting as the management focal point.

The ISO standards acknowledge that the implementation process may require a management assignee. In fact, a designated ISO 9000 coordinator is often of great benefit in assuring that the detailed daily implementation activity has a singular focal point. ISO's term for this required assignee with ISO 9000 responsibility and authority is *management representative*. This person must be assigned by senior management, from within its own ranks, and he or she usually reports directly to the company leadership on all matters relating to ISO 9000 implementation (see Figure 1.12).

The management representative needs to have ready access to senior management and the respect of all functional management. Although the role is primarily one of coordination, it is also one of project implementation leadership, and it helps if the individual has previously performed such tasks. The management representative is not ordinarily responsible for the functional employees involved in the process, but rather works through the functional heads to assure the required levels of performance. Of course, the management representative solves and/or eliminates as many implementation problems as possible but must be capable of obtaining other resources if implementation is in jeopardy. The management representative must be able to identify barriers in time to address them with little program impact. Such timely action requires the support of employees assigned from the functional organizations. Those employees must have confidence in and respect for the assigned management representative.

1.4.5 Management representative qualifications

The management representative plays a very significant role in the successful ISO 9000 implementation process. Some small companies name

Candidates should
- Be a senior-level person
- Be recognized by management and the workforce
- Have successful project management experience
- Have full knowledge of company operations
- Have a working rapport with functional management
- Have a basic understanding of quality system concepts

Figure 1.12 Selecting the management representative.

the senior company manager as the management representative, which is completely acceptable; however, the tendency toward delegation to lesser levels in this situation is not the intention of the ISO 9000 requirement.

Companies frequently assign the management representative task to the senior quality assurance manager. While some quality leaders can perform the task of program management, their training and experience is frequently not keyed to such a schedule-driven activity. Experience has also demonstrated this assignment tends to misrepresent the basic ISO 9000 concept of total company involvement. That is, such an assignment may mistakenly lead employees to conclude ISO 9000 is a quality assurance program rather than a company-level quality system application. Even further, the company's ISO 9000-based quality system may be construed to be the responsibility of the head of the quality assurance function and not the company chief executive and his or her staff.

1.5 Barriers to successful ISO implementation

The barriers to successful ISO 9000 implementation are usually the result of an inadequate company management commitment to the process. Management's approach to resource provisioning may also be related to an inadequate level of commitment to the quality system concept itself. Since the balance of the company takes its lead from the attitudes and responses of management, a sound enlightened management must always take appropriate steps to eliminate barriers rather than exhibiting the very actions that create the problems. Five categories are listed as the most likely barriers to successful ISO 9000 implementation (see Figure 1.13).

1.5.1 Insufficient management involvement

Casual delegation or apparent total abdication of implementation responsibilities by senior management is usually caused by a lack of appreciation for the ISO 9000 standards' benefits to the company. Absence of management involvement may also be the result of the company's leadership not taking the necessary time to examine the ISO quality standard in sufficient detail, and to realize it is *not* just another quality assurance program. Management may also resent the implication of having to

- Insufficient management involvement in the process
- Inadequate resources provided to perform the task
- Inappropriate assignment of low-level personnel
- Working to an unknown or unreasonable implementation plan
- Inadequate acceptance of the need for ISO 9000 by the workforce

Figure 1.13 Barriers to ISO 9000 implementation.

change its approach and style as part of the implementation activity. Management may not have recognized and accepted the fact that the ISO quality system requirement affects the whole company. In short, company management becomes a poor example instead of the leadership it needs to be.

The solution to this problem lies in the presentation of information on why the company and its management will benefit from ISO 9000 implementation. These data should be coupled with peer and executive pressure from those senior managers who are firmly committed and involved in implementation. Making successful ISO implementation a significant factor in the executive compensation package seems to gain a huge swing in personal commitment to the process. Seldom, however, does the company have to use punitive measures to get the interest level up, once the affected managers have all of the necessary data and understand the overall benefits.

1.5.2 Inadequate resources to perform the task

This barrier is not as obvious as the previous one, but exists when management appears to recognize the need for ISO 9000 implementation and even directs it be done, but does not provide the necessary resources for the task. This apathy may be negatively reflected in the assignment of adequate personnel, necessary budget allocations for the task, or provisioning of appropriate support and administrative resources. If ISO 9000 implementation is truly part of the company's quality strategy, it deserves the normal level of management attention and commitment that is characteristic of such a company-level activity. To do less risks implementation success and tells employees that, regardless of what is stated, management gives ISO 9000 implementation a low priority. If competing priorities seem to always outrank the ISO 9000 efforts, then implementation will become an "oh-by-the-way" program (or "Do this if you have some spare time.").

The solution to this barrier is positive and timely action on the part of the management representative to draw attention to the commitment issue and gain an early resolution. The proper selection of a well-respected individual as the management representative dramatically facilitates the resolution of such issues.

1.5.3 Inappropriate assignment of personnel

This problem is also a poorly disguised, yet subtle, way of functional management demonstrating to the workforce that ISO 9000 implementation is not really very important. The assignment of personnel with minimal experience or acknowledged low ability is catastrophic for a program. Worse yet may be the assignment of individuals with a currently ill-defined job, a job in jeopardy of elimination, or people in obvious need of something to do. The ISO 9000 implementation assignment should involve some of the very best personnel within each functional unit—people who have the reputation of being able to get the job done. The company must assure one or two uncommitted functional managers do not scuttle such an important program by their assignees being a problem for the many others trying to do a good job.

The management representative must identify such situations early in the process and quickly remedy them. Resolution is usually achieved by direct contact with the cognizant functional manager or the balance of the senior staff. The other managers will not be receptive to having their assigned functional personnel coping with such problems and, as such, problem resolution will be expedited.

1.5.4 Unreasonable plan and/or schedule

Attempting to implement a plan that does not appear capable of achieving the ISO 9000 quality system goals is readily apparent to all the dedicated employees involved. A situation of that type is counterproductive and doomed to failure. It is a simple fact: Management must assign personnel and resources appropriate to the approved implementation plan and schedule. The plan and the resources must match. There should be no absence or excess of necessary resources. Adherence to the plan becomes the means of measuring implementation progress. Without such a measure, few aspects of the activity would be able to operate in schedule harmony with others. Soon local ad hoc plans and schedule work-arounds would appear to slow the overall activity.

It is a basic tenet that people want to know where they are supposed to be going and what they must achieve in the process. In that regard, the problems associated with an unreasonable schedule are obvious. The frustration of working to a schedule, which is obviously impossible to achieve, breeds early frustration and eventual failure. Giving one's best effort will accomplish less in an impossible situation than in one where the schedule is very tight, but possible. Management must be aggressive with schedules, frugal with resources, but nonetheless reasonable.

Periodic management reviews of the implementation process, which are not only required by ISO 9000 but also by prudent management discipline, should reveal any unreasonable scheduling problems. The management representative will likely bring these to the attention of senior staff long before they severely impact implementation activities. In some cases, management may have to extend the schedule rather than add resources. If such is the case, extension will be a consensus decision.

1.5.5 Inadequate acceptance by the workforce

The workforce may appear to have little or no faith in ISO 9000 implementation activities. This attitude conveys apathy and predicts failure. It appears the workforce expects the whole ISO 9000 activity will go away, if it waits long enough. While at first this may appear to be a responsibility of others and not of management, workforce appreciation of the ISO 9000 standards only comes through management action and/or information transfer. Even though workforce acceptance attitudes are customarily slow to develop in the face of change, negative attitudes are usually traced to fear of what is in store. Although cautious in commitment, employees want the company to succeed because it is clearly to their benefit.

For resolution of this barrier, a proper change management approach must be pursued. Management must acknowledge the previous company and workforce performance was great for the environment of the time. The new environment of worldwide competition and global ISO 9000 quality system baselines, however, calls for the current, very capable company workforce to adapt and successfully embrace new challenges. Workforce awareness of ISO 9000 quality system benefits, challenges, and objectives, coupled with company employee involvement in the process, will put a tremendous amount of additional brainpower on the task. Thus, workforce ownership and acceptance of the changing process will be achieved.

Conclusion

It is important to clearly understand why a company is considering ISO 9000 compliance. Many driving forces exert an influence on this decision. The company must decide if ISO 9000 implementation is important enough to expend resources for proper pursuit of full compliance. The nature of the company's ISO 9000 implementation plan will be based on its primary driving forces for compliance. ISO 9000 implementation must be part of the company's strategic planning activity. As such, a quality policy must be developed and issued by senior management. When coupled with the selected ISO quality standard, the quality policy becomes the basis for the company's quality system. To be successful, management must be committed to the benefits and process of ISO 9000 implementation. If it is important, it should be addressed by senior management as a normal part of doing business.

Deciding to implement the ISO 9000 quality system standards should not be done without management's consideration of the total implementation task. This must be accomplished in accordance with a tentative plan. This text defines an eight-step implementation process for use as a guide in developing the tentative plan, which must reflect company needs and resources. The plan will become the company's primary implementation guide until detailed planning is developed.

Management must share rationale for ISO 9000 implementation with the workforce, since it plays a key role in the implementation success. Employee participation is expected by ISO quality standards. With enough involvement, employees will arrive at a point of ownership in the implementation process and the resultant quality system.

The ISO management representative is assigned to act in support of senior management. He or she does not assume responsibility for functional employees but acts as a coordinator for their implementation activities. This person needs to have ready access to senior management, as well as the respect of all functional management. The representative must remove any barriers to the implementation process, even those from a less-than-committed management. Since the company takes its lead from the attitudes and responses of its managers, they must act to remove barriers, not create them.

Implementation actions required by this module

1. Identify the drivers for ISO implementation that affect the company.
2. Establish what objectives/benefits have been set for ISO 9000, when implemented.
3. Implement an initial training plan to gain some basic ISO 9000 background.
4. Join an ISO 9000 networking activity within the community or on-line.
5. Determine how the ISO 9000 implementation fits into the company's strategic plan.
6. Determine senior management ISO 9000 interest, and develop a plan to resolve negatives.
7. Decide the best ISO 9000 implementation approach and sequence for the company.
8. Develop a list of input variables to be considered in the decision process.
9. Develop a tentative implementation plan, time frame, and schedule.
10. Using the tentative plan, determine the required resources and schedule.
11. Make the decision to utilize ISO implementation as a means of performance improvement.

12. Decide whether to pursue registration, as well as ISO 9000 implementation.

13. Identify or develop the company quality policy and objectives.

14. Determine senior management assignments for implementation responsibilities.

15. Select an individual to be the company's ISO 9000 management representative.

16. Determine how the company will deploy the quality policy to all levels.

17. Establish a method of providing senior management oversight of the implementation process.

18. Establish and identify functional and multifunctional implementation teams.

19. Decide on a method for introducing the ISO 9000 plan to the entire workforce.

20. Develop a plan for the involvement of the workforce in the implementation process.

21. Decide how the implementation status will be communicated to the workforce.

22. Identify any anticipated company-specific barriers to ISO 9000 implementation.

23. Decide how the company will measure ISO 9000 implementation progress.

24. Develop a plan for assuring there is smooth management during the change to the ISO quality system.

Step 2: Assessing Current Company Position

2.1 Preliminary implementation steps

2.1.1 Guidance on selecting ISO 9000 directive standard

2.1.2 Selecting the appropriate ISO standard for the company

2.1.3 Design/development plays a major role

2.1.4 ISO 9001 is the most comprehensive standard

2.1.5 Tailoring the selected ISO 9000 directive standard

2.2 Deciding on the scope of ISO 9000 implementation

2.2.1 Avoiding the problem of multiple quality systems

2.2.2 Variation in scope must have rationale

2.2.3 Use of facility layouts to define exact scope

2.2.4 Scope influences how much the registrar charges

2.2.5 Scope selection is no defense for noncompliance

2.3 What is a valid ISO 9000-based quality system?

2.3.1 Quality system, not quality assurance system

2.3.2 Every system must have a focal point

2.3.3 Some existing systems are close to ISO 9000

2.3.4 Variations in degree of quality system compliance

2.3.5 Identification of all quality system variation

2.4 Extent of existing quality system documentation

2.4.1 Entrepreneurial approach is not repetitive

2.4.2 Degree of existing documentation available

2.4.3 Some documentation is almost always present

      2.4.4 Quality system procedures address system elements

      2.4.5 Work instructions are used to perform tasks

2.5 Organizing/training for shortfall analysis

      2.5.1 Use of functional teams during shortfall analysis

      2.5.2 Multifunctional teams will aid shortfall analysis

      2.5.3 Organizational interfaces must not be overlooked

      2.5.4 Plans for addressing all possible shortfalls

      2.5.5 Dealing with little or no documentation

Conclusion

Questions answered in this module

1. What is shortfall or gap analysis, and why must it always be a formal approach?

2. What is the difference between ISO 9000 directive and the guideline standards?

3. What is the difference between ISO 9000, ISO 9000 series, and ISO 9000 family?

4. How should a company select the appropriate ISO 9000 directive standard?

5. Why is possible design/development activity important to the selection process?

6. What if the most suitable standard covers aspects that the company does not perform?

7. What is the process of tailoring the application of the directive standard?

8. The ISO 9000 directives permit tailoring, but how does one decide to do it?

9. What is there to prevent simply tailoring out all company problem areas?

10. What is a generic standard, and how can it fit all business organizations?

11. How does a company document the scope of implementation of its directive standard?

12. What is registration, and when should contact with a registrar begin?

13. What are the likely charges for registration, and are they fixed or negotiable?

14. How is an ISO 9000-based quality system different from a company's current system?

15. Why do informal quality systems often result in uncontrolled nonrepetitive processes?

16. Why must ISO 9000 quality systems involve all functions, even if not product oriented?

17. Why must all quality systems have a standard upon which to measure success?

18. If a company currently has a successful quality system, does it need to start over with ISO?

19. What is the best way to select personnel and prepare for shortfall analysis?

20. How does a company decide how much of its current quality system can be used to satisfy ISO requirements?

21. What is quality system documentation as opposed to nonsystem documentation?

22. Can existing quality system documents be used to satisfy ISO 9000 requirements?

23. Why should all shortfall analysis teams have all existing documentation?

24. How is partial compliance with ISO 9000 requirements handled?

25. What should be done if there is no documentation but the task seems to be performed?

Step 2

Assessing Current Company Position

Once a company decides to implement an ISO 9000-based quality system, some preparatory actions must be taken. These activities must be considered as the company organizes itself for determining the extent of variance between the ISO 9000 standards and the company's performance. Entering into the variance or shortfall analysis without addressing these activities may well result in having to perform the task several times before it is completed. This module addresses the identification and processing of the preparatory actions necessary for Step 3, the shortfall analysis.

2.1 Preliminary implementation steps

The company must approach these preliminary steps in an organized and thorough manner. Adequate preparation will assure the company that all aspects of the shortfall analysis are consistently addressed. Only under such conditions can the shortfall results be weighed equally in the development of any necessary remedial actions. A casual approach to the consistency and organization of this task will result in a clouded and incomplete shortfall analysis, which will affect the usefulness of the remedial actions. Incomplete actions will be inadequate for developing the company's detailed ISO 9000 implementation plan.

The sequence of performing the preparatory activities is not as critical as assuring that all are addressed. The primary goal in this phase is to conduct the activities with a single, structured approach. The process must be performed in the same manner by all participants.

The first preliminary activity must be the review and selection of the ISO quality system standard that the company will implement. The standard will also be the basis for the comparison between its requirements and the company's actual compliance during shortfall analysis.

2.1.1 Guidance on selecting ISO 9000 directive standard

In the background module, the five ISO quality system standards that comprise the ISO 9000 series were briefly reviewed. It was noted that three of the standards were directive or contractual. One of the three will have to be selected by the company as the basis of its planned ISO 9000-based quality system. The other two standards in the series are guideline documents.

One of these, ISO 9000-1, *Quality management and quality assurance standards—Guidelines for selection and use* was specifically developed to assist in the selection of the proper directive standard and to provide guidelines for its interpretation and use. For background in the decision process, the 9000-1 document also explores various quality principles, quality concepts, bases of ISO quality systems, role of documentation, nature of processes, and so on.

ISO 9000-1 presents a decision method to help determine the most appropriate directive standard for each company. The ISO 9000-1 standard has specifically identified and stated the scope of each of the three directive standards. The entire scope is stated in the title. The scope of each standard is exclusive. On that basis, the examination of the scope/title of the directive standards should be regarded as the best indicator of what the final selection should be.

The other guideline document is ISO 9004-1, *Quality management and quality system elements—Guidelines.* Although it is not specifically designed to aid the company in its selection of an ISO 9000 directive standard, it does provide information as to the interpretation of the terminology used in the statement of scope. Further, it provides guidance for establishing and operating a quality management system that will be suitable for creating the system environment in which ISO compliance can be achieved. This document has become one of the best means of determining and evaluating whether the company has the capability to implement ISO standards. Although 9004-1 is a best practices guideline for a quality management system, it is a clear avenue to successful ISO

9000 implementation and registration (see Figure 2.1). It is regarded as the most useful ISO 9000 document for interpreting basic quality system requirements.

2.1.2 Selecting the appropriate ISO standard for the company

A company must select one of the three directive or contractual standards as its focus for its ISO 9000 quality system. Within the selected standard will be the requirements that the company must satisfy for successful ISO 9000 implementation and compliance. Selection of either ISO 9001, ISO 9002, or ISO 9003 will depend on the nature of the operations for each candidate company, enterprise, or entity.

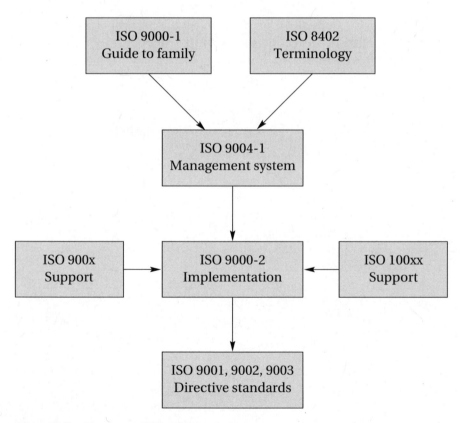

Figure 2.1   Focus on ISO 9004-1.

The titles of the 1994 directive standards are as follows:

- ISO 9001:1994, *Quality systems—Model for quality assurance in design, development, production, installation and servicing*
- ISO 9002:1994, *Quality systems—Model for quality assurance in production, installation, and servicing*
- ISO 9003:1994, *Quality systems—Model for quality assurance in final inspection and test*

As indicated in section 2.1.1, the simplest selection process discriminator is whether the scope/title of one of the standards covers all of the company's basic activities. For instance, if the company provides design or development activity as all or part of its product or service business base, it has only one choice. Within the three possible ISO 9000 quality system directive standards, only ISO 9001 provides the requirements for design and development activities. If the company is one that has no design or development activities, but has production, installation, or services in its charter then ISO 9002 is the most appropriate standard. Finally, if the company does no value-added work to a supplied product or service, other than final inspection and test activity, then ISO 9003 is likely the most suitable quality system standard.

2.1.3 Design/development plays a major role in decision

The process of design and development plays a significant role in the selection decision. Without careful scrutiny, the company may make an inappropriate choice. For example, design and/or development activities may apply to both products and services, as well as to hardware and software. In fact, the actual ISO 9000 product categories that may have design and development activities include hardware, software, processed materials, and services (see Figure 2.2). Thus, companies designing or developing product blueprints, service-based programs, project or process engineering, software design, and test methods and programs, as well as classical product design and development, would all need to implement ISO 9001. Companies without design and development capability, but which are simply discharging or implementing the provided designs or specifications should select the ISO 9002 quality system standard. Frequently, these latter companies are referred to as "build-to-print" companies.

- Hardware—"Tangible, discrete product with distinctive form" (ANSI/ASQC Q9000-1-1994).

- Service—"The results generated by activities at the interface between the supplier and the customer and by supplier internal activities to meet customer needs" (ISO 8402:1994).

- Software—"An intellectual creation consisting of information expressed through supporting medium" (ANSI/ASQC Q9000-1-1994).

- Processed materials—"Tangible product generated by transforming raw material into desired state" (ANSI/ASQC Q9000-1-1994).

Figure 2.2 Categories of products.

ISO 9003 is seldom used for implementation or registration purposes since it has such limited application. Distributors, sometimes referred to as stockists, limited testing companies, and verification services may qualify for use of this directive standard. Experience shows, however, some value-added work is performed even in companies with these limited operations. The performance of any value-added work requires the affected company to select ISO 9002. Examples of limited value-added work might be drilling a cotter-pin hole in a standard stocked bolt, or plating standard washers, or even special product packaging for overseas shipment after testing.

2.1.4 ISO 9001 is the most comprehensive standard

ISO 9001, ISO 9002, and ISO 9003 are a tiered set of documents, which provide the benefit of choosing different levels for a company's intended ISO 9000-based quality system. For example, everything in ISO 9003 is included in ISO 9002, and everything in 9002 and 9003 is included in ISO 9001. Also, ISO 9001 has requirements beyond those in ISO 9002 and ISO 9003 when it addresses requirements for design and/or development. As such, ISO 9001 is the most comprehensive directive. It addresses a total of 20 quality system elements, whereas ISO 9002 covers 19 elements (20 less the 1 for design/development). ISO 9003 has only 16 quality system elements and many of those are of reduced scope (see Appendix A).

The quality system standard chosen for the company may be a customer's contractual requirement. On that basis, it is in the company's best interest to utilize a *well-considered and deliberate* selection process. This way the company is prepared to defend its selection if a customer inadvertently "over specs" on a contract or purchase order. Of course, it may be in the company's interest to first determine if possible capability expansion is the customer's intention. This may also be the company's future objective, and thus customer interest may be the catalyst for moving ahead. If so, knowledge of all the ISO directive standards will be beneficial.

2.1.5 Tailoring the selected ISO 9000 directive standard

ISO directive quality system standards have a provision for the selective tailoring of their requirements. Obviously, the tailoring can not be the result of the company simply not wishing to address a known problem area. Tailoring is appropriate if some of the requirements are not totally applicable to a given company.

The company needs to systematically review the selected standard and determine the exact aspects that are not applicable to its operations. Within the document may be areas of partial application. These may exist within system elements and even within paragraphs. The end result of the tailoring process must be a revised version of the standard that is solely applicable to the candidate company. Within the company facility, the contents of the tailored standard, its scope of planned application, and the scope of its intended implementation must be a perfect match.

The company management must assure standard tailoring is necessary, since it must be constantly defended. The tailoring must be well documented and the transfer of tailored requirements to their actual implementation must be complete. In the face of the rigid review tailoring receives from customer and registrar alike, many companies avoid the process completely. It is, however, permitted by ISO 9000 and is used successfully where it makes sense.

Note: When working with a registrar, one of the first situations to be resolved will be the scope of the company's ISO implementation. The registrar will compare the scope of implementation and the intended scope of registration. Registration will usually parallel the ISO 9000 tailoring chosen by the company. Mutual understanding and acceptance must be determined before any third-party auditing takes place.

2.2 Deciding on the scope of ISO 9000 implementation

Tailoring of both the selected standard and its application are acceptable practices. The tailoring of the scope or extent of implementation is a separate but related decision. Deciding on the exact scope of ISO 9000 implementation depends on a number of factors, all of which are company based and within its control. Management must assure the scope of the implementation is always logical for operations and cost-effective for the company.

As noted, there are occasions when a requirement called out in the standard is simply not performed by the affected company or facility. Examples of such situations may be where a company or facility utilizes centralized corporate procurement/purchasing, remote or corporate warehousing, or corporate software development activities. In such cases, the company is only formally responsible for its direct operational capabilities and should tailor its compliance and documentation accordingly. The compliance documentation needs to cover all of the affected facility's activities up to and including its side of the interface with the corporate or remote unit (see Figure 2.3).

Tailoring may be done by
- Entire quality system elements
- Individual functional organizations
- Facilities, buildings, and areas
- Product and service lines
- Production lines
- Subunits of each of the above

Figure 2.3 Tailoring a standard.

2.2.1 Avoiding the problem of multiple quality systems

There is merit in trying to follow the original intent of ISO TC 176 by applying the selected ISO quality standard to company operations in total. Such an approach is relatively easy for the company to present to both customer and registrar. In some respects it is also less of a problem to management and the workforce than tailored standards application.

Due to the nature of absent or diverse operations and functions, however, a tailored standard and implementation scope may be absolutely necessary. If so, it is simpler for all concerned if the company applies the tailored scope to all aspects of the company or facility, instead of just certain functions and operations. The latter creates confusion.

The situation that should be avoided is the use of two or more distinct quality systems in different parts of the company. It is much easier for management and employees to deal with one basic approach, or one basic quality system, than to struggle trying to remember what quality system standard applies to which product or process. Having one basic quality system also limits training, documentation, and costs. Unless there is some clear demarcation upon which to base a multi-system quality approach, it is recommended the ISO 9000 standard (tailored or otherwise) be *implemented facility-wide*.

2.2.2 Variation in scope must have rationale

If the company does determine it will not fully apply the standard to the facility, there should be some logical way to do so. One example is a division based on distinct multiple product lines, such as having both military and commercial production lines or services within the same facility. Another example is if the candidate company has multiple corporate units within its facility that are non-ISO 9000, such as a regional product repair facility or the corporate research center. Although these units are located in the same basic manufacturing or servicing facility that is seeking registration, there is likely a separate management structure that would set these activities apart. A final example of demarcation might be the application of ISO 9000 to one of two distinct single, customer-based production lines. In these examples, application of the selected standard to part of the facility is understandable and acceptable, but frequently hard to manage.

After review, the management of most companies eventually determines that it will fully implement the selected ISO 9000 standard across all facilities, functions, and product lines; however, the nature and extent of implementation may tax available resources to the point of having to achieve ISO 9000 implementation on an incremental basis. In some cases, companies time their ISO 9000 implementation so the organizations, areas, facilities, or products that support certain customers are pulled ahead in response to a customer-requested registration. This expedited activity can progress while the rest of the company proceeds with implementation at a more manageable pace. The company is faced with addressing multiple quality systems during such a process, but if properly documented, the method is acceptable. It is another case of ISO acceptance of whatever makes the best economical or business sense for the particular company.

2.2.3 Use of facility layouts to define exact scope

When attempting to define and identify the planned scope of the ISO 9000 application, particularly when explaining it to a registrar, many companies use a facility map or plant layout. This shows where the ISO quality system is implemented and what areas are presented for registration. The layout may even show lines right through some functions, such as an engineering function that supports both military and commercial product lines.

In fact, in some cases, the layout may even indicate an individual area or employee as having to divide time between an ISO 9000-based program and one that is not. Of course, there must be records to support such a dual role. Situations like this are frequently found in small companies; however, most have found full ISO 9000 compliance to be a very effective solution to the problem of trying to keep the records straight.

2.2.4 Scope influences how much the registrar charges

At this point, note that in most, but not all cases, the scope of ISO 9000 implementation equates to the scope of a company's requested registration. The way the candidate company defines the scope of its ISO 9000 implementation is usually acceptable to the registrar.

Registrars customarily establish their fees or charges to companies based on several factors. Charges are usually determined on a facility-by-facility basis. Minimum charges, as of 1995, ranged between $1500 and $2500/person/day on-site. The rate is adjusted upward by the workforce size at each facility, the number of distinct product lines, and any other factors that may influence the time required for the registrars to adequately prepare and perform the necessary audits. Charges for audit preparations, report writing, and so on are included in the on-site fees. Off-site time usually is equivalent to the actual time spent at the candidate company. Registrar costs of $10,000–$20,000 are not unusual for large companies (1000+ employees), where two to three auditors may spend two to three days on-site. Small companies may have one auditor for one to two days and cost only $1500–$5000. These numbers for the basic process are presented for reference only. Registration cost quotations are always company-specific or facility-specific.

Travel variations affect registration costs. In addition to the registrars' fees, reasonable travel-related expenses are charged to the candidate company. The distance the auditors must travel to get to the site and the length of stay in the locality will influence the company's total cost.

Since the auditors are going to be on-site anyway, the definition of a facility can be somewhat negotiable. For instance, it may be possible to demonstrate to the registrar that there are several facilities that comprise one basic local company. If the facility locations are in close proximity, this situation can be likely presented and negotiated as one facility with two to three local buildings. Obtaining this type of agreement is particularly likely if the subject facilities are under the same basic management structure.

Diverse facility locations and operations, with unrelated production lines or different types of service activities—even under the same management—will be difficult to structure under a single audit. Likewise, closely located facilities within the same corporation but essentially unrelated will not be accepted as one multiple-building facility. Additionally, connected activities in facilities located in different corners of the state or country, even if under one management structure, will require travel, possible new lodging, and so on, and would not be viewed as a single audit.

Note, however, some companies with multiple facilities, even in different states, have successfully negotiated package deals with registrars. The candidate company should never lose track of the fact that the registration business is a market-driven activity. If a company has multiple facilities that might eventually become candidates for registration, it would be prudent for the company to let that fact be mentioned during any negotiation activities with registrars.

2.2.5 Scope selection is no defense for noncompliance

As noted, a company can not selectively omit aspects of its ISO compliance that it simply does not wish to meet. The prudent company must never consider attempting to identify functions as being outside the scope of its registration application, when they are clearly part of the overall process being considered for ISO 9000 implementation. Unfortunately, this is occasionally attempted by a candidate company with an area or function having known weak performance, poor ISO 9000 implementation, or inadequate system documentation.

The registrar will not approve a company attempting such subterfuge. If such a situation is determined ahead of time, the registrar will likely immediately advise the company that it is not in compliance with the intent of the ISO standards. Obviously, such an attempt would not be condoned by ethical company management and the likelihood of such encounters is very small. As noted, if there are legitimate reasons for exclusions, there is an avenue to address the situation and it would probably not be a problem. It would be well to discuss any planned exclusions with the registrar as early as possible in the application process. Clarity on the application must result in a mutually understood implementation scope prior to any audit.

2.3 What is a valid ISO 9000-based quality system?

The ISO 9000 definition of a quality system is, "the organizational structure, responsibilities, procedures, processes, and resources needed to implement quality management." Quality management is then defined as, "all activities of the overall management function that determine the [company's or entity's] quality policy, objectives, and responsibility." In the broadest sense, the quality system is basically how the company is managed and operated.

2.3.1 Quality system, not quality assurance system

Unfortunately, when the term *quality system* is used, some people initially assume it refers simply to the quality control or basic quality assurance organization or function. The ISO family of quality standards and guidelines makes the interpretation quite clear. When the standards refer to a *quality system* it means the *overall company-level system* of management of all those performance activities that can, in any way, affect the quality of the company's products and/or services. The ISO 9000 definition of a quality system includes activities ranging from marketing research and product development, to procurement and production, to verification and delivery, and to installation and servicing.

Every activity or function in the typical ISO 9000-based quality system is essential for successful company operation. All such functions must be operated and managed with quality of performance, process, and product as the company goal. ISO 9004-1 provides best practices guidelines for implementing a company-level quality management system that is capable of enabling the company to meet the directive or contractual ISO standards. In addition to the requirement for an implemented quality system, the standards require that the system be both documented and effective.

2.3.2 Every system must have a focal point

A successful quality system is always based on a sound, customer-accepted standard, which may or may not be ISO 9000 based. In fact, there are some other excellent quality system standards in use, however, only the ISO 9000 quality system standards have worldwide acceptance. All quality system standards act as the focus mechanism for the quality system itself. Further, the standards become a positive means of assuring adequate identification of all the quality system elements and requirements. No major system omissions are possible if the standards are followed.

Without standards, any form of quality system is usually informal, incomplete, and undocumented. Absence of a standard normally results in an uncontrolled process. Further, without a quality system standard and its attendant documentation, no measurement of compliance is possible—without a documented standard, to what basis does the company measure? The absence of measurement capability stems from having no available documented baseline (see Figure 2.4). Companies with an accepted and implemented quality system standard, for both focus and system element identification, will be capable of developing the means of monitoring compliance. A documented baseline provides the means for an ongoing and repetitive method of operation.

2.3.3 Some existing systems are close to ISO 9000

Some companies have excellent non-ISO quality systems in place. Normally it is because the organizations have embraced the accepted quality system standards developed and used by specific industries. Examples may be found in companies working to support military, automotive, nuclear, and pharmaceutical customers. Even though modified or interpreted in view of the specific industry activities, virtually all of these standards address the same basic quality system elements found in the ISO standards.

Compliance to ISO 9000 requirements for these companies is often a relatively simple matter. Such companies may be able to demonstrate they can meet multiple quality system standards with very little modification to their basic quality system and its documentation. Frequently, these companies present their compliance to multiple standards in the form of a matrix that demonstrates how each requirement of each standard is

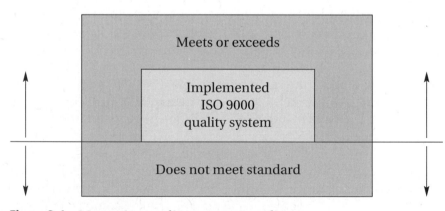

Figure 2.4   Measuring quality system compliance.

covered within the quality system documentation. Such companies either work to the most stringent requirement to cover all requirements, or have a quality plan that has been developed for each customer/product and defines the aspects of the quality system that applies.

Occasionally, the ISO 9000 standards will require an expanded interpretation of a particular industry-based system element. Usually, modifications relate to achieving compatible interpretations of terminology. The interpretation may cause a slightly different application of the system element, such as an identified need to collect and control records.

Industry-specific interpretations normally fit well within the overall ISO 9000 generic approach to basic quality systems. Unfortunately, there is a critical type of variance between some of the industry-based quality systems and ISO-based systems. The variance relates to the narrow interpretation of some industry standards and systems as simply being quality control oriented. Such a limited approach is contrary to the true ISO 9000-based systems, which involve all functions in pursuit of compliance. Thus, the candidate company must interpret its selected ISO 9000 standard as a comprehensive company-level quality system and not as a basic quality control system. The broad interpretation is often spoken of as "big Q [of quality systems] versus the little q [of quality control systems]."

2.3.4 Variations in degree of quality system compliance

The quality system variations will likely fall into one of several categories, including the following:

- No apparent quality system exists.
- Essentially no quality system exists.
- Very basic quality controls in place.
- Quality system and standards are company design
- Quality system is based on a recognized industry standard.
- Quality system is approaching world-class status.

Over time, most companies have developed a quality system that covers some aspects of many elements. Such an approach is often encountered in small companies where they have implemented what they deemed appropriate for the situation or problem encountered.

During the forthcoming shortfall analysis activity, the performance and documentation results will have to be reviewed against the requirements of the selected ISO 9000 quality system standard. The company will assess its current position in relation to compliance with the ISO quality system requirements. It is quite likely there will be a variety of quality system compliance situations encountered. The most likely situation is that the quality system will not be totally implemented by each of the company's functional organizations. The second most likely situation is that the system is implemented in varying degrees by, and within, each of the individual functional organizations. The third possible situation is the quality system implementation is suboptimized for the benefit of one or more organizations, often at the expense of the total system.

2.3.5 Identification of all quality system variation

Fortunately, ISO 9000 expects examination of each and every quality system requirement by each and every function to assure all aspects of all requirements are addressed. The equalizer in situations of variable quality system compliance is that planned multifunctional focus, on the selected ISO 9000 standard, will permit developing a level baseline across the company's total quality system. The standards application process will be the vehicle for identifying areas for improvement. Eliminating noncompliant elements will result in system upgrade and a leveling of performance at a position of full quality system compliance. Further, the ISO 9000 family also supplies guidelines for the company to use in achieving a common interpretation and approach during the review and upgrade process.

Company management must be certain that all functions and organizations become actively involved in shortfall analysis. When setting up the review process, the company must ensure that participation includes the total company functional and operational structure. As discussed earlier, in many companies this may need to be accomplished by a senior management mandate. Hopefully, it is simply facilitated by management and workforce awareness of ISO 9000 implementation benefits.

2.4 Extent of existing quality system documentation

The company probably found a variable existence and degree of quality system implementation within its operations. Variation in the amount, integrity, usefulness, and utilization of any related quality system documentation is likely to be 10-fold (Figure 2.5). Typically, the variation of a company's available quality system documentation may extend from having virtually no governing system documentation available to having essentially full system documentation in use. Some companies attempt to perform the quality system tasks but have little or no documentation, while others have documentation but it is not followed. The other extreme is where one company neither performs the task nor has documentation, while another company has both a compliant quality system and acceptable documentation. The potential variations within the company and/or its individual functions must be resolved.

Many companies are surprised at the extent of their current quality system documentation. The coverage may be much closer to being compliant to the selected ISO 9000 standard than was originally anticipated by management. This somewhat unexpected surprise provides management with considerably greater confidence than when the ISO implementation decision was originally made. Even so, most companies have more problems with the extent and adequacy of their documentation than any other aspect of the ISO 9000 implementation process.

Quality system	*Nonsystem*
1. Quality policy	1. Employee expense forms
2. Quality manual	2. General office memos
3. Quality system procedures	3. Company/union contracts
4. Work instructions	4. Hiring policies
5. System specifications	5. Legal briefs/cases
6. Purchase orders	6. Product pricing analysis
7. Process specifications	7. EEO documentation
8. Statistical programs	8. Health care forms
9. Quality plans	9. Employee salaries/rates
10. Test specifications	10. Patent documentation

Figure 2.5   Quality system versus nonsystem documentation.

2.4.1 Entrepreneurial approach is not repetitive

Many companies encourage an entrepreneurial approach to managing and operating the company. On the surface this may appear to be quite progressive and certainly the degree of employee empowerment is beneficial. Each employee needs to know, however, the extent of his or her empowerment. In the absence of some level of documentation structure and guidance, this approach degenerates into each participant making his or her own interpretation of all requirements. The company's operational activities are then complicated even further, since, in unanticipated situations, each individual decides acceptable company performance and results.

This lack of firm direction causes operational processes to vary each time they are exercised. In this environment, decisions are usually made without knowledge of what process variation or remedial actions were encountered and handled earlier in the flow. This situation is true even if the end product of the process eventually meets the customer requirements or company product specifications. The activity still amounts to an uncontrolled and therefore nonrepetitive and nonoptimized process. Since company operations are essentially all based on processes, an uncontrolled approach in each process becomes very costly (Figure 2.6).

The ISO 9000 standards require both the presence of governing quality system documentation *and* workforce adherence to the documentation. They include provisions for responding to system and documentation adjustments and improvements. Adherence to the ISO quality system causes the company to be constantly moving toward the optimization of its quality system, its related operational processes, and the very documentation that requires the movement toward optimization. This concept depends on the company developing and utilizing full quality system documentation, representing its optimal approach to total operations and activities.

2.4.2 Degree of existing documentation available

At the individual company level, the degree of existing documentation tends to fall into three general categories.

No documentation. The least likely category to be encountered is when the company has virtually no documentation. This situation is ordinarily

Account servicing	Process development
Accounts receivable	Product delivery
Calibration control	Product design
Component screening	Product improvement
Customer service	Product inspection
Data security	Product packaging
Document control	Production scheduling
Employee services	Promotional contacts
Equipment installation	Proof testing
Field support	Records control
Financial planning	Reliability analysis
Hiring activities	Resource allocation
Internal auditing	Safety awareness
Inventory control	Software development
Management review	Transportation service
Management training	Value analysis
Methods analysis	Vendor selection
Payroll management	Waste reduction

Figure 2.6   Typical business processes.

associated with very small companies, but the likelihood of a successful company operating under these limitations is very low.

Complete documentation. The next most populated documentation category includes those companies with a fully documented quality system and, as with the system itself, is likely to be the result of ongoing compliance to a recognized quality system standard. Experience shows that large companies or subunits of large companies tend to have complete or nearly complete documentation of their entire quality systems. They have found that because of the number of employees involved in operating the quality system, adequate documentation is mandatory for assuring an effective level of system/process control. Many of these large companies have used the ISO 9000 standards as a baseline from which they have moved toward becoming a world-class quality system company (see Figure 2.7). Augmenting the basic ISO 9000 documented quality system is becoming increasingly popular as companies move to achieve greater internal efficiencies and increased market share.

Partial documentation. The most frequently encountered category when examining a company's quality system is where some documentation exists. Many times the first organized company efforts to look for documentation convinces the ISO management representative that no valid documentation exists. If any exists, it is assumed to be outdated, not applicable, of token worth, or apparently unknown to the workforce. The company, however, must not be satisfied with a cursory look, since any documentation will benefit the implementation process.

2.4.3 Some documentation is almost always present

Further examination will likely reveal a number of existing documents. Only those that are quality system oriented will likely transfer into the

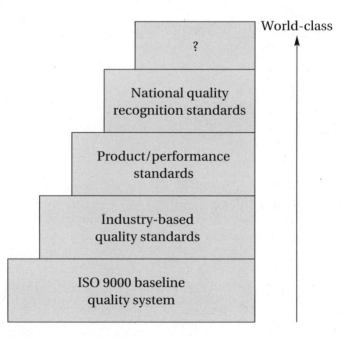

Figure 2.7   ISO 9000 baseline plus.

new or revised quality system. Certain organizations and functions tend to have a greater level of existing documentation than others.

Even documents not currently used, such as policies, procedures, and instructions that hold historical information on company operations, problems, and solutions are of value. Such documents are excellent sources to use during the upcoming shortfall analysis. They probably hold a great deal of company operational history from some point in time. They will certainly be beneficial in assuring former problems are not repeated, or solutions to former problems are not forgotten. Experience indicates there is always someone in the company who can provide valuable background data, by using the old documents as the basis for his or her memory exercise. Gather all such existing documents from all functions and give them to the individual or team assigned to shortfall analysis.

The degree and existence of acceptable, upgraded valid documentation is also quite variable. This is usually traced to one of the following:

- Operational nature of specific organizations or functions
- Local and cognizant management interest
- Recent management changes
- Frequency and currency of customer audits
- Other perturbation drivers

It is conceivable for a company to have one function with virtually no quality system documentation and a similar unit with excellent documentation. This situation can even exist within a particular operational subunit or functional activity. There is always a reason for such variation, and it can generally be traced to the requirements levied or expected by the cognizant management.

The prudent ISO management representative must assure every organization identifies and contributes any and all documentation to the shortfall analysis. Such universal functional support is essential, even if it exposes unacceptable lapses in document currency and/or obsolescence. Before the company can achieve ISO 9000 compliance, these situations will have to be resolved, so early realization of these problems is actually an advantage.

2.4.4 Quality system procedures address system elements

In preparation for the shortfall review, companies must collect any existing quality system documentation, such as policies and procedures, which *may* reflect current or past compliance to a recognized quality standard. Of particular benefit is the presence of any quality system procedures, which indicate how the company intends to comply with the system elements of the particular quality system standard being addressed (see Figure 2.8). In many cases, these quality system procedures can be directly used, or with only minor changes, to satisfy ISO 9000 elements.

2.4.5 Work instructions are used to perform tasks

Companies should not overlook the large category of documentation that is classified as work instructions. Even small companies or otherwise poorly documented companies have some level of basic instructions in use. These are usually job or task related and may provide guidance on many basic company activities (see Figure 2.9).

The ISO 9000 family of quality system standards recognizes work instructions as an essential type of operating level documentation. The detailed job-related operating activity is the least likely to undergo major changes even in an ISO 9000 environment. It is entirely possible many of the current work instructions can be moved intact (or with little change) directly into the documentation structure being used or developed to meet ISO 9000 requirements. Many companies find they have most of

General procedures	*Subordinate procedures*
• Quality system	• Quality planning
• Design control	• Document changes
• Purchasing	• Receiving inspection
• Training	• Material handling
• Contract review	• Design validation
• Document/data control	• Design review
• Product identity/traceability	• Purchasing data
• Inspection control	• Corrective action
• Quality records	• Statistical procedures
• Management responsibility	• Inspection/test procedures

Figure 2.8 Examples of quality system procedures.

- Tool selection and use guidelines
- Nondestructive test methods
- Computer data entry
- Marketing calls documentation
- Contract review checklists
- Drawing release procedures
- Internal audit checklists
- Training evaluation forms
- Processing change requests
- Purchase order release instructions
- Processing shipping documents
- Equipment start-up and operation procedures
- Laboratory analysis procedures
- Production planning changes
- Incoming inspection methods
- Records retention instructions
- Corrective action analysis
- Customer complaint processing
- Software configuration checklists
- Shipping release instructions

Figure 2.9   Examples of work instructions.

the work instructions necessary for ISO 9000 compliance. They simply must develop the balance of the documentation and its system structure.

Some companies convert or directly use the operating instructions provided with equipment purchases, as internal company work instructions. Nothing in the ISO 9000 standards prevents a company from such use. As with any other quality system document, these instructions must have proper identification and status within the company's quality system. Such instructions must be available to the affected employees and they must understand the instructions as related to their job assignments.

2.5 Organizing/training for shortfall analysis

Prior to actual shortfall analysis, the company must have identified, located, and collected all available existing quality system documents. Once collected, these documents will then need to be categorized as to their expected usefulness during shortfall analysis. They may appear to be quite satisfactory, requiring few if any changes to comply with ISO requirements. On the other hand, they may be suitable for historical background only. The documents should be sorted into one of the following categories.

- Useful current documentation needing little or no change
- Useful current documentation but with required changes
- Obsolete documentation but with useful data
- Useable documentation but as reference material only
- Incomplete, but valid documentation
- Nonexistent documentation

These documents should be sorted and given to the functional and multifunctional shortfall analysis teams or individuals. It is better to provide documents that may be of questionable use than to have a team establish a firm shortfall where helpful documents may exist. A quality system document may be useful to more than one team or shortfall analysis activity.

2.5.1 Use of functional teams during shortfall analysis

For the purpose of performing shortfall analysis, a functional team may have several members or only one, depending on the resources, the schedule, and the size of the task. It is recommended that each functional team plan for a full review of each element in the selected ISO standard. This review should be planned for even those elements not appearing to have direct application to some of the functional activities. For instance, the design or engineering function should go beyond its obvious charter to also examine requirements for elements such as contract review, quality records, training, and so on.

Since ISO 9000 requirements apply to the total quality system, there are often support and corollary activities that will reveal themselves during an element-by-element review by all functions. When the shortfall review teams make the necessary performance comparisons, they are in a better position to assure that both direct and implied ISO 9000 requirements are being considered. For example, a direct requirement for keeping records also has implied requirements for the following:

- Identification of what is considered a record
- Need for a record collection method
- Assignment of responsibility for the particular record mentioned
- Means for input to record storage
- Establishment of record retention periods

If all of the implied requirements are not considered within every function when determining shortfalls, the ISO 9000 implementation plan will be superficial. The company may be placed in the position of having to perform a significant amount of in-process rework of its new compliance methods and documentation.

2.5.2 Multifunctional teams will aid shortfall analysis

There is decided value in assuring the company utilizes both functional and multifunctional teams during shortfall analysis. In fact, this type of approach is beneficial throughout the entire ISO 9000 implementation process. As noted, the functional teams are important since they can concentrate on the particular ISO 9000 requirements that affect the function they represent. The use of multifunctional teams, or individuals with multifunctional knowledge and experience, however, provides a solid base for assuring all structural aspects of the requirements are comprehensively reviewed.

Multifunctional efforts also provide assurance that the structural and interface aspects of the quality system elements are thoroughly reviewed and addressed. Structural elements are those requirements within the standard that tend to bridge all functions. As an example, elements such as corrective action, training, internal quality auditing, management review, and document control affect all functions. A detailed multifunctional review makes certain all requirements for interrelated functional activities are identified and addressed.

Another multifunctional area that companies often fail to address is how they manage the interfaces between their functional organizations. Most companies have found that ISO 9000 implementation forces them to examine the ways in which they can make these interfaces as transparent to process flow as possible. In so doing, a wealth of potential time and money savings in the overall process flow is discovered.

2.5.3 Organizational interfaces must not be overlooked

The interface issue can also be addressed as it affects every employee within the company. No matter what the task, all individuals—just as with each group, division, department, or company—have both a supplier who performs the work that flows to them and a customer to whom their own work is forwarded. It makes no difference whether the person works in company administration, the shop, the laboratories, the field, the offices, or any other company area. All have, and are, suppliers and customers. ISO 9000 specifically requires the interrelations of all functions and individuals who are part of the quality system to be defined. As such, the plan for the shortfall review should assure that these internal supplier/customer interfaces are not overlooked. They must be examined as necessary to ensure that ISO 9000 system elements requirements are satisfied.

In small companies, it is not unusual for a well-experienced, well-versed individual (or several individuals) to perform the existing document collection and shortfall analysis by him or herself. Assuming it is performed properly, this approach can be successful. Certainly less time is required and the results should be satisfactory for the purpose intended. When the eight-step implementation process is used by small companies, the basic preparatory activities described, including the functional and multifunctional influences must be considered and accommodated. See Appendix C for more details.

Experience has often demonstrated that the total shortfall preparation responsibility should not be assigned to the quality assurance function. Of course, the results are heavily dependent upon the individual(s) selected, but there is usually not a comprehensive knowledge of company-wide functional documentation residing in the quality assurance organization.

2.5.4 Plans for addressing all possible shortfalls

The company wants to accomplish the shortfall analysis thoroughly and efficiently. It has selected personnel from all functions and assigned them to various aspects of shortfall analysis. These employees must be made aware of what is expected of them and how to achieve it. To assure this outcome, key organizational methods and tools need to be developed and standardized for use by the shortfall teams. They must first determine whether the basic requirement of the ISO standard is being addressed. Then they must decide whether the methods used by the company actually meet the standard. The next step will be to determine whether the particular task or process is documented. Finally, the team must decide if the available documentation is effective for the purpose intended.

In order to assure a successful result, the ISO management representative or an assigned shortfall analysis coordinator will need to address the following aspects.

- Directive standard selected and available.
- All existing documentation collected.
- Systematic plan and analysis methods developed.
- Participants selected, trained, and assigned.
- Method of documenting analysis results devised.
- Existing documentation distributed to teams.

The representative will also need to do the following:

- Develop for team use a systematic plan and detailed methods for reviewing the company performance and documentation against the requirements of the selected ISO standard.
- Determine the method of documenting the results of the shortfall analysis. A comprehensive and definitive approach to reviewing and recording shortfalls is essential for developing the company's detailed implementation plan.
- Assign participants their role(s) and provided training or orientation on the planned shortfall analysis task. They should learn how shortfall analysis is performed, how shortfalls are documented, how to deal with ISO requirements where the company has no documentation at all, what type of summary report is expected, and so on.
- Provide participants with the means of contact for the functional focal points and the names of team leaders, members, and the management representative. Also provide team meeting details and schedules.
- Give teams all the existing documents that have been collected, any checklists or forms developed for use, and any other preliminary data necessary for the shortfall analysis.

2.5.5 Dealing with little or no documentation

The company should always use the most knowledgeable and capable representatives available from the functional organizations for the shortfall analysis. This is especially important because some of the organizations will have little or no documentation for all or some of the processes they perform. Thus, the reviewers need to utilize their experience and knowledge of how their functional organization performs the undocumented task and determine whether the current means of performance meets ISO standards—if it were documented. If not, what is the specific shortfall? Is the shortfall satisfied anywhere else in the company? The answers to all such questions are facilitated by employees experienced in their respective function.

In most situations where there is no documentation, the basic requirements in the standard will be addressed, in some fashion, by the current performance method. There is, however, no guiding documentation available that assures the performance is a repetitive process. Sometimes basic or informal local work instructions may be available, but they are usually insufficient to provide enough control to comply with quality system requirements.

Conclusion

ISO has developed three directive standards that have been accepted worldwide as baseline quality system standards. The first action in assessing the company's current position is to decide which of the directive standards is most appropriate for the company operations.

Although it is generally expected the company will implement the selected ISO standard, in total, at any given facility, the scope of company implementation is up to the company and its customers. If not implemented in total, the limited scope must be identified. Limited scope may be based on the nature of company programs, competing customer requirements, other contractual quality standards, company economics and resources, and so on. Company areas or functions selected for ISO implementation must meet the applicable requirements of the standard in their entirety. The implementation scope must also be in accordance with the selected registrar's quality system approval requirements.

The company must comply with the standard's definition and interpretation of what constitutes a basic quality system. The major difference with the ISO interpretation and other quality standards is that ISO 9000 assumes the quality system is the responsibility of all the company functional units. It is not, as with some quality standards, a quality control system with the quality assurance department as its primary functional caretaker. ISO 9000 also requires the quality system to be documented, implemented, and effective before company compliance can be judged acceptable. The company should provide orientation for employees on its planned ISO 9000 quality system.

The shortfall analysis compares each requirement of the selected ISO quality standard with what the company is currently doing. The majority of companies preparing for the shortfall analysis have found a quantity of suitable documentation available for consideration during the review process. The company is often operating reasonably close to actual compliance with the basic quality system requirements of the ISO 9000 standard. Although additional documentation may be required, management is often pleased to find the company is familiar with the nature of the elements in the standard.

A systematic approach to the shortfall analysis process is clearly needed. The shortfall review must be comprehensive to be a means of defining any necessary remedial actions. The shortfall analysis must be performed by experienced and trained personnel, operating as teams or individuals, and as experts in their specific areas. Remedial actions in response to shortfalls become the input for the detailed implementation plan.

Implementation actions required by this module

1. Obtain a set of ISO 9000 or Q9000 series of quality system standards.

2. Consider obtaining additional, appropriate ISO 9000 family guideline standards.

3. Become knowledgeable with the content of the three primary ISO directive standards.

4. Examine the directive standards for stated requirements in all applicable elements.

5. Use ISO 9000 guidelines to select a directive standard suitable to the company.

6. Decide if the company will implement all aspects of the selected standard.

7. If tailoring of the standard is planned, determine the anticipated scope.

8. Assure that there is a logical basis for defining the scope of the tailoring.

9. Contact several registrars to discuss the planned scope and the company's facility.

10. Keep open the option of working with two to three registrars until final selection.

11. Examine the nature and extent of implementation of the current quality system.

12. Collect all existing quality system documentation, even if it is not current.

13. Categorize all collected documents as to their potential use for ISO 9000 compliance.

14. Establish and train functional and multifunctional shortfall analysis teams.

15. Provide all teams with copies of the selected standard and all existing documentation.

16. Determine the nature and method of performing and documenting the shortfall analysis.

17. Develop a plan for addressing situations where no documentation exists.

18. Assign and staff the shortfall analysis teams for the actual shortfall review.

Step 3: Determining Shortfalls

3.1 A systematic approach to determining shortfalls

3.1.1 Methodology for performing shortfall analysis

3.1.2 Using the selected standard as a source of requirements

3.1.3 Dealing with unstated or implied requirements

3.1.4 Determining compliance when the task is intermittent

3.1.5 Assigning personnel for the shortfall analysis

3.2 The major shortfall is usually documentation related

3.2.1 Looking for levels one and two documentation

3.2.2 The presence of company level three documentation

3.2.3 Operating direction of levels four and five

3.2.4 What to do if there is no documentation

3.2.5 Involving the workforce in the shortfall analysis

3.3 Guidance documents for directive standards

3.3.1 Many guidelines are available for shortfall use

3.3.2 Guideline focused on ISO 9000 interpretation

3.3.3 Guidance for industry-based ISO 9000 quality systems

3.3.4 Specific guidance for key system elements

3.3.5 Assistance with ISO 9000 terminology

3.4 Techniques for assuring a complete shortfall analysis

3.4.1 Shortfall analysis must include all elements

3.4.2 All functions must look at all elements

3.4.3 Use checklists to assure all key aspects are examined

3.4.4 Checklists can take various approaches

3.4.5 Using externally prepared input examples

3.5 Preparing to develop the detailed implementation plan

3.5.1 The total implementation task is taking shape

3.5.2 Organizing all of the collected shortfall data

3.5.3 Preparing final shortfall data for input into the plan

3.5.4 Still time for potential user involvement and input

3.5.5 What every identified shortfall must have

Conclusion

Questions answered in this module

1. What is the definition and purpose of the shortfall analysis?
2. How can a standard be directive but not prescriptive in its requirements?
3. Why are the same requirements in the standard often interpreted differently?
4. How can generic requirements be specifically applied to any organization?
5. What is the difference between direct and implied requirements?
6. Why is it essential that all direct and implied requirements be identified?
7. Why must the results of the shortfall analysis be identified in significant detail?
8. Are documents available to assist the company in interpreting requirements?
9. Why do nationally recognized quality systems appear to be so similar?
10. If the required task is basically performed per the standard, can a shortfall exist?
11. Why are shortfalls usually associated with the adequacy of quality manuals?
12. Why are most identified ISO 9000 shortfalls associated with documentation?

13. What approach should be taken if there is essentially no documentation?

14. Why should formal audit functions be avoided in performing shortfall analysis?

15. Should the teams that collected the existing documentation do the shortfall analysis?

16. To what extent should the workforce be involved in shortfall analysis?

17. What is the best way to get assistance from the ISO 9000 family of guidelines?

18. How can the company assure that it has identified all existing shortfalls?

19. Can suitable checklists be developed or purchased to assist in shortfall analysis?

20. How must the collected shortfall data be organized for use in the implementation plan?

21. Why should the shortfall analysis team also suggest remedial actions?

22. In what format should the final shortfall analysis data be for use in the implementation plan?

Step 3

Determining Shortfalls

The previous module covered the preparatory steps required prior to performing a company's shortfall analysis. This module examines the activities associated with the analytical process. The goal of shortfall analysis is to determine and identify any variance between ISO requirements and company performance. Shortfall analysis has been described by several other terms, such as *gap analysis, compliance variance, documented gap*, or simply the *shortfall.*

The shortfall analysis process must be thorough and precise because the results become the basis for the company's detailed implementation plan. Any oversight in determining a company's shortfall will result in an omission in compliance. Such oversights cause either last-minute panic or noncompliant audit findings, both of which are unacceptable and unnecessary.

3.1 A systematic approach to determining shortfalls

In the second module, the nature of how the company must organize its approach to the shortfall analysis task was explored. Both functional and multifunctional teams or individuals must be assigned to address the related functional and structural quality system elements. To assure this, many companies use a responsibility matrix to establish the primary and support areas of management responsibilities (see Figure 3.1). Whatever the precise nature of the company's shortfall review process, it must be a systematic and thorough approach. It must result in the systematic identification of all company variances to ISO requirements.

110

Elements \ Functions	Management	Administrative	Contract review	Engineering	Purchasing	Operations	Manufacturing	Quality assurance	Industrial engineering	Human resources	Facilities	Customer service
Management responsibility 4.1	●	●	■	■	■	●	■	■	■	■	■	■
Quality system 4.2	●	●	■	●	●	●	●	●	●	■	▲	●
Contract review 4.3	●	■	●	■	■	▲	■	■	■			■
Design control 4.4	●	▲	▲	●	■	■	■	■	■	■		■
Document and data control 4.5	●	■	▲	●	■	●	■	■	■	■	▲	●
Purchasing 4.6	●	■	■	■	■	●	■	■	●	■		●
Control of customer-supplied product 4.7	■			■	●	■	▲	▲	▲			●
Product identification and traceability 4.8	●			▲	■	■	●	■	■			▲
Process control 4.9	●	▲	▲	■	■	■	●	●	●	●	■	■
Inspection and testing 4.10	●	▲	▲	■	▲	■	■	●	■	▲	▲	▲
Control of inspection, measuring, and test equipment 4.11	●	▲	▲	■	■	■	●	●	●	■	■	■
Inspection and test status 4.12	●	■		▲	■	■	■	●	■			■
Control of nonconforming product 4.13	●	■		■	■	●	●	●	■	▲	▲	■
Corrective and preventive action 4.14	●	■	■	■	●	●	●	●	●	■	■	●
Handling, storage, packaging, preservation, and delivery 4.15	●		▲	▲	▲	■	●	■	●		■	●
Control of quality records 4.16	■	●		■	■	■	■	●	■	▲	▲	■
Internal quality audits 4.17	●	■	▲	■	●	■	■	●	■	■	▲	●
Training 4.18	●	▲	■	■	■	■	■	■	■	●	▲	■
Servicing 4.19	●	■	●	●	■	●	■	■	■	■	■	●
Statistical techniques 4.20	■			■	■	■	■	●	●	■		■

Legend: Major role ●   Support role ■   Reviewing role ▲

Figure 3.1 Typical responsibility matrix by element.

3.1.1 Methodology for performing shortfall analysis

By now the candidate company's management has selected the ISO 9000 quality system standard it plans to implement. Since the choice of standard has been made and all the preparatory activities of Step 2 have been accomplished, the company is ready to begin shortfall analysis.

The personnel assigned to the shortfall analysis task must be experienced and have a solid understanding of the company's overall operation. The successful performance of their tasks depend on the following factors:

- Specific assignments
- Proper resources
- Knowledge of documenting shortfalls
- Shortfall methodology

Specific assignment. Personnel must

- Be assigned a specific system element, paragraph, task, process, and so on.
- Be well versed in their assigned task or process.
- Have a schedule.
- Know if they are working on teams or as individuals.
- Know if they report to their functional manager, the ISO management representative, or both.

Proper resources. The assignee(s) must have the following:

- Selected ISO 9000 directive standard
- All ISO 9000 guidelines that are applicable to the assigned task
- All available company documentation that relates to the assignment
- Access to all other company documentation
- Access to the cognizant management and workforce in the area assigned

Knowledge of documenting shortfalls. The assigned individual must

- Know the standard method of documenting results, including the use of special forms.
- Know the degree of detail expected in the statement of shortfall.
- Be able to explain the relationship between the documented shortfall and the proposed remedial action.

Shortfall methodology. The assignee(s) must be aware of the proper steps for investigating possible shortfalls. Thus, they must

- Know the requirements of the directive standard.
- Examine whether the company actually performs the required task.
- Determine whether the task is performed to the requirements.
- Decide whether the documentation addresses the task.
- Determine whether the documentation meets the requirements of the directive.
- Decide if both the task performance and the documentation are effective for the purpose intended.
- Examine processes for compliance or shortfall to any applicable, current, and documented procedures.

The people assigned to the shortfall analysis need to be meticulous as they examine each applicable element, paragraph, and line in the directive and documentation. They require training on the approach to take when there is no documentation. They must know when the focus of the review is on performance and when it is on documentation. Finally, they need to be thoroughly convinced that their level of performance is critical to the development of the final implementation plan.

3.1.2 Using the selected standard as a source of requirements

The company's search for shortfalls must begin with the search for stated requirements. The quality system requirements are stated within each of the system elements in the directive standard selected. Reviewers must read and analyze the selected standard on a complete section-by-section, line-by-line, and even word-by-word basis. This dissection must be made while keeping in mind the total picture of a well-defined basic quality system.

The requirements in the selected quality system standard are directive, not prescriptive. As such, the standard generically states what is required, but it does not provide specific direction as to how the requirement must be satisfied. To assure no aspects are overlooked, the requirements in the standard must be viewed from several approaches, each of which offers new considerations for determining the exact nature of the requirement. Once the requirement has been clearly defined, the reviewer determines whether the company complies or falls short of compliance. The following discussion provides insight on the factors contributing to proper interpretation of the requirements.

Dealing with the standards' generic nature. The ISO 9000 quality standards are written in such a way as to be equally applicable to all companies, organizations, and entities (see Figure 3.2). The exact methods used to satisfy the requirements are dependent on the nature of the company attempting compliance. Only management, supported by the workforce, can determine the best approach for the company to use. Personnel from two different companies, reading the same stated requirement, may "see" different requirements. Interpretation of requirements relates differently to each company.

Each reviewer or analyst will always be using his or her own company's frame of reference when comparing the requirements with current performance. As such, the resultant list of applicable requirements, shortfalls, and solutions will always be specifically tailored to the reviewer's parent company. With each such analysis, the genius of the ISO 9000 generic standard approach is proven again.

Handling the interpretation of a vague requirement. Many requirements are quite clearly expressed in the selected standard, leaving the reviewer with little doubt as to what is expected. For example, ISO 9001 paragraph

Business	Vehicle	Process controlled
Manufacturing	Staff/machines/tools	Machining
Academia	Staff/course preparation	Instruction
Insurance		Claims handling
	Staff/equipment	
Hotels	Staff/material	Housekeeping
Retail	Staff/displays/goods	Stock rotation
Newspaper	Staff/source input	Preparation to print
Airlines	Staff/equipment	Aircraft servicing
Hospital	Staff/equipment	Emergency room

Figure 3.2 Generic nature of standards (using ISO 9001 process control example).

4.1.2.3, states that "the supplier's management with executive responsibility shall appoint a member of the supplier's own management" to function as the company's ISO management representative. The requirement is satisfied by a clear single action. The standard then goes on to explain the responsibilities of the appointment.

Other requirements, however, may be stated in such a way as to provide for considerable leeway in deciding the exact application. For instance, ISO 9001 paragraph 4.5.3 on document and data changes states, "where practicable, the nature of the change shall be identified in the document or the appropriate attachments." In this case, the reviewer must deal with when it is or is not practicable to identify the change directly in the document; and exactly what are the appropriate attachments. The standard is intentionally vague in this situation to permit the candidate company some leeway in determining how it will meet the basic document and data change identity requirement. This allows for variation in acceptable compliance methods used in unrelated business activities, such as required for software development, bridge/building construction, and automotive test design.

Companies can sort out the proper application and interpretation of vague requirements in a number of ways (see Figure 3.3).

1. *Examine requirement in context.*

   The initial step to understand the requirement must be to examine it in the context of the overall standard, as well as the specific wording within the paragraph or subparagraph. The stated

---

- Look for clear and obvious statements.
- Consider statements in context of text discussion.
- Determine how statement applies to company operations.
- Project an approach that would meet requirements.
- Examine ISO 9000-2:1993 for interpretation.
- Use other applicable ISO 9000 guidelines.
- Utilize any commercially available references.
- Determine what makes sense for the company.

Figure 3.3 How to examine ISO 9001 requirements.

activities are usually reflective of a process, and when examined as such, the logic of the sequence aids in the interpretation.

2. *Subject already addressed by company.*

   The next step is to examine the requirement in relation to how the candidate company manages or stipulates that aspect or phase within its own quality system. Again using the example from paragraph 4.5.3 of ISO 9001, it may be clear that within the company operations, there are situations where changes are shown (or could be shown) within the document. It may also be there are other times when the changes cannot be shown in this manner. The same is true for whether or not the company uses attachments to indicate a document change. Reviewers can now interpret the requirement in their own frame of reference. The most suitable means of complying with the requirement may now be determined. A consistent approach for identifying document changes may be the preferred method, but variation by functional document may also be acceptable.

3. *Have reviewers interpret requirement.*

   When reviewers are involved in such an in-depth analysis, often they can visualize suitable compliance methods even if the requirement is not currently being achieved within the company. For example, the need for noting document changes may be satisfactorily accomplished by something as simple as underlining the specific lines that have been affected by the latest change. Indeed, this simple technique is frequently used by companies as an acceptable method of meeting the standard. The ISO 9000 generic approach permits whatever compliance method the candidate company regards as most appropriate for its situation. The key is that it must be a *compliance* method.

4. *Use ISO guideline documents to aid interpretation.*

   The appropriate guideline may provide information as to how the ISO 9000 directive requirement may be interpreted and/or satisfied in a best practices environment. The guideline documents cover many of the ISO directive subjects, and often can be used to gain sufficient information to make suitable interpretations and decisions. Some of the most pertinent guideline documents will be discussed in section 3.3.

From these examples, the shortfall may be written either as a general problem area with no apparent solution, or as a specifically identified problem with a potential means of resolution. The actual identification of the particular problem, as well as its possible resolution, may be based on an ongoing company operational reference. Above all, reviewers must always use a logical company-based approach to the shortfall definition process. Even when the company simply does not perform the required task, selection of a new compliance method must still be logical to company operations. Shortfalls must be written in such a way as to permit ready identification of possible remedies.

3.1.3 Dealing with unstated or implied requirements

In addition to those requirements that are directly stated in the ISO 9000 directive standard, reviewers must be experienced enough to detect the many implied requirements within ISO standards. While intended to result in compliance actions, these implied requirements are not stated in the standard and must be seen as requirements only by implication. For example, ISO 9001 paragraph 4.9 states, "Records shall be maintained for qualified processes, equipment, and personnel." The simple statement "records shall be maintained" conveys the obvious requirement to maintain records; but it also implies the identification of what documents will be considered as suitable records, and how specific records for qualified processes, equipment, and personnel will be maintained.

Expanding these implied requirements to a secondary or support level, it should be evident that once suitable records are identified, there must also be a system and responsibility for collecting, storing, and maintaining them. Another implication is the need to define how the other requirements for records are affected by any process, equipment, or personnel changes. Thus, a requirement for "records" invokes a whole battery of implied requirements for identification, development, collection, responsibility, control, storage, retention, and so on. The reviewers must be astute enough to assure that the shortfall analysis addresses the company's total variance. A simple statement reflecting the absence of records will not be sufficient to determine the scope of the specific shortfall. The remedial actions that must be developed and included in the detailed implementation plan depend on the thoroughness of the stated shortfall.

3.1.4 Determining compliance when the task is intermittent

It is often difficult to perform shortfall analysis when the task being reviewed is intermittent. Thus, it is difficult to observe a required task being performed on a real-time basis. An example is the management review of the quality system. The requirement in the standard is stated in such a way as to require considerable judgment in determining compliance. ISO 9001 paragraph 4.1.3 indicates, "The supplier's management . . . shall review the quality system . . . to ensure its continuing suitability and effectiveness." In this case, the requirement is quite clear but the determination of compliance is likely to be an extensive investigative task. The intermittent nature of the activity, and the possible inability to observe it being performed, causes heavy dependence on document and records review.

In order to properly perform the shortfall analysis when the task is intermittent, reviewers must determine whether there is causative documentation to require such a review and whether there is evidence of the reviews taking place. Part of the shortfall may be that there is an absence of evidence that the task is actually performed.

Even if there is recorded evidence that management reviews the quality system periodically, are suitability and effectiveness of the quality system adequately addressed? Is the quality system actually suitable and effective? In other words, is the management review effective in achieving what is intended? In this situation, reviewers must

- Determine if there is a procedural requirement for management review of the quality system.
- Examine for any evidence that the reviews take place as required.
- Assess whether the suitability and effectiveness of the quality system are indeed addressed at the reviews.
- Defer the question of overall system effectiveness to the management representative.

The question on whether the required end result of system effectiveness has been achieved is one that must be judged by the total quality system shortfall.

3.1.5 Assigning personnel for the shortfall analysis

Some companies use a modified internal quality system audit program to determine shortfall. Although this approach is ordinarily quite thorough, it tends to be very time-consuming. In this application, it usually breaks down due to the absence of concrete objective evidence and the absolute data needed for typical internal quality audit findings. If, however, the company is simply converting its quality system from one standard to another, and it is selectively used, an internal quality audit approach does provide some well-derived shortfall data for any necessary actions. Normally, internal quality audit activities are used to confirm compliance and are not used as early in the implementation process as shortfall analysis.

In Step 2, it was suggested that all of the company's functional organizations examine each of the requirements of the ISO quality system standard for application to their operations. Just as a company addresses requirement compliance based on its frame of reference, so will the individual function. Thus, the use of functional teams or individuals with a broad scope of reference is an excellent means of assuring all shortfalls are identified. In addition, the broader reference base will benefit the company in deciding how to actually address the documentation shortfalls encountered.

3.2 The major shortfall is usually documentation related

As noted in Step 2, all available documentation for use in the shortfall analysis activity should be collected. Even partial procedural coverage of any ISO 9000 quality system requirement provides for less of a shortfall and a point for initiating shortfall definition and resolution.

During the shortfall analysis, the reviewers have been attempting to match the requirements of the ISO 9000 directive standard with the company's performance. Whether the reviewers have moved from requirement to performance to documentation, or prefer to pursue the process as requirement to documentation to performance, is simply a matter of choice. Whatever method is selected, the reviewer will typically find that the task is more frequently performed than it is documented. Whether the performance or the documentation meets the ISO 9000 requirements must be decided on an individual case basis. Regardless of the reviewer's approach, the problem of inadequate or absent documentation will be the primary source of recorded shortfalls. The following information should aid reviewers in dealing with the problem.

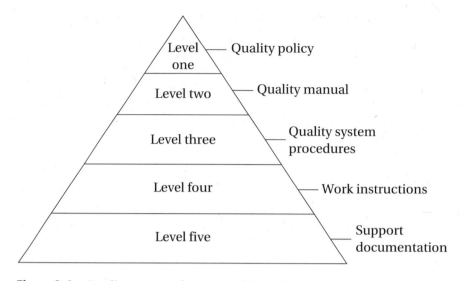

Figure 3.4 Quality system document hierarchy.

3.2.1 Looking for levels one and two documentation

The accepted ISO 9000 quality system document hierarchy involves the quality policy, a quality system manual, basic quality system operating procedures, detailed work instructions, and support documents. These are usually described as levels one through five (see Figure 3.4).

The quality policy is typically a single-page document, and is usually included in the front of the quality manual. Since the company is probably implementing the ISO 9000 family of documents as a new requirement, it is unlikely the company will have an existing quality system manual that is closely related to the selected ISO standard. As with the quality system, many companies may have a quality system manual, which is based on some existing non-ISO quality standard. Other quality manuals may be based upon the quality system approach developed by the company.

Generally, the quality system elements of non-ISO-based quality standards cover essentially the same basic system elements as the ISO 9000 standards; however, the extent and intent of individual system element requirements vary considerably. As such, the identified shortfall in the quality system manuals will likely relate to absence of the entire manual, no ISO 9000 focus, or coverage for all or part of some elements. Thus, the shortfall on the quality manual may be one of the following:

- Complete absence of quality manual
- Total omission of one or more system elements
- Partial omission of one or more system elements
- Inadequate coverage of existing elements
- Manual focused on non-ISO system standard
- Combination of all or some of above

Of course, the best situation to find is the presence of a quality manual that is completely acceptable to the ISO 9000 requirements. With a company new to ISO 9000, that is unlikely. Other than full acceptance, the next best situation is when the primary variance is simply how the existing quality manual addresses the same system elements as are found in an ISO 9000-based quality manual. This situation only exists when the company is compliant with a recognized quality system standard that approaches the scope of an acceptable quality system from the same broad operational base as do the ISO 9000 standards.

One of the purposes of the quality manual is to state the company's policy on accomplishing each of the quality system elements identified in the selected ISO 9000 standard. The manual must address the company policies that relate to quality; the nature and scope of the company quality system; and the company's plans and basic methods for accomplishing the requirements of each quality system element. The task of the shortfall reviewer assigned to assessing quality manual compliance is to determine, element by element and policy by policy, where shortfalls exist. The reviewer must then specifically identify where the shortfalls are relative to the standard. *Note:* the typical company quality system manual is quite focused as to purpose, scope, and content, and is not ordinarily an extensive document.

Levels one and two in the ISO documentation hierarchy are usually the easiest tiers for the company to evaluate because they are virtually all policy oriented. The detailed documentation associated with quality system implementation is customarily provided by the related system operating procedures and work instructions. These documents are found in hierarchy levels three through five and offer a higher risk for definitive shortfalls.

3.2.2 The presence of company level three documentation

Typically, the primary shortfall is the variance between the system element requirements of the standard and the company's detailed quality system operating procedures. Although it may be an extensive task, in each case, the requirements from the ISO standard must be compared to the company's performance and documentation line by line. The results of the comparison determine the extent of shortfall on quality system procedures. Any of the following situations are possible.

- Problems are carried over from quality manual shortfall.
- Documentation of quality systems is incomplete.
  —Procedures only address some elements.
  —Procedures are clearly quality function based.
- No implemented document/data control system exists.
- Ownership of system is not evident in procedures.
- Structure and content of procedures are vague and confusing.
- Procedure availability is poor, and there is inadequate training and/or usage.

If the company is fortunate, the existing quality system documentation may be directly used for demonstrating compliance with no documentation shortfall at all. Such a situation would be the exception. More likely, incomplete documentation requires some revision. Of course, documentation of any sort always helps to resolve company shortfalls.

3.2.3 Operating direction of levels four and five

In the typical company, work instructions are quite often the most readily available form of quality system documentation. Even companies with poor overall documentation usually have some work instructions to assure the operation of their production or service processes.

Most company work instructions are likely to be task oriented. By themselves, they may not provide any significant level of system element compliance; however, by examining them after they are categorized in relation to each of the ISO quality system elements, the basis for all or part of an operating procedure may become apparent. Work instructions often are the detailed methods and means of implementing the operating procedures. Thus, any use of existing work instructions will minimize the efforts needed to remedy procedural shortfall.

3.2.4 What to do if there is no documentation

The most difficult shortfall situation for any company is when it has virtually no documentation at all. This shortfall can range from absolutely no documentation to where the existing documentation has only a few areas of total omission in its coverage. As previously discussed, the total documentation omission may be by complete elements, sections of elements, or by not having any current applicable company document.

The absence of applicable documentation may be due to two possible situations: (1) The required task or process is performed but there is no causative documentation; or (2) The task is not performed. Seldom is there documentation when the task is not performed. Frequently, both the performance and the documentation are insufficient to meet ISO requirements.

Absence of documentation is a situation that causes the team or reviewer to refocus the shortfall comparison from the standard versus actual documented company performance to the standard versus undocumented company performance. This comparison acknowledges a documentation shortfall and moves to determine whether there also exists a quality system performance shortfall. The following questions must be asked.

- Is the specified action performed at all?
- Is the task partially performed?
- Is the task performed to ISO requirement?
- Is there any informal documentation available?
- Does the workforce understand the current task?
- Has the workforce had any training? Can the workers help?
- Can the task performance shortfall be defined?

The reviewer must ask, "does the company actually perform the process/task stipulated in the ISO 9000 standard?" If so, "does the method and level of performance meet the intent of the standard?" If both answers are yes, then engage the affected workforce to help identify the extent and nature of documentation shortfall. If either or both of the answers is no, the reviewer must systematically analyze the line-by-line requirements to see where shortfalls exist. The attendant documentation shortfalls will usually parallel the performance shortfalls.

Frequently, specific aspects of a required task may not be performed at all because the task has no causative documentation. For instance, ISO 9001 paragraph 4.6 states, "The supplier shall review and approve purchasing document...prior to release." It may be that the purchase orders are indeed released but there is absolutely no compliance with the requirement to "review and approve purchasing documents for adequacy of specified requirements prior to release." The shortfall is quite clear: Some type of review and approval is required but not performed. Therefore, the shortfall must reflect a vacant need for a purchase document review to be developed, documented, and implemented.

Reviewers should not attempt to initiate corrective action during their analysis but rather leave such activities to the implementation process. The reason for taking this position is the total corrective action package often influences interrelated activities. In fact, even if the specific requirement in the standard is addressed, the final remedial action for the overall system element may result in some change in compliance. When the total company shortfall is available, the best approach for complete resolution will be incorporated into the detailed implementation plan.

3.2.5 Involving the workforce in the shortfall analysis

If the reviewers determine a specific ISO directive requirement is not being performed, and there is no company requirement for it, then all identified variances must be meticulously listed so as to permit definitive remedial action. In so doing, the reviewers must design or create a scenario that does meet the standard in order to have a basis for writing the variance. In some cases, performing this exercise may require the aid of additional technical support personnel. Complete absence of the company addressing a requirement is rare, however, and the usual situation causes reviewers to record only gaps in performance compliance. Remember that documentation shortfall is the most frequent problem.

Reviewers should question the process participants and users to help define the shortfall as finitely as possible. Experience shows that users of any existing documented procedures can make extensive contributions. This is particularly true when the reviewers are attempting to determine if the existing documentation is adequate to achieve compliance.

In many cases, the shortfall is not one of performance compliance to the ISO quality system standard, but rather the absence of causative or directive documentation and any records to demonstrate compliance.

Reviewers should attempt to ask everyone involved in performing the operation for a list of process steps. When defining the shortfall, reviewers must be certain all possible variations are considered, and should discuss any new documents with the process users. This assures that specific aspects of the process that users believe need to be covered are considered.

Further, in the absence of any documentation, prudent shortfall reviewers speak directly to the process operators, and enlist their aid in determining what is actually performed and therefore what is actually undocumented. These operators are the only employees who can bring the facts to the recording. They may be the only individuals who can list and describe the undocumented process steps. In these situations, it is not unusual for most job or task definitions to have been communicated by word of mouth. Frequently, the absence of documentation is partial or intermittent within the process, and only users are capable of expeditiously identifying these gaps. Simply listing the process steps, with whatever description the operator/user can provide, may give sufficient information for the reviewer to define the specific compliance shortfall.

3.3 Guidance documents for directive standards

The ISO 9000 guideline and supplemental documents are still termed *standards*. Even so, they are not intended to be used in a directive sense or applied to contractual situations. They complement the directive ISO 9000 standards.

The primary purpose of the guideline standards is to help determine the proper interpretation and application of the directive or contractual standards. The methods described in the guidelines cannot be considered mandatory since there may be numerous other acceptable ways to effectively comply with the requirements. The guideline documents provide a best practices approach to meeting the requirements.

3.3.1 Many guidelines are available for shortfall use

There are over 20 supplements and guidelines in the ISO 9000 family available to any company contemplating ISO 9000 implementation. Those identified as supplements provide guidance in the application of the directive standards to certain commodity-based products. The documents identified as guidelines provide overall guidance on the interpretation and application of ISO 9000 requirements for the quality system, system elements, or aspects of element content. Several of the most valuable guidance documents for use during the shortfall analysis have already been examined in Step 2 (ISO 9000-1 and ISO 9004-1). Some other applicable guidelines are reviewed in the remainder of this section. Appendix B provides a complete list of ISO 9000 family supplements and guidelines.

3.3.2 Guideline focused on ISO 9000 interpretation

There is a guideline document that gives significant benefits to interpreting and implementing the ISO 9000 directive or contractual documents. ISO 9000-2, *Generic guidelines for the application of ISO 9001, ISO 9002 and ISO 9003* was specifically written to provide guidance as to what is expected by the ISO 9000 directive standards. This document should be available to each shortfall analysis reviewer within the candidate company. Although late to the ISO 9000 scene, this 1993 document has received widespread acceptance as a detailed guide for assistance in the interpretation of directive standards.

ISO 9000-2 provides specific compliance guidance on each quality system element requirement in the directive. It uses the same numerical, paragraph-by-paragraph references as the directive standard. Each stated requirement within each system element is examined, and the expected TC 176 implementation response is defined for users. If there is any question whether the current performance method meets the directive standard, ISO 9000-2 provides definition of the expected best practice methods for compliance. Even if the candidate company does not perform the task in the manner recommended by the guideline, the information offered is usually sufficient to decide whether the company is compliant, or what actions are required for it to be so. Every candidate company can benefit from the use of ISO 9000-2 during the shortfall review process since it

- Covers all 20 primary elements of ISO 9001.
- Provides for selective application to ISO 9002/3.
- Provides interpretation and clarification of requirements.
- Explains what is expected on tasks and in documentation.

- Presents guidance on compliance methods.
- Gives examples of acceptable compliance approaches.
- Explains some areas of possible overkill.

3.3.3 Guidance for industry-based ISO 9000 quality systems

All ISO 9000 guideline documents are generically written. As such, even the described guideline documents, which address many aspects of system element compliance, are still not company specific to the degree desired by many intended users. TC 176 has determined that company-specific or even industry-specific guidelines are virtually impossible to develop. Certainly such specific guidance could not be done on an international basis, as would be required by the ISO 9000 TC charter. Although such an undertaking is impossible, TC 176 did pursue and develop a series of basic product-specific or commodity-specific guidelines.

In addition to the hardware standards reflected in many of the guidelines, there are now commodity guideline documents dealing with software, processed materials, and services. The commodity-based supplement standards are: ISO 9000-3, *Guidelines for the application of ISO 9001 to the development, supply and maintenance of software;* ISO 9004-2, *Quality management and quality system elements, Part 2— Guidelines for services;* and ISO 9004-3, *Quality management and quality system elements, Part 3—Guidelines for processed materials.* These additional interpretive aids help companies apply the selected ISO directive standard to their commodity-unique activities.

3.3.4 Specific guidance for key quality system elements

The ISO 9000 guidelines mentioned so far tend to address generic interpretation and application of either basic quality system concepts or overall system requirements. Other ISO 9000 guidelines are available that address specific aspects of the individual quality system elements. Although these guidelines are primarily designed for use by companies already implementing ISO 9000 standards, they are beneficial during shortfall analysis. These guidelines address specific aspects such as operating, managing, and staffing internal quality auditing programs; calibration and use of measuring and test equipment; configuration management activities; developing quality manuals and quality plans; quality improvement; and project management.

Of particular interest is ISO 10013, *Guidelines for developing quality manuals*. It addresses the purpose, structure, content, and issuance of company quality system manuals. Since the quality manual plays a central role in the company's compliance with the directive standard, the reviewers assigned to the shortfall analysis task on the company manual would likely benefit from its use.

Whatever business the company conducts, guideline standards are available for use in the ISO implementation process.

3.3.5 Assistance with ISO 9000 terminology

If terminology encountered in the standards appears to go beyond standard dictionary usage, ISO 8402, *Quality systems terminology—Vocabulary* provides the official definition and usage of quality-related terminology. This document offers guidance on the accepted worldwide definition and usage of nondictionary quality system-related terms found in all ISO 9000 directive and guideline documents. Specifically, ISO 8402

- Provides a glossary for the basic ISO 9000 standards.
- Defines commonly used terms in ISO 9000 standards.
- Organizes terms into structured categories.
- Provides added term explanations in its notes.
- Cross-references related terms.
- Utilizes an alphabetized listing for quick and easy access.

Consensus approval of ISO 9000 standards often involves some compromise and common usage may not be so common everywhere in the world. To assure consistency of application, all ISO 9000 documents must follow the prescribed use of ISO 8402 terms before the documents' acceptance and release.

3.4 Techniques for assuring a complete shortfall analysis

As noted, the shortfall analysis must be performed in a systematic and thorough manner. This assures all aspects of company noncompliance to the selected standard are identified in sufficient detail to define the necessary remedial actions. Thus, to assure a complete shortfall review, it must

- Include all system elements.
- Assure all subelement paragraphs are covered.
- Examine all functions at all elements.
- Utilize functional and multifunctional teams.
- Use appropriate standards and guidelines.
- Use checklists to assure that requirements are reviewed.
- Use outside references as appropriate.

Absence of shortfall detail leads to absence of a thorough implementation plan.

3.4.1 Shortfall analysis must include all elements

A successful shortfall review thoroughly addresses each individual quality system element within the selected standard. Each element, paragraph, and line are examined. If the company approaches the shortfall analysis with the goal of it being a complete controlled review, then there is little chance of an omission. It is relatively easy to control coverage at the total level when there is no selectivity or preferences built into the schedule.

This requirement has been stated earlier but bears repeating. The failure of many companies to actually accomplish the shortfall review process at the proper level of detail causes many costly recovery activities during the actual ISO 9000 implementation.

3.4.2 All functions must look at all elements

The review is best performed by using representatives from all functions. Frequently, companies are deeply involved in ISO implementation, perhaps even preparing for a visit from registration auditors, when they discover they have overlooked something (for example, the engineering, marketing, or human resources functions have not documented and measured their training activities). In virtually all such cases, the failure can be traced to the company assuming that only certain system elements apply to a given function. System elements usually have some application to the majority of company functions and/or functional units. The element-by-element review can be performed by either functional or multifunctional teams (or individuals). The actions needed to recover from such a shortfall analysis oversight usually cause multifunctional ramifications anyway, so the resources are better applied in a preventive mode. Extensive documentation changes are normal in a recovery mode.

3.4.3 Use checklists to assure all key aspects are examined

Checklists addressing each quality system element or chosen subject can be developed by the appropriate shortfall analysis teams, and used by all functions. Although the use of checklists assures a common systematic review, they are primarily a baseline approach above which the reviewers may still wish to venture. The content of checklists can be derived from any of the following:

- The directive standard using company-selected key points
- Available company system reference documentation
- The content of selected ISO guidelines
- Commercially available quality system checklists.

Several specific checklist techniques applicable to the ISO 9000 shortfall review are described in the following sections.

3.4.4 Checklists can take various approaches

Checklists can be developed for whatever system, element, task, or process is being examined. These tools can also be developed at any level of detail required by the individual shortfall review. Use of the ISO 9000 guidelines and other references permit reviewers to focus a resultant checklist on whatever subject content and detail are desired. The following examples of checklists reflect only several bases from which the company may derive its own checklists.

Checklists with directive words. The various components of the requirement base are stated in each system element of the directive standard. The requirements are stated in sentence form, or at least parenthetically.

Each specific required action will ordinarily be communicated by directive words such as *shall* and *must.* Knowing this, a checklist can be developed that is based on all such directive words found in the standard. This simple technique is ordinarily used as a shortfall analysis starting point.

Action verb checklists. A more thorough checklist approach relies on the requirements in the directive standard being specifically stated as required actions. The exact nature of any directed action will be conveyed by an action verb. A simple list of all the action verbs in the selected directive standard is essentially a checklist of all the stated requirements. The company must assure the task associated with each required action is identified, defined as to company application, and addressed by all affected company functions and organizations.

Some action verbs are either linked or may affect a number of areas, so the company must assure all possible applications are reviewed. Examples of this linkage include, ISO 9001 paragraph 4.14, "The supplier shall *establish* and *maintain* documented procedures for *implementing*" and "the supplier shall *implement* and *record*" (emphasis added). Any shortfalls identified in this manner will be well based and well focused. As always, when performing the shortfall analysis, the company must assure both direct and implied requirements are addressed.

Documentation-based checklists. This is a list of all the stated requirements for quality system documentation found in the selected standard. The nature of the stated documentation requirements was examined in Step 2. Obviously, many of the documentation requirements will also be found in conjunction with the action verb checklist. Their use here provides another viewpoint from which to assure all shortfalls will be detected during the review process.

3.4.5 Using externally prepared or commercial examples

Another technique to assure the shortfall review is as complete as possible is to use externally available examples of ISO 9000-based documentation and checklists. Such examples can be purchased or may be acquired from sister companies or any other industry affiliation. Hard copy form or disk versions are available. Remember that these versions of "acceptable" documentation and checklists must only be regarded as examples. By their very nature and source, they were not developed for a specific company. They were developed either for use by the originating company or as a generalized, generic document with potential market-place appeal.

Although the fact is frequently overlooked by eager companies, users must still develop the necessary tailored content for applying the examples to their company. Note that these sample documents may provide the shortfall reviewers with some additional ideas on how to interpret ISO 9000 quality system requirements. These examples do not apply directly to a given company, especially if the company name is simply changed on the sample procedures.

Occasionally companies abuse these examples by trying to directly use them as evidence of their existing quality system. Even worse, some companies try to change their quality system to fit the sample. These companies will eventually come back to the accepted process of docu-menting their own system. There is no proven, acceptable shortcut to actually becoming involved in the shortfall analysis process. Sooner or later, the company must learn the requirements of the standard and what it will take for the company to achieve a compliant approach suit-able to its operations.

3.5 Preparing to develop the detailed implementation plan

If the company has conducted the shortfall analysis in a thorough and proper manner, it should have developed a complete list of all of the finite omissions and gaps in its compliance to the selected ISO quality system standard (see Figure 3.5).

Step 4 covers the development of the final or detailed implementa-tion plan, wherein this entire shortfall list will be addressed for resolu-tion. Before reaching that point, several shortfall data sorting tasks must be accomplished. Any organization of the shortfall analysis results will make them more useable for the implementation plan. Also, these orga-nizational efforts must be completed to help facilitate development of the necessary remedial actions.

> - Eliminate any duplications but save unique variations.
> - Organize based on system elements or categories.
> - Decide upon a lead organization for responsibility.
> - Develop suggested remedial action for each shortfall.
> - Establish time required to work remedial action.
> - Determine shortfalls that must be worked in series.
> - Retain subdivisions for input to the implementation plan.

Figure 3.5   Organizing shortfall analysis results.

3.5.1 The total implementation task is taking shape

Assuming the shortfall analysis was done multifunctionally, the company will likely have a shortfall list affecting all functions and organizations. Every compliance shortfall that must be remedied during the implementation process should now be identified.

The initial examination of the total results of the shortfall analysis will be the first time the company has a good indication of the total implementation task ahead. The company leadership, management representative, team leaders, and all other participants will now see the total volume and scope of the task. In raw form, the list may appear overwhelming, but it can be systematically addressed.

3.5.2 Organizing all of the collected shortfall data

There are many things that the shortfall review teams can do to categorize the contents of the bulk list. These include the following:

- Determine if the shortfalls are in system, documentation, or both.
- Avoid generally stated shortfalls except to categorize them.
- Divide shortfalls into specific problems.
- Divide problems into subproblem causes.
- Determine the discrete tasks required for resolution.
- Review the tasks with assignees to assure shortfall closure.

Such actions will result in an output suitable for molding into the detailed implementation plan.

Eliminate duplications. The first step is to screen the shortfall list for duplications that may have developed by having multiple teams or individuals looking at the same requirements. Potential duplication is far better than omission. In the process of eliminating duplication, the company must assure the filtration screen still retains those valid variations that are actually due to different applications, baselines, or functions.

Sort by system element. The next step is to organize the bulk shortfall list into categories based on the system elements of the selected quality standard. Even such a basic move will begin to provide structure. If appropriate, the company must be careful to identify the shortfalls to more than one system element. As an example, the acceptance of purchase orders or contracts from a customer may involve compliance with both ISO 9001 paragraph 4.3 on contract review, and, if there is requirements flow down to the company's suppliers, paragraph 4.6 on purchasing.

Assign functional responsibility. Finally, the company needs to decide on a lead organization, team, or individual for managing and organizing each shortfall category. This is frequently an obvious choice if the company has functional organizations with the same title as the pertinent system element; however, some companies have functional titles and structural variations that require studied selection. Compounding the selection, some elements in the standards are not clear as to a primary function for responsibility. For example, ISO 9001 paragraph 4.8 on product identification and traceability or paragraph 4.5 on document and data control could be assigned to various functions. If the shortfall analysis has utilized a management oversight function, as suggested in Step 1, then it is usually the same function that directs the structuring of the shortfall results.

3.5.3 Preparing final shortfall data for input into the plan

Another possible step for organizing the shortfall data is to determine what apparent remedial action will be suitable for resolving the variance. If the shortfall has been performed at the necessary level of detail, a clear definition of each resultant remedial action will be easy. The availability and use of tentative remedial actions facilitates drafting a detailed, final implementation plan.

The same shortfall analysis individual or team that originally identified the variance is usually best suited to provide the tentative remedial actions. Frequently such actions are considered by the team as part of the process of clearly defining the shortfall. In addition, the team will have extensive knowledge of the necessary detail for appropriate decisions. The analysis team often records the discreet shortfall in such a way as to permit the tentative remedial action to simply be the antithesis of the shortfall. For instance, "there is no assigned person or process for approving engineering procedure changes" becomes "define a process and assign a person to approve engineering procedure changes."

Each draft remedial action needs to be examined so as to estimate the time required for its resolution and implementation. Some shortfalls may result in remedial tasks that can be resolved in a day; others may take a week; and so on. Having some idea of the time requirements for each tentative remedial action will permit the implementation plan coordinator to realistically structure and schedule activities. The shortfall reviewers are usually in the position of presenting a reasonably sound time estimate.

The review team must identify those anticipated remedial actions that may be worked in parallel with others. Of course, this also identifies those remedial actions that must be worked in serial order. For example, ISO 9001 paragraph 4.5.2 on document and data control, approval and issue would likely be worked before paragraph 4.5.3 on document and data changes; however, paragraph 4.4 on design control can be worked at the same time as paragraph 4.6 on purchasing.

This type of serial order review may need to be subdivided and performed within each quality system element or responsible functional area. The order developed at this point is a best estimate since the eventual order will depend on the final overall implementation plan.

3.5.4 Still time for potential user involvement and input

As noted, the reviewers should avoid simply stating no documentation exists. Since most user-operators own or operate all or part of about six to eight processes, it is prudent to involve this population in the shortfall analysis. The knowledge of this group should be employed to define a process as it is actually performed. In the absence of documentation, the users can contribute by simply listing each process step. If this approach was not taken during the shortfall analysis, there is still time to use the affected workforce advantageously as tentative remedial actions are identified.

The ISO 9000 standards state company documentation should only be to the extent necessary for the satisfactory performance of the task. The implementation plan coordinator will require some level of detail as to what constitutes the extent necessary. Since the users will be the target audience for any resultant system documentation, these employees may be the best source for such information. By requesting that the users list each step when the process is undertaken, the shortfall organizing activity will be the recipient of one or more skeletal lists for each process. Even in such nebulous terms, with some minimum refinement, the implementation planners will get remedial actions having reasonable scales of content and time.

3.5.5 What every identified shortfall must have

Organizing anticipated remedial tasks and identifying anticipated time allotments for them helps the company develop its final implementation plan. All identified compliance shortfalls must have a tentative remedial action, a time and resource estimate, and a recommended assignee. These submittals are given to the detailed implementation plan coordinator.

Conclusion

The shortfall analysis process compares the requirements stated in the selected ISO 9000 quality system standard with the actual company performance. The analysis must be designed so the shortfalls are completely identified, usually through a detailed line-by-line comparison. To accomplish this comparison, the company must utilize the generic requirements of the standard as the basis for evaluating the extent of company-based compliance and variation. The need for full interpretation of the generic requirements can be accomplished by use of both the directive standard and the numerous ISO 9000 guideline documents available.

The company must assure the shortfall review detects and defines every variation from compliance to the directive standard. Numerous methods for achieving a systematic and complete shortfall review can be used. These include the ISO 9000 guidance documents, system element-by-element analyses, functional and multifunctional teams, identifying both direct and implied requirements, current and other existing company documentation as resources, checklists suitable for the company business, user workforce involvement, and any other approach that will increase the confidence that all shortfall variations have been identified and documented.

The company with no existing documentation in all or some of its processes will find the shortfall results to be both performance-deficient and documentation-deficient. To assess the situation, the shortfall reviewers must acknowledge the documentation variance, and use the process owners to help examine it. The company may or may not find that the process, although undocumented, is close to meeting the requirements of the selected standard. User involvement is a significant tool in clearly identifying shortfalls, as well as in evaluating proposed remedial actions.

Prior to the development of the detailed ISO implementation plan, the company must be certain all of the shortfalls have been identified and organized into remedial actions that are sufficiently definitive for inclusion in the plan. The final task of the shortfall analysis teams is to categorize the resultant remedial actions. The categories should permit assignment of responsibility, an approximation of the required time for completion, and a basis for the company to evaluate the necessary resources. Once these activities are completed, the company will have the necessary information to develop the final or detailed ISO implementation plan.

Implementation actions required by this module

1. Assure the trained shortfall analysis team understands the planned approach.
2. Identify and obtain ISO 9000 guideline documents related to company operations.
3. Assure that team members interpret requirements from the company viewpoint.
4. Train the shortfall teams to use the ISO 9000 guidelines to aid interpretations.
5. Using the selected ISO 9000 standard, review each requirement for its application.
6. Assure all direct and implied requirements are identified and considered.

7. Apply each requirement to the organization in a manner that makes the most sense.

8. Identify and record performance and documentation shortfalls in specific detail.

9. Develop a plan for how teams are expected to approach the absence of documentation.

10. Utilize the workforce to help construct absent or incomplete documentation.

11. Identify and implement methods that assure the shortfall analysis is complete.

12. Consider the use of various forms of checklists and examples to assure thoroughness.

13. Collect all shortfall analysis data to begin the required sorting process.

14. Assure that all shortfall analysis data are in the identified format for use.

15. Use the shortfall analysis teams to perform the data-sorting process.

16. Require shortfall teams to provide a suggested remedial action for each shortfall.

17. Utilize the affected workforce as an acceptance review for the remedial actions.

18. Have teams develop tentative time schedules based on their knowledge of tasks.

19. Make sure specific remedial actions have identified resources and responsibilities.

20. Consider retaining the same team members throughout the entire implementation process.

Step 4: Developing the Implementation Plan

4.1 Necessary input to the plan

    4.1.1 Converting shortfalls into remedial actions

    4.1.2 Remedial actions must specifically define a task

    4.1.3 Important near-term considerations for the plan

    4.1.4 Significant aspects in assuring a successful plan

    4.1.5 Including ongoing changes in the plan

4.2 Laying out the company's ISO 9000 implementation plan

    4.2.1 Managing plan development

    4.2.2 Initial activities not reflected in the final plan

    4.2.3 Activities that must be included in the final plan

    4.2.4 Planned review and audit activities

    4.2.5 Preparation activities for customer or registrar audit

4.3 Facilitating development of the implementation plan

    4.3.1 Assure implementation plan is continuous process

    4.3.2 The input for planning activity must be timely

    4.3.3 Managing process participants from functions

    4.3.4 Ongoing management involvement and approval

    4.3.5 Continuity of personnel expedites successful process

4.4 The marks of a successful implementation plan

    4.4.1 The plan must appear capable of success

    4.4.2 Are details sufficient to permit planned adherence?

    4.4.3 Is the schedule linked to available resources?

    4.4.4 Is management involvement apparent in the plan?

    4.4.5 The plan must be capable of completing the objective

4.5 The role of the ISO 9000 implementation plan coordinator

4.5.1 Confidence in the leader assures the cause

4.5.2 Assuring management awareness of planning process

4.5.3 Assuring functional management is still responsible

4.5.4 Coordinator assures commitment and priority

4.5.5 Success of plan development rests with the coordinator

Conclusion

Questions answered in this module

1. Is it essential to have a company implementation plan or will functional plans do?

2. Why are the most successful ISO 9000 implementation plans project management based?

3. Who should be responsible for basic ISO 9000 implementation plan development?

4. What prevents simply assigning a task and a completion date to an individual?

5. Is there an optimum ISO 9000 implementation schedule?

6. What if the customer has specified an unrealistic ISO 9000 compliance date?

7. Why is it critical to get every possible implementation task scheduled in the plan?

8. Must the implementation plan maintain the same level of detail as in the shortfall analysis?

9. What is the most extensive activity found in the typical implementation plan?

10. What are the most critical actions that must have near-term completion schedules?

11. Can the ISO 9000 plan be used to identify, assign, and schedule non-ISO tasks?

12. Are there differences between ISO 9000 plans of small and large companies?

13. Is it a problem to plan major company changes during ISO 9000 implementation?

14. Is there any benefit to scheduling company implementation in phases, blocks, or tracks?

15. Should all related ISO 9000 training, employee involvement, and so on be in the plan?

16. Should all activities through the customer/registrar compliance audit be scheduled?

17. Are there aspects that facilitate plan development and/or assure plan success?

18. Who must accept and approve the company's final ISO 9000 implementation plan?

19. What is the role of the management representative in ISO 9000 plan development?

20. What means should be scheduled for incremental review of the implementation progress?

21. What responsibility does functional management have to assure plan compliance?

22. What basic indicators can be used to predict the success of an ISO 9000 plan?

Step 4

Developing the Implementation Plan

Developing a sound ISO 9000 implementation plan is the keystone for assuring a comprehensive and effective ISO 9000-based quality system. The objective of this module is to guide in the definition, organization, and development of such a plan. The first consideration is to maintain the same systematic approach the company used during the shortfall analysis. The second consideration is to continue the same level of detail into all aspects of the implementation plan. The more definitive the aspects of the planned tasks, the more assurance the company will achieve the desired result. Performing the actual ISO 9000 implementation activities, as directed by the plan, will be covered in Steps 5 and 6.

4.1 Necessary input to the plan

Step 3 assessed the company's current compliance position in relation to the requirements of the selected ISO quality system standard. In so doing, the shortfalls were identified. Closing Step 3 activities showed how the shortfalls were organized into specific remedial actions. The goal was to easily use the remedial actions as discreet identifiable activities in the implementation plan.

4.1.1 Converting shortfalls into remedial actions

Having an organized base, representing the total population of potential remedial actions, allows the management representative or plan coordinator to apply a structured project management approach to the plan's development. The detailed definition of tasks, responsibilities, and resources from Step 3 permits proper allocation and placement into the plan. It also allows for the development of a well-considered schedule. Such a comprehensive and organized approach results in an ISO 9000 implementation plan that is both comprehensive and acceptable to company management and the workforce.

It is assumed the company has identified all compliance variances during the shortfall analysis process. For the purpose of developing the detailed implementation plan, not only is clear identification of the shortfalls required, but so is their translation into tentative remedial actions. The company must assure each shortfall has received full attention and resolution by its inclusion in the tentative remedial actions lists. These are best developed by the cognizant shortfall analysis team or individual. The proposed actions should be offered as the shortfall participants' best approach for achieving full ISO 9000 compliance.

For the implementation process to be successful, the basic plan must also include all proposed actions anticipated within each organization and function. There must be only one implementation plan, but it must include all actions necessary for compliance.

Experience shows there is a significant amount of functional interrelation. Each function must provide the proper level of attention when defining the proposed actions. If this is not done completely, the total interrelation among all of the detailed actions will be lost. This will guarantee last-minute attempts to recapture the absent relationships. Managing the interrelations within the quality system is a direct requirement of ISO 9001 paragraph 4.1.2.1.

For sound plan development, some idea of the required resources and time of each remedial activity must be identified. This helps the planning coordinator develop the implementation plan.

4.1.2 Remedial actions must specifically define a task

The more definition the company can achieve in identifying, formulating, and determining the scope of the proposed actions, the more suitable the overall implementation plan will be. When the plan is being coordinated, these tentative actions may be modified or refocused. Potential interactions must be considered during the actual tasking, scheduling, review, and approval of the final implementation plan.

A nondefinitive remedial action causes problems for the plan coordinator. Without proper definition, the action's scope, probable duration, and required resources can not be determined. In short, the plan developers have no real information upon which to plan or schedule. A nondefinitive remedial action is usually the result of a poorly defined shortfall and must be considered as a failure on the part of the respective team or individual.

For example, a proposed remedial action that simply states, "address shortfalls in purchasing" or even "correct shortfalls noted in the purchase order release process" is virtually useless. In order to properly address either one, the implementation plan developers must first return to the task of determining the actual shortfalls in purchasing.

The management representative should have assured the appropriate definition was a mandatory product of the original shortfall review. To recover, another shortfall activity will be required. By necessity, the reexamination may even involve some of the very individuals who should have correctly performed it initially. Of course, once the shortfall has been properly determined, there still exists a need for defining the appropriate remedial actions. Unfortunately, this is what was supposed to happen during the original shortfall analysis process and such rework must be considered as waste.

4.1.3 Important near-term considerations for the plan

Company management may not have developed a quality policy, quality objectives, and a quality strategy before the onset of ISO quality system implementation. Successful ISO 9000 compliance assumes such policy-based actions have been accomplished as a normal part of the company's business activities. The company leadership must take the necessary steps to resolve this deficiency, and may do so before the shortfall analysis detects the problem. In fact, such is usually the case because so much of an ISO 9000 quality system depends on these manifestations of management leadership.

If the company has not previously developed a quality policy, quality objectives, and so on, it must schedule their accomplishment in the early phases of the plan. Many companies actually begin their planned actions with the development and documentation of these level-one strategic planning activities. Unfortunately, many companies completely overlook the ISO 9000 requirement for these management quality positions. ISO

9001 paragraph 4.1.1, addresses the issue when it states the company quality policy must be, "understood, implemented, and maintained at all levels of the organization." This means every employee must be involved in the quality policy deployment.

The means and methods for successful deployment must be in place and effective within the documented quality system. The forward-thinking company builds time within its detailed implementation plan for the full development, documentation, understanding, implementation, and maintenance of the quality policy and its related documents. These efforts must be performed early in the implementation activity since they affect the remainder of the proposed actions.

As presented in Step 3, another key input to the implementation plan is the identity of those planned actions that can be worked in parallel, perhaps even within the same function. Also identified are those that must be worked in serial order (Figure 4.1). As the coordinator starts to develop the detailed implementation plan, it will be apparent that many actions may be worked in both categories for at least part of the time. For instance, all organizations can work on the system element document and data control in parallel as they identify their candidate documents. Prior to the completion of this activity, however, organizations must have serially established their control system responsibilities, structure, and related document formats.

4.1.4 Significant aspects in assuring a successful plan

It is very beneficial if the individuals who were involved in determining shortfalls and tentative remedial actions are also involved in developing the contents of the implementation plan. These are the people who are most familiar with the exact nature of the shortfall and the actual rationale for the proposed remedial actions. Having them address and schedule those same actions results in considerable savings in time, money, and effort.

If such continuity is not possible, the management representative or implementation plan coordinator should build time into the plan for new participants to be brought up to speed on their tasks. Hopefully, the company has followed the earlier premise and has approached the entire implementation activity as a process. If so, the continuation of ISO 9000 implementation personnel (or their in-process replacements) will not greatly impact resources and scheduling. Turnover of personnel can be easily tolerated among those people working on teams, but the

Parallel

1. Write documentation for nonserial elements.
2. Apply quality policy across all functions.
3. Provide awareness/training to affected functions.
4. Address a structural element with a multifunctional team.
5. Perform internal quality audit of individual elements.

Series

1. Assign system omission to function, document, train, and implement.
2. Develop document/data system, and document, train, and implement.
3. Establish training needs, perform training, evaluate, and record.
4. Develop material specs, use them to select supplier, and include them on purchase orders.
5. Create a quality procedure, its supportive instructions, forms, tags, and so on.

Figure 4.1 Working remedial actions in parallel/series.

role of people assigned as individuals is particularly affected by any such inprocess replacement. The impact on the schedule due to employee replacement and transitioning may cause the prudent company to reconsider personnel reallocation. The problem of personnel replacement is not a major consideration in small companies, because the limited resources tend to assure the involvement of selected individuals will be continuous.

As suggested in the basic assessment discussion in Step 1, the involvement of senior and middle functional and structural management is an essential operational constituent of the implementation plan. Performance evaluations and reviews must be scheduled to assure management awareness, involvement, support, and the provision of required resources. These management reviews are as important for plan development as for plan implementation.

A functional area that performs unsatisfactory, and therefore delays the company's implementation tasks and schedule, is clearly the responsibility of the related functional managers. They will usually be aware of the performance of their representatives when activities relate to aspects of the function. Periodic company-level management reviews included in the implementation plan, however, will assure that all appropriate managers have a sound awareness of how their people are performing in relation to the total plan assignment. It is the practiced coordinator who schedules such monitoring activity directly into the basic implementation plan. In fact, the minimum schedule points for management review and approval are each time the plan transitions from one implementation phase to another.

Even though they are not directly related to any ISO 9000 shortfalls, there are a number of other activities that must be scheduled into the implementation plan. In almost all cases, these activities result from management decisions to include various parallel efforts. Often these activities are the indirect result of the company's ISO 9000 initiatives and are best accomplished in conjunction with the plan. These activities may include implementation of basic company or functional organizational changes, corporate quality policy and objectives, management training, and other prudent actions.

In addition to these indirect activities, a number of directly related ISO support activities must be scheduled into the implementation plan. These include creating an overall employee awareness of the ISO 9000 standard, the planned company ISO implementation process, the registration process, and company progress against the implementation plan. In addition, some scheduled ISO supportive actions should result in assuring key influences are kept up-to-date. These influences include the corporation, sister companies, the customers, and affected labor unions. For example, if support personnel have been loaned to the company, the cognizant corporate source will need to track scheduled release.

Other supportive activities to be scheduled include: the identification and nature of any orientation/training necessary to support implementation; any changes to identified operational aspects such as standard forms, tags, and charts; any related facility changes/methods; the time required for staggered or incremental introduction of changes; and the development of the means and techniques for measuring implementation effectiveness.

4.1.5 Including ongoing changes in the plan

Up to this point, typical ingredients that must be molded into a sound company ISO 9000 implementation plan have been addressed. If, however, a company's management has determined the existence of some major problem or improvement areas that it feels must be resolved before or during ISO 9000 implementation, then these activities must also be scheduled into the plan. An example of such a change would be the installation of a computerized engineering database. Since frequently these major company changes affect relatively few aspects of ISO 9000 implementation, many of the ISO activities can be accomplished in parallel.

On the other hand, experience shows it is prudent for the company to limit major or significant operational changes during ISO implementation. If possible, changes should be limited to only those necessary for compliance to the ISO standard. A company trying to achieve compliance to a moving system baseline usually experiences coordination problems and accompanying delays. Once implemented and documented, however, the ISO 9000-based quality system is an excellent means for incorporating subsequent changes.

Since they go beyond the basic ISO 9000 implementation task, these change decisions are clearly ones that must be made by senior management. If, however, changes are to be worked in conjunction with the ISO 9000 implementation, it is wise to schedule them in the basic ISO 9000 implementation plan.

4.2 Laying out the company's ISO 9000 implementation plan

The company is now ready to develop the actual ISO 9000 implementation plan. Most of it will be based on the specific remedial actions that have been defined in the shortfall analysis. In fact, the development of the plan has probably not been a point-in-time occurrence. It is more likely the plan has been going together sequentially for some time, as the results of the shortfall analysis and focus activities have been realized.

4.2.1 Managing plan development

As noted, the company's overall ISO 9000 implementation activities are truly a defined process. Carrying the concept further, the company actually uses a sequential subprocess to lay out the implementation plan. By using such a process concept, the plan is easy to conceive, develop, and manage. The plan coordinator will eventually schedule many supportive subprocesses within the basic implementation plan. In fact, the resultant plan is simply a project management-based representation of the overall implementation process.

The person ultimately responsible for the development of the detailed implementation plan is the ISO management representative. Some companies also assign an implementation plan coordinator to assist. This is particularly true if the management representative does not have specific project management experience. Of course, the final implementation plan requires the concurrence of senior and functional management. The detailed tasks, schedules, and responsibilities must be worked out ahead of time by the management representative and his or her implementation team. In reality, management's review and approval of the plan will likely occur incrementally, perhaps as scheduled in the tentative plan itself.

One aspect of the plan that is the most influenced by senior management is the scheduling of the final completion point or ISO 9000 implementation date. As noted, the date may have been established due to customer pressure, corporate direction, or some other fixed requirement. At that point, everything in the plan is basically a time scheduled setback from the fixed completion date. The arbitrary nature of outside influence on the selection of the company's ISO 9000 implementation date sometimes puts enormous pressure on resources. If such is the case, before building the complete plan to an unacceptable date, senior management should consider attempting to negotiate a more reasonable date with the customer.

Ordinarily, the customer is simply interested in having its supplier companies pursue ISO 9000 implementation. Experience shows that near-term due dates are usually set by the customer to influence management at a given supplier company to initiate ISO implementation. In this case, the due date is usually selected to encourage prompt action and is arbitrary. Thus, the customer may be willing to discuss and renegotiate the stated compliance date.

The ideal scheduling situation is for the company to proactively begin its own ISO 9000 implementation process before any customer request. The proactive company can select a compliance date that permits the most effective use of its available resources. As expected, this type of approach is usually well received by customers. Most customers like it when one of their existing suppliers implements an ISO 9000 plan. They are particularly impressed when they can see progress to a planned schedule. Under these conditions, most customers accept the supplier-determined implementation plan and completion date.

When in such a proactive mode, the prudent company must recognize that an implementation plan of too long a duration becomes inefficient. It could end up costing more money than one which has very little cushion in the schedule. Setting the completion date aside, the optimum implementation schedule for any company depends on the volume of identified compliance shortfall and the company's ability to respond with resources. It also relates to the presence of an existing documented non-ISO 9000 quality system. Thus, the optimal schedule for the detailed implementation plan depends on the following:

- Possible adherence to a recognized quality system
- Degree to which a current system is documented
- Volume of identified compliance shortfall
- Resources and time required for remedial actions
- Size of the company and its resources
- Level of resources the company can commit
- Pressure from the customer/market on implementation

Depending on company size and degree of compliance shortfall, companies working to an efficient proactive plan have achieved implementation in 4–16 months. With some existing documentation, a few very small companies have even achieved compliance in as little as two months. For similar-sized companies, it all depends on the extent of compliance shortfall.

4.2.2 Initial activities not reflected in the final plan

Since the ISO 9000 implementation plan reflects the company's overall process of moving toward compliance, it is difficult to identify any phases in the plan except in a general way. For the purpose of discussion, however, it will be assumed the process can be defined as a sequence of phases. The following phases may be integrated, overlapping, or worked in parallel/serial order. They may be influenced by a quality system element or by company organization. They often depend on the nature of the company's application of resources. Each company's plan is developed based on its own situation. Therefore, each company plan is different. On such a basis, the following designated phases are to be regarded as simply overviews of implementation work in progress.

As noted, the first phases were developed and implemented as the result of the tentative plan discussed in Step 1. These first phases resulted in the company's decision to proceed with ISO 9000 implementation; the determination of available resources; the shortfall activity; and the development and organization of tentative remedial actions required for resolution of the identified shortfalls. These preparatory phases were primarily investigative and were without the benefit of knowing the total volume of actions that will eventually be needed for full and successful ISO 9000 implementation.

4.2.3 Activities that must be included in the final plan

The completion of the preliminary phases is the company's entry into the phase that involves developing the actual detailed implementation plan. The tentative plan has guided the company activity through all preparatory phases and will now be superseded by the detailed implementation plan (Figure 4.2). As noted, it is only at this point that the company is finally in the position to identify all of the remaining remedial actions. The final implementation plan is then developed to schedule and accomplish the remedial actions. The plan will also address other associated actions now known to be required for company compliance. These include the following:

- Actions with senior management responsibility (for example, quality policy)
- Total or partial system element omission (for example, quality auditing)
- Addressing absence of documentation for quality system elements
- Supportive implementation activities (training, etc.)
- Internal review and verification audit activities
- Preparations for customer/registrar audit activities

Tentative plan *(Preliminary phases)*	*Detailed plan* *(Final phases)*
Decide on implementation.	Screen/select remedial actions.
Provide awareness to workforce.	Develop detailed plan and schedule.
Plan resources/draft schedule.	Assign responsibilities/actions.
Select management representative.	Address system omissions early.
Select ISO standard.	Perform documentation process.
Form teams for shortfall.	
Obtain current documentation.	Accomplish training/proving.
Train personnel for shortfall analysis.	Implement and evaluate actions.
Perform shortfall analysis.	Verify and validate compliance.
Develop tentative remedial actions.	Perform any remaining actions.
	Prepare for, and pass compliance audit.

Figure 4.2   Preliminary phases end at detailed implementation plan.

With these total considerations in mind, the company must now construct a final implementation plan that assures all of the remaining phases are accomplished. These remaining activities can be categorized as follows:

- Primary shortfall-related remedial actions
- Necessary nonshortfall-related supportive activities
- Necessary company activities required to verify the remedial actions have been satisfactorily implemented
- Activities associated with the registration process

The first category includes the plans for scheduling and implementing all remedial actions. These activities can be grouped into three major planning subheadings.

1. Planning related to system element omission
2. Documentation of the quality system
3. Supportive implementation activities

Planning related to system element omission. The first activity is customarily the least extensive of all. It involves bringing the company's basic quality system to a point of addressing all of the quality system elements of the selected ISO standard. In most cases, companies do have a quality system that essentially covers the basic elements, although, such coverage may be poor.

If the company has voids or gaps in its basic system element-by-system element compliance, resolution must begin immediately. This is necessary to avoid impacting subsequent tasks. In the case of an outright functional omission, not only will an organizational assignment need to be created, but also the attendant resources, objectives, staffing, and management will need to be considered in the plan.

One of the most frequently encountered system element omissions is the ISO 9000 requirement for the internal quality audit activity stated in paragraph 4.17 of ISO 9001. Other cases of complete system element omission tend to be unique to individual companies and often include the following paragraphs: 4.5 document and data control; 4.11 control of inspection, measuring and test equipment; 4.12 product identification and traceability; 4.14 corrective and preventive action; and 4.16 control of quality records.

In most cases, the system element omission is not the absence of total elements, but rather the partial coverage of subelements. During shortfall review, many companies identify significant variances within many of the system elements. For example, in reviewing ISO 9001 paragraph 4.18 on training, many companies are only partially compliant. This is usually due to those portions of the requirement involving records of the training needs analysis, the performance of the required training, and the evaluation of the process. Records for these activities are either not addressed or only partially addressed. With the basic organizational structure and responsibilities of the 4.18 element established, full compliance can be achieved with minor functional additions. These required changes can then be incorporated in conjunction with the documentation process.

Documentation of the quality system. Moving from the least-extensive implementation phase to what is usually the most-extensive phase, the company encounters all of the remedial activity that relates to the documentation of its quality system. All documentation that was identified as absent or in need of revision during the shortfall analysis process will need to be created or modified, and implemented. The company plan must address achieving full documentation of the quality system.

Steps 2 and 3 reviewed considerations that relate to the extent or level of required documentation. As the nature of the implementation plan is considered, there are several points worthy of further mention. First, the documentation must be based on what the company actually does in compliance to each element. Second, the existing documentation in the form of quality system procedures, work instructions, and support documents should be used to the extent possible. Third, those quality system elements where little or no documentation is available should be addressed by trying to capture what is actually being performed.

The implementation plan coordinator must schedule the following tasks.

- Identification of the type or level of documentation
- Development or modification of the contents of the documents/procedures
- Development of the structure and writing of the required documentation
- Review and approval of the documentation
- Release and proof test of the documentation
- Employee training associated with new documentation
- Verification of the effectiveness of the documentation

Completion of these tasks should result in a newly written, structured set of effective quality system procedures and work instructions.

The documentation phase usually involves all of the functions and organizations within the company. Implementation of most documentation involves a multifunctional coordination, review, and approval subprocess prior to the documentation being released to the user organizations.

It is convenient to work actions for certain quality system elements in support of one another. Working related system element activities in parallel is called *tracking*. It is frequently performed with the aid of a subcoordinator for each documentation track. The tracking concept may or may not fit into a given company's implementation plan, but it is worthy of consideration.

For example, activities relating to ISO 9001 paragraph 4.5, the document and data control system, must be planned and worked early in the implementation schedule. A basic document and data control system needs to be in place for early use by all other system element documentation efforts. In support of this activity, each function must be scheduled to identify the documents it will place in the company's data control system. Interestingly, the same concept can be used when the functional organizations determine the quality records to be placed in the quality records control program, per ISO 9001 paragraph 4.16.

On that basis, a single documentation track can now be defined that includes compliance to both the affected system elements—document and data control, and control of quality records. In fact, the ISO documentation practitioner finds that these system elements can be both planned and effectively worked together. Linking elements by their similarity, the related company structure, or the assigned responsibility permits a number of companies to pursue implementation through the concept of related documentation tracks. Although such a structure is unique to the ISO 9000 implementation plans of each candidate company, the typical generic approach to the concept offers the company another option for scheduling implementation activities. The following lists typical generic tracks.

1. 4.5 document and data control, and 4.16 control of quality records

2. 4.3 contract review, 4.6 purchasing, and 4.7 purchaser-supplied product

3. 4.13 control of nonconforming product, and 4.14 corrective and preventive action

4. 4.4 design control, and 4.19 servicing (in service-based businesses)

5. 4.8 product identification and traceability, and 4.9 process control

6. 4.10 inspection and testing, and 4.11 control of inspection, measuring, and test equipment

7. 4.1 management responsibility, 4.17 internal quality audits, and 4.18 training

8. 4.15 handling, storage, packaging, preservation, and delivery, and 4.19 servicing (in product-based businesses)

Note that this list has omitted element 4.2 quality system. By its very title, this element covers all other system elements, functions, and tracks. For coordination, however, 4.2 is usually placed in track 6.

The track concept is only one approach candidate companies can use to create an implementation plan that has structured coordination with the documentation process. Other scheduling and documentation arrangements are likely beneficial. The company must decide what is the best approach for building its documentation plan. Further discussion of documentation methodology is presented in Step 5.

Supportive implementation activities.   Many other activities need to be considered, developed, and scheduled as part of the detailed implementation plan. One of these is the required ISO-related training. Training in the ISO 9000 concepts and applications is required for virtually all employees as the result of new quality system methods and documentation, expansion of employee involvement in many ISO 9000-related activities, and use of audit and verification activities by the company, customer, and registrar. The company must also plan to accommodate any training variances associated with differences within each functional organization. Thus, training is required due to the following:

- The company's newly implemented quality system standards
- The company's newly embraced quality system compliance methods
- The governing documentation for the compliance methods
- Other new supportive documentation for the system
- Probable expansion of employee involvement activities
- Anticipated auditing and compliance verification activities
- The company's pursuit and achievement of registration

Requirements for the initial employee orientation on ISO 9000, specific task and documentation training, auditor/auditee training, and periodic employee updating on implementation progress were already described. Now actions to achieve these tasks need to be defined, developed, and scheduled. In addition to these informational and awareness training activities, planned user involvement in draft document review and proof testing of new procedural concepts must be included in the implementation plan. As discussed, training should always be scheduled at a point where it is immediately beneficial to recipients.

If the shortfall analysis reveals the absence or incompleteness of a formal internal quality audit program, the appropriate remedial actions must now be planned and scheduled. They must include not only the creation or modification of the function and its documentation, but also its internal auditor training program. This program must include and schedule on-the-job auditing. Auditor training must be scheduled early in the implementation process so that the trained auditors will be available for the subsequent ISO 9000 compliance verification activities.

There are probably a number of other supportive activities that need to be considered for inclusion in the implementation plan. The company will have already developed a list and definition of these actions. The company must assure no required action is overlooked in scheduling. Something as simple as the possible need for having new ISO 9000 quality system forms, tags, and charts will require a lead time and, as such, are candidates for scheduling in the implementation plan.

4.2.4 Planned review and audit activities

As activities in the implementation plan are completed, the company must plan and schedule both reviews and final acceptance. Occasionally, these steps can be performed once, and the task is completed. More often, planning for incremental acceptance of the compliance verification actions provides better assurance. A company must never rely on a single final verification and acceptance review as its first serious examination of implementation success. Such an approach assumes first-time perfection in a developmental activity, and it is clearly a poor time to discover major problems.

All ongoing implementation monitoring by company management and its representative must be included in the plan. In addition, most companies schedule a formal review process that entails user self-audit, cognizant management audit and approval, implementation team review and approval, internal quality audit, and some version of an independent examination and acceptance.

This last company-level verification effort may be defined and scheduled to be as encompassing as necessary. In a small company, it may be performed by the ISO management representative or even functional implementation coordinators. A large company may use the company's new formal internal quality audit process as the primary approach. Whatever methods are used, the entire review and verification process needs to be scheduled in the plan. Verification is often scheduled by company function and area as well as by quality system element. Do not overlook the fact that the quality system verification process is also a mandatory ISO 9000 requirement, and is used to demonstrate system effectiveness before full compliance may be considered.

As noted, periodic management reviews of the quality system are both mandatory and essential. These reviews serve as an ongoing measure of performance against the planned implementation tasks and schedules. These management reviews must be specifically scheduled in the implementation plan. These reviews are critical to the process schedule as periodic management acceptance gates.

4.2.5 Preparation activities for customer or registrar audit

If the end point in the implementation plan is a customer or registrar compliance audit, the company must assure it has thoroughly examined all aspects of its compliance before the outside audit. The schedule for these activities should provide ample time for the company's internal quality auditors to complete at least one audit cycle of all system elements prior to any outside audit. The coordinator should also build time into the schedule for the necessary liaison and attendant company preparation that is typical of any visitor audits. Further, it is prudent to allow time in the schedule for some possible additional remedial actions that may be identified during the company's preparatory audits.

The company should incorporate a formal independent final acceptance audit into its ISO 9000 implementation plan. This is an excellent means of preparing for the customer or registrar visit. It provides systematic assurance that no aspect of compliance has been overlooked. In addition to declaring the company in compliance, the scheduled audit(s) also exposes the company's management and workforce to the auditor/auditee environment. By scheduling the activity in all functional areas, it permits company personnel to practice being audited. The benefits gained from this experience can only be fully appreciated by being a visiting auditor at a company which has not done so.

During an audit by any outside agency, it is in the best interest of the company to plan and schedule the training and use of company internal quality auditors as company facilitators. In so doing, the company takes advantage of the fact its auditors will likely know more about the total ISO 9000 quality system than anyone else in the company. This subject is explored in Step 8.

4.3 Facilitating development of the implementation plan

The company can benefit from reviewing several significant planning factors, if it recognizes and addresses them ahead of actual plan development. These facilitating factors are essentially carryovers from the shortfall assessment and remedial action definition activities discussed in Step 3. They include the following:

- Ongoing management involvement and approval
- Assure implementation plan reflects a continuous process
- Assure required input sequence is developed and issued
- Timely input to the planning activity
- Functional management responsible for participants
- Continuity of participating personnel

4.3.1 Assure the implementation plan is a continuous process

The primary method of facilitating plan development is to make certain there is no gap within the total process of ISO 9000 implementation. Once the implementation process starts, the company must maintain it in a continuous mode to derive the most benefit. At this point in the overall implementation process the company should have moved through the development of ISO 9000 background; the assessment of current position; the shortfall analysis; and the development of the final implementation plan. In most cases, this last step starts with the earliest inputs available from the shortfall analysis and data-organizing activities. By making the development of the implementation plan a natural follow-on to the earlier activities, several other subsequent implementation activities benefit.

4.3.2 The input for planning activity must be timely

Another significant factor that facilitates the development of the implementation plan is the timely input of all the required results of the shortfall analysis. Frequently, the interdependency of the input can result in many remedial actions that can not be used or placed in the plan until other delayed input is available. It is the responsibility of the ISO management representative—or the implementation plan coordinator—in conjunction with the responsible functional managers, to identify any delays as early in the plan development process as possible.

4.3.3 Managing process participants from functions

If circumstances of delinquent input to the plan can not be quickly resolved, senior or functional management assistance must be brought to bear on the problem. A request for action should never occur until the management representative has contacted the functional managers directly responsible. The necessary corrective action is not complete, however, until a satisfactory result has been achieved. This is the only positive way to prevent or minimize potential schedule delays. Carrying this shared responsibility concept into the development of the implementation plan is essential to achieving the company's commitment date for full compliance.

4.3.4 Ongoing management involvement and approval

As noted, senior and functional management should be closely monitoring the implementation process through to full ISO 9000 implementation and acceptance. This can be assured by establishing and scheduling management approval of the shortfall analysis and resultant planned remedial actions as the only accepted basis for their input into the implementation plan. By linking management involvement to actions that must be scheduled in the final plan, the level of senior attention needed to guarantee continued success of the process is virtually assured. Thus, management approval is an ongoing activity. These management reviews will

- Provide senior management with periodic updates.
- Assist the management representative in schedule compliance.
- Become significant milestones for the program.
- Become update targets for responsible functional managers.
- Assure implementation team attention and time lines.
- Reveal problems for senior management attention.
- Provide forum for direct adjustment of resources.
- Meet ISO standard requirement for management review.

Management review and approval activities continue throughout ISO 9000 quality system implementation because the very plan presented for management acceptance by the management representative will include scheduling of these same acceptance activities. This involvement is reinforced by actually obtaining management input approval to include the scheduled management reviews in the basic implementation plan. Thus, senior management essentially approves the scheduling of its own involvement.

4.3.5 Continuity of personnel expedites successful process

Continuity of personnel in the overall implementation activity is beneficial. The same teams or individuals are used to assess the company's current compliance position; perform the shortfall analysis; organize the shortfall data for use; and develop the tentative remedial actions. The benefits of this type of participant linkage can be increased by using these same personnel to help develop the implementation plan. Consequently, the resultant plan will reflect a smooth transition from the preparatory phases to the remedial and verification phases.

Many companies also use these same key individuals on implementation teams. Fortunately, the need for the company to successfully implement the ISO 9000 standards was instilled in these same people early in the process. By their continued involvement, they can now help carry this supportive position through to full ISO 9000 implementation and compliance. The goal should be to make the transition between the preparatory phases and the development and implementation phases as transparent as possible. This interface transparency will have many other benefits during the actual plan implementation. These are discussed in Steps 5 and 6.

4.4 The marks of a successful implementation plan

Participants should regard the plan as a road map through the intricacies of the implementation process. If the plan is followed, it will result in a smooth transition to the ISO 9000 environment. Assuring a successful plan means

- Users must perceive the plan as logical for the purpose intended.
- The planned results must appear practical and useable to the user workforce.
- The plan must be sufficiently detailed to guide all necessary tasks.
- The schedule is appropriate for the task load.
- The schedule is accepted and linked to the resources provided.
- Visible periodic management reviews are present in the plan.
- The plan must provide a means of achieving its objective.

The implementing team's confidence in the plan is an essential ingredient in gaining its endorsement. The implementation team must fully understand what is required and how to achieve it.

4.4.1 The plan must appear capable of success

The first mark of a successful plan relates to it being logical for the purpose intended and the anticipated output being acceptable to end users. The plan's contents must be capable of being accomplished by all participants and suitable for the task of ISO 9000 implementation.

While the plan must appear to be logical and beneficial to the company, the real evaluation will be made after it has been totally executed. Initial success, then, is really focused on whether the participants believe following the plan will achieve the desired goal. In order to satisfactorily discharge the requirements of each specific assignment, the planned actions must be understandable, practical, and useful to the identified end users. The planned procedural concepts, the nature of training, how changes are to be managed, user input to the process, and so on, all build confidence. The plan must provide a quality system that not only meets ISO 9000 standards but is also of clear advantage to the company. If such a result is even remotely in question, the implementation plan developers will have failed in their task.

4.4.2 Are details sufficient to permit planned adherence?

A second mark of a successful plan is that it contains enough detail to assure that all necessary compliance aspects are covered. A superficial coverage of tasks, obvious omissions, or the ganging of actions in the plan will cause the implementing personnel to fear those unknowns that may yet be discovered. Although some unknown or incomplete actions may occur within even the best plans, it is when employees can anticipate some of these situations that confidence is destroyed. All planned actions must be divided into discreet tasks. Each contributory subset must have a defined scope, a responsible assignee, a specific schedule for completion, proper resource allocation, and the identification of interfaces. With these data, the employees assigned to the process will have the confidence needed for bringing implementation to a reality.

4.4.3 Is the schedule linked to available resources?

The third indicator for judging a potentially successful plan is the appropriateness of its scheduling. The schedule is critical to whether the involved personnel will fully support it. No matter how well the plan is laid out, if the scheduled time allocations do not appear to have any chance of being met, the implementing personnel will have little heart in it. A schedule with no clear chance of attainment dooms the plan from the start. The schedule must be linked to the resources, even if marginally, for the company team members to really believe their best efforts will have some chance of yielding the desired results.

4.4.4 Is management involvement apparent in the plan?

The fourth measure of a potentially successful plan lies in the degree of in-process management review that is built into it. These periodic reviews must be visibly scheduled at strategic points, wherever management or peer acceptance of the incremental results is deemed appropriate. Known review and approval points will assure both a management examination of schedule compliance and the adequacy of resources. Typical in-process monitoring activities include the answers to the following questions.

- Are all required actions being achieved?
- Are all approved schedules being met?
- Are the affected users proofing all documentation?
- Are all procedural reviews integrated into the plan?
- Are all accepted documents properly released and controlled?
- Is the adequacy of implementation complete and acceptable?
- Is the system compliance audited and accepted?

Having built-in management reviews assures that the affected functions, teams, and individuals must at least periodically report their schedule status to the company's senior levels. All such evaluations should be in accordance with the scheduled requirements. The review may also be an avenue for presenting the need for additional resources to a management base that is capable of providing relief.

Scheduled management reviews are incentives to keep the implementation process on the planned schedule. Nobody wants to be in the position of having to explain his or her failures to the management. Further, the functional management with oversight responsibility for compliance will not wish to expose its schedule problems to senior levels. These concerns often lead to a flurry of activity and attention by managers and participants just prior to the scheduled senior review. With such reviews built into the plan, it also keeps the implementation effort from being forgotten in the course of performing other business-related activities. Many of the implementation plan participants have assignments other than ISO 9000, and the priorities of the management-directed ISO 9000 implementation effort must be maintained. If any schedule relief or adjustment is made in the plan, it should only be done by the responsible senior management. It is certain that when detailed reviews are part of the plan, management is clearly a participant in both word and deed.

4.4.5 The plan must be capable of completing the objective

The fifth and final measure of success of the plan is it must cover the implementation process results through to the point of total acceptance and approval by the corporation, a customer, a registrar, or another third party. In the absence of external involvement, the plan may even be accepted by the company's internal quality audit function.

The evaluation activities that lead up to final acceptance are no less important or valid because they may have been scheduled throughout the implementation activities. The following in-process measures are samples of incremental success.

- Meeting all required actions
- Achieving all approved schedules
- Proofing all procedures by users
- Assuring the integration of all procedural reviews
- Issuing and controlling released documentation
- Completing and accepting training
- Proving and accepting the adequacy of implementation by functional organizations
- Auditing company performance to new system elements

To support the process of incremental acceptance, the company's ISO 9000 implementation plan must have built-in auditing and compliance evaluation measures. These must continue up to the point of independent final acceptance and approval.

4.5 The role of the ISO 9000 implementation plan coordinator

The management representative may select a person to act as the implementation plan coordinator. This individual(s) must be accepted by both the affected management and the user workforce. An effective plan coordinator

- Achieves acceptance by management and workforce.
- Demonstrates overall project management capability.
- Assures assignees are capable/suitable for the task.
- Closely monitors schedule compliance in all areas.
- Quickly identifies problems for resolution.
- Monitors resource levels for performance adequacy.
- Keeps management aware and involved in the process.

4.5.1 Confidence in the leader assures the cause

Confidence in the leader is important, because if the participants believe in the leadership, then they can accomplish the task as planned. If the individual is well recognized and well regarded, as based on past successes, then the principals will regard him or her as the obvious person to speak to about any process barriers. Knowing company management has assigned a capable person to lead the development and implementation of the plan carries a great deal of influence when schedule dates and other plan commitments are due or in jeopardy. This is particularly true if the coordinator also demonstrates full respect for the participants' knowledge and experience; their ability to contribute directly to the plan; and the fact that they are working under considerable pressure from functional management.

4.5.2 Assuring management awareness of planning process

Although the management representative has the responsibility for developing and managing the implementation plan, the assignment is not designed to replace oversight and management by the responsible functional manager on each affected process. The implementation plan coordinator must truly act as the title implies. Certainly one of the coordination activities will be to keep management aware and involved. The representative must not rely solely on the scheduled senior management reviews as the means of assuring awareness. Use of management review points in the schedule, progress reports to functional bases, resource status reports, problem reports, as well as personal discussions with responsible managers must be high on the list of assignments for the implementation plan coordinator.

4.5.3 Assuring functional management is still responsible

The periodic management reviews built into the implementation plan are normally initiated prior to plan development. They permit senior management approval of the developmental activity. Of course, as with plan implementation itself, the coordinator must be prepared to act during the interim periods to identify and remove any barriers to the development activities.

These actions support the normal management structure. The coordinator can not replace the functional managers. It is the latter who supply the personnel and other resources to accomplish the task. Keeping management aware of the progress of the developmental activity is to assure the functional managers have all the information they need to manage their personnel in the plan development effort. When the plan coordinator or management representative has identified a problem beyond his or her ability to resolve, it is the responsibility of the functional or senior management to resolve. Experience shows the functional managers are responsive in this situation because they do not wish to relinquish control of those people assigned to them and for which they are responsible.

4.5.4 Coordinator assures commitment and priority

Since the coordinator is assigned the specific task of developing the detailed plan, he or she also becomes the person ultimately responsible for monitoring the overall level of resources committed to plan's development. The coordinator also has the added incentive from knowing he or she is also responsible for the plan's implementation. In this assignment, the coordinator must identify what appears to be a lack of adequate effort or the absence of resources from any sector.

If there is an initial or in-process absence of priorities or resources, the coordinator must do whatever is necessary to restore commitment. Since the functional managers are the source of the assigned personnel, it is they who must assure the proper level of resources. Further, the assigned functional personnel respond to the priorities of their management, and it is usually the same management who may be providing conflicting priorities. Even though the coordinator should attempt to identify and resolve plan development problems whenever possible, it is unlikely the functional people will deviate from the priorities of their own management. On that basis, the coordinator must have the priorities resolved by the functional manager or request senior-level assistance. Other functional managers who have firmly committed their resources can often act as a catalyst in resolving situations of this type.

4.5.5 Success of plan development rests with the coordinator

The management representative or plan coordinator must assure the implementation plan offers complete coverage for the task. The capability of the plan to achieve its goals depends on the definition of each supportive/subordinate process. The coordinator must assure remedial actions are of sufficient scope and detail to guarantee that the assigned implementation personnel will completely understand them. Further, the assignees must have the necessary capability and resources to perform to the plan.

Although senior management reviews of tasks, schedules, and resource commitments can be used as the coordinator's ultimate hammer, it is still the coordinator who must put it all together and develop a plan. The real measure of success will be the fully developed implementation plan, achieved in accordance with the previously approved schedule and resources. Common mistakes to avoid during ISO implementation include the following:

- Absence of senior management involvement and leadership
- Omitting implementation as part of the company-level quality strategy
- Regarding ISO 9000 as just another quality assurance program
- Absence of a detailed, multifunctional project management plan
- Incomplete shortfall analysis causing schedule and/or dollar loss
- Failing to verify and validate all remedial/compliance actions
- Over- and underdocumenting the company quality system
- Ignoring use of available employee resources and not gaining employee ownership for the process

Conclusion

The development of a sound, detailed implementation plan is critical to successful ISO compliance. The plan is developed to resolve the shortfall variances between the requirements of the ISO standard and the company's existing quality system. The plan must convert all of the identified shortfalls into definitive, remedial actions that are capable of leading to acceptable ISO compliance. No two companies will have exactly the same shortfall analysis results or the identical company environment in which to implement the remedial actions. Therefore, every plan is different.

In laying out the detailed implementation plan, it must assure no aspect of the shortfall is overlooked. Every identified shortfall must be converted into a definitive action. Some of the most significant actions that may be required relate to the complete omission of a quality system element, the omission of parts of one or more elements, or the absence of acceptable system documentation. Other aspects of the implementation plan should address supportive training, user review, auditing to assure compliance, and preparations for a successful customer or registrar compliance audit.

The company must have confidence the plan will be entirely suitable for accomplishing the implementation of the selected ISO quality standard. The management representative must (1) make certain all inputs to the plan are made in a timely manner; (2) assure every remedial action is scheduled for completion; (3) schedule periodic management reviews as part of the plan; and wherever possible, (4) assure that the same individuals stay involved in the entire process.

The company must guarantee that a number of key success indicators are identified and incorporated into the plan. The marks of a successful plan include the following:

1. The plan being developed is logical for the purpose intended.
2. There is sufficient definition to accomplish the tasks.
3. The schedule is appropriate for the available resources
4. An adequate amount of in-process management review exists.
5. The plan covers all activities through to the external verification of compliance.

The management representative's role is quite significant in assuring the company achieves successful compliance. The nature of the ISO 9000 implementation plan development and execution relates closely to typical project planning activities. The management representative works through both senior and functional management to assure the implementation plan is suitable and timely for its intended purpose.

Implementation actions required by this module

1. Decide who is responsible for developing the ISO 9000 implementation plan.
2. Develop the ISO implementation plan as a project management–based activity.

3. Decide if a customer's requested compliance date is achievable or if it needs to be negotiated.

4. Determine the company's optimum implementation schedule and compliance date.

5. Systematically collect and input all ISO 9000-related actions for scheduling into the plan.

6. Assure every identified action from the shortfall analysis is defined and scheduled.

7. Assure the use of those methods that facilitate ISO 9000 plan development.

8. Priority schedule those critical actions that must be completed in the near term.

9. Decide whether to include non–ISO-related activities in the implementation plan.

10. Assure planned actions will achieve full ISO 9000 compliance when implemented.

11. Integrate planned actions to assure a continuous incremental completion process.

12. Assure scheduling of all training, employee involvement, and so on directly into the plan.

13. Schedule the mechanism to approve and monitor the implementation plan.

14. Be certain that functional management responsibilities are built into the plan.

15. Assure implementation plan activities result in customer acceptance of compliance.

16. Invoke those plan-related aspects that will increase the likelihood of success.

17. Verify that implementation plan users have confidence that it is achievable.

18. Schedule points in the plan where periodic progress reports are made to the user workforce.

Step 5: The Documentation Process

5.1 Operating to the implementation plan

5.1.1 Activating the writing process

5.1.2 Intended documentation hierarchy and structure

5.1.3 Knowing what to write and how to write it

5.1.4 Maintaining schedule discipline

5.1.5 Removing barriers to success

5.2 The ISO 9000 family documentation requirements

5.2.1 Requirements from directive standards such as ISO 9001

5.2.2 Documentation recommendations from ISO guidelines

5.2.3 Specific wording of documentation requirements

5.2.4 Assure that documentation covers the standard

5.2.5 Documentation as operational guidance

5.3 Specific company documentation considerations

5.3.1 Hierarchy and structure of a documented system

5.3.2 Linked documentation structure

5.3.3 A procedure for writing procedures

5.3.4 Addressing the documentation control system

5.3.5 Review and release of documents

5.4 Aspects to consider when writing documentation

5.4.1 Documentation must deploy the quality policy

5.4.2 Creating constancy of purpose

5.4.3 Control and continuity of the quality system

5.4.4 Documentation as a means of communication

5.4.5 Documents for the workforce must be useable

5.5 Developing the company's quality manual

5.5.1 Purposes of the quality manual

5.5.2 Structure of a quality manual

5.5.3 Contents of a typical quality manual

5.5.4 Preparation and development of the quality manual

5.5.5 Issue and control of the quality manual

Conclusion

Questions answered in this module

1. Why do ISO 9000 standards have a reputation for requiring seemingly too much documentation?

2. How is complete documentation of the company quality system determined?

3. What steps must company follow when writing system documentation?

4. What type of instructions or training should candidate authors receive?

5. What is the management representative's role in the documentation process?

6. Why is maintaining schedule discipline important in the writing process?

7. How are the basic documentation requirements defined in the directive standards?

8. Are there any documentation guidelines available within the ISO 9000 family?

9. Is there any specific wording expected in a company's ISO 9000 documentation?

10. Who should develop and approve the ISO 9000 level one quality policy document?

11. Is a company vision, mission statement, and quality strategy required by ISO 9000?

12. What is expected in the quality manual? How long should it be?

13. Are there recommended formats for quality manuals or quality system procedures?

14. Must the content of the quality manual parallel the content of the ISO standard?

15. What is the content difference between the quality manual and quality system procedures?

16. Must all system documentation adhere to the same format or can there be variations?

17. Can the corporate quality manual be included as part of a facility's quality manual?

18. How are proprietary data secured in a manual that may go outside the company?

19. Can illustrations such as flowcharts, graphs, and tables be used to aid document communication?

20. Must small companies have a manual, system procedures, and work instructions?

21. What must be documented when system elements are simply not performed?

22. Is having a method for developing procedures essential?

23. Does ISO 9000 provide guidance in establishing document and data control systems?

24. To what extent should there be user involvement in document development and approval?

25. Why is controlled distribution important for quality system documentation?

The Documentation Process

For most companies undergoing ISO 9000 quality system implementation, the documentation process carries the greatest degree of management concern. This is usually the result of myths or rumors overstating how extensive the company's documentation must be. As noted, ISO standards are quite clear in their statements about documentation. For instance, they indicate the documentation should

- "Be stated simply, unambiguously, and understandably."
- "Ensure common understanding."
- "Limit documentation to extent pertinent to application."
- "Document in systematic and orderly manner."
- "Address complete quality system."

On that basis, the amount or volume of documentation is not considered when judging compliance.

The 1987 directive ISO standards were the first to list the requirement stating "the elements, requirements, and provisions adopted by a company for its quality management system should be documented in a systematic and orderly manner." The 1994 directive standards have gone on to state, "the range and detail of the procedures... depend on the complexity of the work, the methods used, and the skills and training needed." As a result of this position, all company documentation shortfalls to the selected ISO quality standard were identified in Step 3, and a plan for their resolution was developed in Step 4. Step 5 now begins the activities of the company's ISO 9000 plan. This step concentrates on the portion of any identified shortfall that relates to quality system documentation.

5.1 Operating to the implementation plan

As the ISO implementation plan was developed, the management representative (1) assured that all tasks were identified; (2) worked with the parties responsible to achieve them; and (3) monitored their scheduled completion. This orderly approach was summarized in the initial or tentative implementation plan. After the shortfall analysis identified the extent of necessary remedial actions, these were detailed in the final implementation plan. For most companies, a major portion of their plan involves steps to rectify the shortfall in quality system documentation.

5.1.1 Activating the writing process

The initial step is to ensure that all persons, whether writing as part of a team or individually, fully understand the implementation plan as it applies to documentation. All participants should work to the same goals and objectives, which are discussed later in this module. Affected personnel, including their managers, must be exposed to the requirements and implications in the documentation portions of the plan, particularly as they relate to the nature of their specific responsibility. This orientation should involve all managers who are responsible for a quality system function; who have accepted the direct role of managing a team or plan phase; and who have members of their workforce involved in the process.

This orientation and review is an opportunity to resolve participants' questions and concerns. It may be the first time some individuals have been assigned to the process, while with others, it may be a continuation of previous activities. The goal of these sessions is to help participants understand the planned documentation process. This orientation session is not a training program on how to write documents. Delivery of such training is presented later in this module.

5.1.2 Intended documentation hierarchy and structure

The management representative should present to the documentation writers, the company's planned documentation hierarchy, structure, and linkage. These aspects will either be based on the existing documentation or on a new approach. Using a pyramidal, hierarchical documentation structure for all elements ordinarily helps authors visualize how the assigned documents will fit into the quality system.

Each author must understand (1) where his or her document(s) fits into the planned structure; (2) its relationship to other subjects or documents; (3) with whom or what organization coordination and review must take place; and (4) to what document(s) it is subordinate or superior. Thus, the following questions must be answered. Does each author

- Understand the documentation plan?
- Have qualifications for the assigned task?
- See where the assigned document fits structurally?
- Have knowledge of the procedure for procedures?
- Understand document control coordination points?
- Have knowledge of the best communication means for the target audience?
- Understand the need to convey quality policy?
- Have the ability to interface with users for input and review?

Unless written prior to ISO 9000 interest, level one documents should be written and reviewed by a management team early in the process. Often level one documents are written ahead of either the shortfall analysis or a written implementation plan, since their need is clear and they require direct senior management involvement. As suggested in Step 3, if these documents are not available, they will easily be identified in the shortfall analysis. If not in existence, the development of a management vision, quality policy, and quality manual needs to be expedited. These important documents must be developed to guide all remaining implementation and writing activities.

Since the quality manual is somewhat unique, it is separately addressed in Section 5.5 of this module; however, all of the discussion involving documentation development normally applies to the quality manual. It may be a newly created document or, if adequate company procedures exist, it can be a based on a summary of procedures.

5.1.3 Knowing what to write and how to write it

Logically, most of the documentation writers are selected for this assignment based on their writing ability. As such, instruction is usually limited to how to write specific-purpose documentation. The details of determining the target audiences, communicating with them, what to include in the documentation from a data transfer viewpoint, deployment of the quality policy, user involvement in review and approval, and so on are covered in later sections of this module.

The management representative should stress to the authors that, they should not start to write a document, procedure, or work instruction without examining all the parameters that are part of the documentation process. Premature actions incorrectly assume that these authors know all things intuitively. They would likely be writing to satisfy only themselves. The management representative must assure each document accomplishes what is intended. Further, each must be consistent and supportive of the company's overall approach to documentation.

The contents of this module must be conveyed to all documentation authors before they begin writing. This is a mandatory task for the management representative. Problems avoided are never going to impact the implementation schedule.

5.1.4 Maintaining schedule discipline

The management representative and the cognizant functional management must convey to the authors the importance of maintaining schedule discipline even in the documentation process. All authors are directly involved in maintaining ISO implementation plan schedule.

Since the approved implementation plan was developed to accomplish the documentation process efficiently, adherence to the plan by the writing teams and individual authors is a shared responsibility with their functional management. By assigning the writers to the documentation process, management has clearly established priorities for these personnel, which should not be violated. Any barrier to the priority or its accomplishment should be quickly identified and resolved. Each writer is quite dependent on the others, since in a well-integrated plan, a failed assignment affects all the other schedules. If the resources are inadequate, the management representative or the cognizant functional manager must be told immediately. An absence of schedule discipline will cause certain failure, and will result in significant schedule extension or a restart.

5.1.5 Removing barriers to success

Unplanned schedule variation is not the only constraint faced by the management representative or plan coordinator. These barriers to success come in many forms, such as inadequate resources, conflicting priorities, lack of skills, inadequate management support, policy conflicts, personal incompatibilities, and so on.

By definition, all barriers must be resolved to achieve success. The management representative has been chartered to remove these barriers, whatever their source. Documentation authors must be confident that when they quickly identify problems they will be quickly resolved. This confidence and teamwork is critical to success.

5.2 The ISO 9000 family documentation requirements

The most logical place to look for ISO 9000 documentation requirements is in the quality system standard selected by the company. Unfortunately, the standards do not provide much information, except to require the quality system to be fully documented. The generic nature of the standard leaves much to the users' interpretation. The following sections attempt to extract whatever requirement information is available.

5.2.1 Requirements from directive standards such as ISO 9001

The directive documents provide some insight in many of their quality system elements. The text of the elements usually specifies the overall nature of the expected documentation. The standards state what is required in a generic sense, but do not explain how to determine or develop documentation. This nonprescriptive approach is often frustrating for individual companies. Each wants to be in full compliance with the ISO 9000 standard and yet must decide the nature and extent of the system documentation required for its business.

As noted, the ISO 9000 solution to this dilemma is for each company to decide what makes good sense for its operations. The system documentation should cover the methods and steps used by the company to assure compliance with the selected standard. In other words, the methods and steps needed to achieve a controlled and repetitive process should be incorporated in the quality system documentation. Each policy, operational method, task, and process should be documented to the extent necessary to assure it is always performed in a controlled and repetitive manner.

The most frequently stated requirement for documentation is in the text of most ISO quality system elements. It simply indicates, "the supplier shall establish and maintain documented procedures." This statement expects the company to be quite thorough but it offers no help in determining the nature and extent of documentation. ISO 9000 requires that companies have whatever documentation is needed to establish, operate, and control an effective quality system.

Another documentation requirement, listed in the text of most quality system elements, is for the existence of records suitable to demonstrate satisfactory quality system performance. The company can examine the records requirements in its selected standard for clues about expected governing system documentation. Records are expected to be either direct examples of the governing documents or evidence of their use. Since the standards only state records will be retained, it is up to the individual company to determine suitable records for its operation.

5.2.2 Documentation recommendations from ISO guidelines

As noted in Step 2, the ISO guideline standards are not directive. They provide best practice approaches that can be considered for compliance within each quality system element. The methods described are simply suggestions, and the individual company may have equally acceptable and effective means of achieving compliance. Compliance methods may be unique to individual company operations. The keyword in judging acceptance of compliance methods is *effective*.

Where the basic directive standard is vague, the guideline document may clarify what is an acceptable approach. Some of the supportive guideline documents for specific industries are as follows: for software, ISO 9000-3; services, ISO 9004-2; or processed materials, ISO 9004-3. These standards provide additional documentation information. Also, a few of the standards are specifically designed for documentation matters, such as guidelines for: quality manuals, ISO 10013; quality plans, ISO 9004-5; configuration management, ISO 9004-6; and quality auditing, ISO 10011. A detailed list of titles and numbers is in Appendix B.

5.2.3 Specific wording of documentation requirements

ISO 9000 directive standard ISO 9001, *Quality systems—Model for quality assurance in design, development, production, installation and servicing* has the most stringent documentation requirements. A number of key indicator words are repeatedly mentioned. Using these key words, documentation requirements are listed in over 100 places in ISO 9001. The wording of these requirements tend to fall into five categories (Figure 5.1).

1. *Category one* is where the stated requirement is to identify. The word *identify* (also *identified* and *identification*) is ordinarily used to direct users to document the assignment of responsibility, the selection of processes (or parts thereof), and the listing of tasks. This requirement is not difficult to interpret, and the company should be capable of understanding how to meet it.

2. *Category two* of the documentation requirements is more difficult to interpret. The primary word is simply *document*. It is used in most of the quality elements. It leaves the nature and extent of the documentation open, although some guidance in application may be found in the particular element described.

3. *Category three* is used like the first category and frequently appears interchangeable. The requirement word is *define*. It tends to be used when the system element addresses aspects of policy and management, workforce involvement, direction or tasks, and process flow. Users' interpretation should permit this requirement to be properly handled except where the usage appears to be essentially another way of saying document.

- *Identify* is used to direct the assignment of responsibility and to select processes, best tasks, and so on.
- *Document* establishes the need to provide procedural coverage for a subject, activity, action, or element.
- *Define* is used when aspects of policy, management, tasks, direction, involvement, and processes are clarified.
- *Establish and maintain* are typical of words used in combination, and they usually refer to a process or its documentation.
- *Record* establishes a requirement for the identification, development, and maintenance of records related to causative documentation.

Figure 5.1 ISO 9000 family documentation requirements.

4. *Category four* includes situations where words are used in combination, the most common set being *establish and maintain.* Combinations are apparently used when addressing causative documents of some type. To state "establish and maintain documented procedures" does not provide clear guidance as to the nature and extent of documentation. Here again, the company is faced with determining what is most suitable for its operations.

5. *Category five* refers to those documents that the company plans to retain as records. The wording in the standard requires the term *to record,* and provides basic guidance as to what and when to record. If the company has documented the quality system element where the requirement for records is listed, the selection of those records it wishes to retain is a simple business-based task.

It must be emphasized that the exact wording is of less importance than the basic requirement for full and complete documentation of the quality system. As noted, the quality system must be documented to the extent necessary to assure proper and effective operation and control.

5.2.4 Assure that documentation covers the standard

The company can not deviate from compliance with all applicable elements of the selected directive. For instance, each of the 20 elements of 9001 must be addressed. Elements that do not apply to the company should be so noted and explained in the quality manual (for example, customer-supplied product is an element, which is frequently inapplicable for many companies).

The company is responsible for the nature and method of its application of the documentation requirements. The application must be a thoughtful, tailored process. Many companies involve the workforce users. As noted, workforce involvement creates awareness, ownership, and an increased chance of successful ISO 9000 implementation and compliance.

A company should not attempt to buy commercially available quality system documentation and use it directly. Materials from sample format books, other companies, or other corporate units will not be directly applicable to the user company. Although sometimes useful for documentation compliance ideas, these inputs are either very generic or tailored to another company. Experience shows demonstrating acceptable company compliance directly using such documentation is unlikely.

The company's quality system governs its operation and its success, so it is worth the time it takes to assure the system is properly established and documented. The company may use any method required to make a sound decision on the nature of the documentation for each element. This decision-making process must be performed at both company and functional levels. The goal will be to determine the optimal means of achieving and documenting compliance. The process forces the best decision to be made for the specific company.

5.2.5 Documentation as operational guidance

The ISO 9000 family views the quality system as the means for operating, assuring, and improving company operations. A quality system is satisfactory only after full documentation has been accomplished. An undocumented quality system can exist, but its value for continuity, repetitiveness, and improvement is difficult to demonstrate. If the quality system is fully documented, reflecting the best-known approach at the time, and the documentation is followed, then the system should be capable of yielding a satisfactory product or service every time.

The company's built-in control of the quality system is basically its compliance to its own documentation. By following the system as documented, all elements within the system are equally controlled. Control is achieved by simply following the documentation! The standards consider any unplanned variation from a documented quality system as an absence of a repetitive process, and therefore system failure. This is a wasteful and costly activity and a violation of the ISO 9000 requirements.

> • Documentation establishes, operates, and controls the system.
> • System documentation addresses all elements.
> • Documentation covers all operational processes.
> • All functional activities must be described.
> • Documentation captures improvements in system.
> • Control from documenting the complete quality system.
> • Controls are specified in detailed documentation.

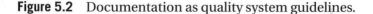

Figure 5.2   Documentation as quality system guidelines.

As improvements fine-tune the system, the changes are captured in the documentation. Thus, the company is constantly optimizing both the system and its documentation. The improved practices are documented and become the basis for even more improvement. As such, the documentation becomes both a reference and a guide for the company's operation. Used effectively, documentation can assure both constancy and improvement of processes (see Figure 5.2). ISO direction for system documentation must not be judged a burden but rather as an opportunity and vehicle for company performance improvement.

5.3 Specific company documentation considerations

ISO 9004-1 states, "All elements, requirements, and provisions adopted by an organization for its quality system should be documented in a systematic, orderly, and understandable manner." Thus, a structured approach is needed. One accepted format for achieving structure is the hierarchical system. The company must decide the structure of its documentation prior to the point of actual writing. The company should assure all of its operational needs and capabilities are considered by determining to what extent it plans to use existing documents and any current document structure.

5.3.1 Hierarchy and structure of a documented system

The quality system documents can be placed in a natural order of importance, termed the *hierarchy of quality system documentation*. The commonly accepted structural levels provide useful data for the company.

Level one. This is the highest level of documentation in the structural hierarchy. The company's quality policy and related quality vision, mission, objectives, and strategy are all examples of level one documentation. The primary document in this level is the quality policy. It is developed and approved by senior management and sets the baseline for quality-related company operations, quality policy deployment, and the quality system itself. The quality policy must always be documented to facilitate its full awareness and deployment throughout the company. All other quality system documents are essentially derived from the policy.

The quality vision is a subset view of management's overall vision for the company. The quality vision should document senior management's position as to where and what it would like to achieve for the company's quality system. Usually the wording of the quality vision references a given year, the customer, the industry, and the company's overall performance. The company quality mission refers to action needed in achieving the quality vision. The quality mission statement may involve such actions as implementation of new quality approaches, concepts, training, and so on.

The final category of level one documentation includes the company's quality objectives and strategies. These documents are described in the tactical or strategic plan and are used to guide the implementation of the quality policy. The quality strategy is frequently implemented over a shorter period than the mission, and identifies the quality-related actions. Quality strategies are the company's planned moves toward policy fulfillment.

Level two. The next document in the structural hierarchy is the company's quality manual. This is generally regarded as the sole occupant of level two, however, it may be elevated to level one by inclusion of the quality policy. As noted, the quality manual should apply the company's quality policy to all of the quality system elements. Further, the manual should provide focus for the quality system by defining the company's methods and means for compliance to each system element in the selected ISO standard. The quality manual is also used to describe the nature of the company's overall quality system. It is the primary vehicle for initiating deployment of the quality policy to all company operations. Once the manual sets the quality policy for all elements, subordinate quality documents must complete full policy deployment.

Finally, since the quality manual presents the company's plan for compliance with the standard, the manual is usually the document of most interest to customers and auditors. Demonstrating planned compliance to the ISO 9000 standard is essential for judging adequacy of the company quality system.

There are occasions when the company may prefer to exclude certain aspects of the quality manual, such as when distribution outside of the company is planned. In such cases, the company may elect to use two versions of its quality manual, one for internal use and one for external use.

A manual that is developed exclusively for internal operations is designated as the *quality management manual*, and may cover more than just the elements of the quality standard. A manual sent solely to external customers as evidence of planned compliance to the quality standard is termed the *quality assurance manual*. Ordinarily such a document does not contain proprietary data. Most companies utilize only one quality manual. If a copy is sent to a customer or other third party, a contractual arrangement is used to assure the privacy of any proprietary data.

Level three. The primary level three quality system documentation is the company's quality system procedures. The ISO 9000 standards make a point of stating that these are "documented procedures." This distinction allows for the fact that many countries regard a procedure as a method of performing a given task, which may or may not be documented. The procedures usually address their subject activities from the position of who, what, where, when, why, and how. The documented quality system procedures direct users to apply the policy to specific subjects or elements.

It is not unusual to have several quality system procedures for each element of the standard or each quality manual section. These procedures are the key to operational success, and, in addition to policy deployment, demonstrate the detailed nature and control of the quality system. Usually system procedures are not used to define detailed work assignments or individual job tasks. When supplemented by referenced work instructions, quality system procedures cover all aspects of the quality system, including all functional and structural elements. In addition, quality system procedures are the means of documenting the major changes to the quality system, particularly as related to policy interpretation and application.

Level four. This category of documentation is primarily comprised of work instructions, which are essential to cover all aspects of company operations. Work instructions provide direction on the performance of specific activities. These quality system documents are basically job oriented, and provide instructions on detailed tasks, processes, tools, and equipment, or are job-classification related. Work instructions often reference level five documents.

Level five. This type of document is normally a form of support documentation for the company's processes. Flowcharts, specifications, matrices, plans, forms, and tags fall into this level of the hierarchy. These level five documents are required to complete the full documentation of system operations. They often become part of the related records.

A document sometimes placed in level five is the quality plan. This is a specific quality system approach for a given customer, project, contract, or product. Quality plans are often specific contractual arrangements between customers and their suppliers when unique processing is required. The quality plan designates which aspects of the affected quality system will be used or modified for processing products or services. It is a tailored approach or modification of the existing quality system, and ordinarily does not create any requirements not already covered by the ISO 9000 standards.

5.3.2 Linked documentation structure

The prudent company should investigate the structural concept of linked quality system documentation. This is a method that assures the ability to track the handling of requirements in two directions—to the requirement source or to the point of its implementation. The benefits of documentation linkage include the ability to establish and trace all related documents for any given element, task, process, or job. Linkage can be accomplished by various means (see Figure 5.3). The ISO quality standards do not direct any specific method. Some companies use a system of in-text referencing to the superior or the subordinate procedures, or to both. Other companies have found a simple in-text restatement of the policy or subject from the higher order document works well. Still other companies list the governing documents at the beginning of an affected procedure, and list references to subordinate documents at the end.

Perhaps the simplest and most common method of implementing a linkage system is by a company-level document numbering system. This method often uses a basic number, established by subject or element, for superior procedures and dashed numbers or decimals for subordinate documents. Thus, work instruction numbered A101-1 is clearly related to a procedure numbered A101.

5.3.3 A procedure for writing procedures

While having a procedure for writing procedures may appear to be overkill and perhaps even unnecessary, brief reflection offers a valid

- Direct reference to superior or subordinate documents by title and/or number
- Alphanumeric code providing source or linkage data and revision level
- Numeric code providing source or linkage data and revision level
- Decimal linkage providing source or linkage data and revision level
- Combinations of the above methods
- Example: Q603.2b, where Q means QA; 600 means purchasing related; 03 is procedure three in category; .2 is work instruction 2 for procedure 03; and b is second revision to work instruction

Figure 5.3   Examples of document linkage.

need for it. Without a documented procedure, all new company documentation would be quite variable, likely disorganized, and of questionable usefulness. Universal application and adherence to such a guide assures a standardized approach throughout the company. This governing document covers the company's approach to structure, format, and content of each level of documentation. It also addresses basic headings, such as purpose, scope, method, and so on; guidance on header blocks, such as title, date, number, release, revision, and so on; and use of subheadings, paragraphs, numbering, underlining, charts, and graphs (Figure 5.4).

Some documents may require a varied format because of the nature of their use. A specification, a work instruction, and an operating procedure will each present different information and may need to have a unique format. Within each document category, however, planned standardization is still appropriate. Variations in documents may be due to the following:

- Pre-existing documentation where change is not cost-effective
- Use of customer-supplied documents per contract requirements
- Functional variations, such as material, process, and product specs
- Data nature of system procedures versus work instructions

Organization		Title/Subject			Number	
Unit issuing	Approved by		Data	Revision		Page

- *Policy or policy reference*
  Governing requirement

- *Purpose and scope*
  Why, what for, area covered, exclusions

- *Responsibility*
  Organization unit responsible to implement the document
  and achieve the purpose

- *Actions and methods*
  List what needs to be done. Use references, if appropriate.
  Keep in logical sequence. Mention any exceptions or specific
  areas of attention. Consider the use of flowcharts. (This paragraph is more extensive in quality system procedures.)

- *Documentation and references*
  Identify which referenced documents or forms are associated
  with utilizing the document, or what data have to be
  recorded. Use examples, if appropriate.

- *Records*
  Identify which records are generated as a result of using the
  document.

Figure 5.4 Typical format for a quality manual or quality system
procedure (reference ISO 10013:1995).

- Use of manufacturer's documents as work instructions
- Use of statutory/regulatory documents as required
- Work instruction variations due to application

Also, any special documents that require standardization for best interpretation (for example, organization charts) need to be addressed in this
procedure for writing documentation.

The subject procedure should also cover the plan for linking types
and levels of documents. This may be achieved by any means that
assures the capability to trace a requirement to implementation or an
implementation action to the point of the basic requirement.

Affected aspects of document release should be covered in the procedure, such as initial document review, final approval cycle, document numbering, document control system, development of a distribution list, nature of change control, and revision identification. As the document writing guidance is developed, the company should consider a policy of referencing other existing documentation (for example, document control procedures) as the preferred means of covering subjects. This approach prevents the proliferation of unnecessary document volume.

5.3.4 Addressing the documentation control system

Prior to the release of any new documentation, the company must determine, define, and implement its system of documentation control. It must specify the company's method of approval for document release. Before final approval of the system, all document types should be reviewed for any unique methods of control. Once the new control system is approved, issuing each new document should be accomplished in accordance with its provisions.

A basic documentation control system usually addresses identification, coordination, review, approval, and distribution. A single governing document control procedure will likely provide overall guidance on each aspect, with specific details covered in related work instructions (see Figure 5.5).

- Identification of all company documents to be controlled
- Establishment of control function(s)
- Use of a master list for all controlled documents
- Method for document development, coordination, and review
- Method for document approval, input to the system, and release
- A way to introduce, process, and control document changes
- Means of knowing and/or demonstrating revision level control
- Means of currency/controlled distribution to assignees

Figure 5.5   Basic document and data control system.

Another benefit of revision level control is when it can be used to eliminate undue proliferation of supportive documents, such as tags, forms, aids, and so on. Controlling proliferation is important, since, in addition to the cost of release and control, each document also requires instructions and training for proper use. A document and forms control clearance function provides a review of each new document proposed for general use.

Establishing records control and retention may be performed as part of the documentation control program or as a separate function. It is appropriate to determine record retention needs when the documentation system is established or upgraded. Including potential records requirements in the basic document may assure affected documents are written in such a way as to become suitable records. Users must never be required to transfer data to a records form when the data have been previously recorded elsewhere. Whenever possible, records must always be actual, completed, and retired documentation. As with all documentation, the communication media may be electronic, microcopy, or hard copy.

5.3.5 Review and release of documents

The assigned document writer is usually responsible for the informal coordination of his or her document with potential users. This helps to assure the document is suitable for its target audience. Further review and approval must be accomplished by the writing team, management representative, and functional and company management levels prior to issue. The nature of the review is based on the type or class of the document, such as specification, operating procedure, work instruction, and so on. Other aspects may affect the level of review, such as whether it is used in only one functional organization or if it is related to specific functional or structural elements.

The individuals approving documents for release will also vary depending on the nature of the document. Most companies use either centralized or functional approval, while still others are beginning to use process owner approvals. All problems and concerns must be resolved and all signatures/approvals must be obtained prior to document release. Only at that point can the document control system register it as official and permit its release. The author is normally responsible for assuring resolution of all comments from the review process. Major issues may require elevation for management decisions.

5.4 Aspects to consider when writing documentation

There are several additional aspects that must be addressed and for which each author must be responsible. Thus, the documentation must

- Deploy the quality policy to all areas and levels.
- Reflect the entire element structure of the quality system.
- Create a constancy of purpose for the entire workforce.
- Provide control and continuity of the quality system.
- Communicate data specifically to intended users.
- Provide useable information for user application.
- Be dynamic, current, and reflective of processes.

A constant approach to the documentation process can only be achieved if the management representative or the designated documentation coordinator involves all participants and authors in assuring planned focus.

5.4.1 Documentation must deploy the quality policy

The quality policy deployment flows from the policy into the quality manual. The policy is then applied to all the elements found in the selected system standard. From the broad base of the company's quality manual and all the affected quality system elements, the policy deployment flow continues through the system procedures and work instructions. Complete deployment of the quality policy occurs when the workforce uses the total quality system documentation to perform all aspects of company operations.

By its existence, the documentation is a visible commitment on the part of company management that it intends to have an acceptable and effective quality system. This documented commitment should be evident to both customers and employees. A fully documented and effectively operating quality system is a commitment of company intent and resources. This commitment must be accepted and supported by all employees.

Employee support is facilitated by having the policy commitment in the documentation that employees use to fulfill their assignments. In writing new procedures, each author must use the quality policy and appropriate sections of the quality manual as guides. If done correctly, the resulting document should be a positive, informative directive, which conveys the application of the company's goals and objectives as presented in the quality policy. Successful companies find adherence to their basic quality system documentation is the best means of implementing their quality policy, objectives, and strategy.

5.4.2 Creating constancy of purpose

When the company is operating to a documented system, reflecting the optimal approach to its methods of performance and compliance, a very focused effort is guaranteed. The quality system, as controlled by the documentation, has created a company constancy of purpose. Every individual is focused and committed to the same overall policies and objectives. This is a tremendous force for the company's success. Employees can assume responsibility and control as a process owner, simply by effectively following the quality system documentation.

The management representative must assure the documentation writing and review process establishes and conveys this constancy of purpose. If company success is to be achieved by following procedures, then the deployment actions discussed in Section 5.4.1 must be in harmony throughout the documentation. This harmony can be achieved only if the authors understand the company's policies and objectives. The authors must be able to capture the essence of the policies and objectives. Doing so helps achieve the constancy of purpose so vital to the company's success.

5.4.3 Control and continuity of the quality system

All documentation writers must include built-in controls that will result in the repetitive process desired. The management representative must assure the adequacy of such controls is addressed during the documentation review and acceptance process. These controls can be derived by different approaches including the following:

- Listing all tasks and processes with assigned responsibilities
- Proper sequencing of tasks, process steps, and constituents
- Specifying parameter values for proper task and process flow

- Defining functional and structural system element linkages
- Requiring explicit verifications, tests, inspections, audits, and so on
- Including process redundancy or monitoring methodology
- Using parallel or comparative actions such as replicate testing

The most obvious control is that achieved by the company documenting the entire quality system. Such coverage assures no portion of the company's overall performance and compliance is overlooked.

When the quality system documentation is followed by the workforce and an optimized repetitive process is achieved, not only control, but also a form of quality system continuity is created. This process stability can be combined with the results of continuous process improvements, which are captured in the documentation change process. The apparent conflict of having stability with provisions for change, assures continued success or system continuity through periods of company instability. Adherence to documentation that is continuously capturing improvements can be an operational benefit. With a documented system as the stabilizing force, coupled with the system's built-in ability to adjust its documentation to both positive and negative changes, system continuity is maintained.

The prudent company will certainly accept the fact that its constancy of purpose, process repetitiveness, system control, and continuity are all dependent on a documented quality system. Further, the dynamic documentation, with its ongoing changes reflected, is the best overall management control system any company can have.

5.4.4 Documentation as a means of communication

The whole purpose of documentation, underlying all other uses, is the transmission of information. Each type of document is used to communicate different types of data, in the form of requirements, information, guidance, instructions, and so on. To assure successful data communication, document authors must be familiar with both the base of information to be transferred and the capability of the potential users. The authors essentially control this communication process, although data transfer may be augmented by selective user training. The target audience must be clearly identified and understood, not as the authors believe it to exist, but as it really does exist. Regardless of the potential user, it is the authors' responsibility to assure the information being transferred by the documentation is valid, unambiguous, and understandable to the target audience.

Data transfer goals must be established. In so doing, document writers must consider the following:

Before writing

- Who is the target audience/customer?
- What types of data am I trying to convey?
- Am I qualified to communicate such data?
- Does the audience have related background?

During writing

- Will the data transfer benefit from user input?
- Can the data transfer be facilitated with diagrams, flowcharts, and so on?
- Are the written data valid, unambiguous, and understandable?
- Can the document be improved with user review?

The authors can also simplify complex subjects by using diagrams, tables, flowcharts, matrices, and so on. This is accomplished by selecting the best method of presenting the required information. If the selection is sound, it will permit users to obtain the essentials needed without having to search through the entire text. Other techniques that can be used to enhance data transfer include grouping data; highlighting headings; using capitalized or italicized key words, breakout bullets, or dashes; placing key data in blocks or circles; and underlining important concepts. All of these communication techniques are completely acceptable per ISO quality standards.

5.4.5 Documents for the workforce must be useable

The ISO management representative or documentation coordinator must assure all documentation has been developed through a process that involves and is supported by potential users. They must understand the documentation and be able to implement it. If employees have been an integral part of the development process, the company will achieve the dual goal of employee understanding and ownership.

Never underestimate the benefits of user involvement in the documentation development process!

Companies that start the implementation process with little or no documentation have a greater likelihood of needing user involvement than those companies that have a high degree of documentation. Absence of a documented system requires that the people most familiar with the existing process get involved. Information from the process participants is likely to be both factual and accurate. In such situations, documentation understanding and ownership are easily accomplished.

Even when the basic documentation is reasonable enough to be easily converted to ISO compliance, prudent company management will involve users. Most companies provide for user review and comment before issuing any documentation. The best review is through interviews and discussion with potential users. Direct involvement gains user ownership!

If employees understand the documentation but do not utilize it, they are registering their belief that the quality system, as documented, is either inadequate or inappropriate. Their concerns may be with the system or with the documentation, but usually these concerns are inseparable. Clearly, such problems must be resolved immediately. Although some real system problems may exist, often the problem simply stems from the employees' lack of involvement in the process.

Another consideration for the documentation coordinator and author is assuring document usability. Although some methods for achieving usability have been covered, the management representative should consider additional approaches for assuring documentation effectiveness, accuracy, and usefulness. These include informal user feedback (before or after document issue) or using a post-issue, proof test concept. Most companies follow up after the document has been in use for a period of time to assure it is satisfactory for the purpose intended and is considered user-friendly.

A final word of caution for the management representative or documentation coordinator: It is imperative that the documentation be periodically reevaluated in relation to its intended use. This is normally for the direction and operation of specifically assigned aspects of the company's quality system. The documentation must be written for the target company audience and not for the satisfaction of the authors, the coordinator, or the auditors—a point of which some companies, customers, and registrars need occasional reminding.

5.5 Developing the company's quality manual

The quality manual is the most frequently discussed form of quality system documentation in the typical ISO 9000 compliance activity. Thus, the activities and considerations associated with the manual's development are presented in this separate section.

Many companies have product manufacturing and quality assurance manuals that cover basic inspection and testing, or even just the activities of the quality assurance function. Such manuals are only part of the documentation necessary for ISO 9000 compliance. ISO 9000 standards require the company to operate to an ISO-based quality system that includes all the functions which affect quality. Consequently, a comprehensive, companywide quality system manual must be developed.

5.5.1 Purposes of the quality manual

A firm requirement for a quality manual is clarified in the 1994 revisions of the standards. These revisions were necessary because quality manuals are absolutely essential. A company needs a quality manual for its internal company use, as well as for presentation to customers and third party reviewers.

The major purpose of the quality manual is as the company's primary definitive form of documentation below the quality policy (see Figure 5.6). The manual conveys the policy into all of the elements of the quality system. The manual directs and documents the quality system. It communicates the quality requirements by translating those of the selected ISO quality standard into the company's documented quality requirements.

The quality manual must address the company's policy on compliance with all the system elements that are required by the selected quality system standard. The company policy and general compliance methodology that relate to the requirements of each element of the standard must be described in the manual. The quality manual descriptions may then be used to present or demonstrate that the company's quality system intent is adequate to satisfactorily address all the requirements of its selected quality standard. As such, the customer or a third party can determine whether the quality system methodology, if fully implemented, appears capable of meeting the standard.

- Communicate the organization's quality policy procedures and requirements.
- Describe and implement an effective quality system.
- Provide improved control of practices and facilitate assurance activities.
- Provide the basis for auditing the quality system.
- Provide continuity of the quality system and its requirements.
- Train personnel in the quality system requirements and methods of compliance.
- Demonstrate compliance with ISO 9001, 9002, or 9003.
- Demonstrate compliance of the company's quality system in contractual situations.

Figure 5.6 The purpose of a quality manual (reference ISO 10013:1995).

The quality manual is the primary bases for system control and auditing. If the manual reflects the essence of the intended quality system, then the manual can also be an excellent database from which to apply auditing as a control function. Auditing then becomes a control function required by the very quality system it audits. Both the adequacy of the manual's described system for meeting the ISO 9000 standard, and the company's compliance to the quality system described in the manual can be judged. The results of such audits can be used to improve the quality system and, therefore, the operation of the company.

The quality manual may also be used as a tool for training company personnel. Since the manual is the primary agent for quality system implementation, it is also the key to the content of the quality system documentation. The basic content provides a vehicle to train personnel from all company functions in the basic requirements and operation of the quality system.

A final purpose for the manual that deserves comment is its use as the primary method of assuring quality system continuity. The same parameters which cause the manual to be the basis of the company's quality system definition and implementation, also cause it to be the primary player in maintaining the overall continuity of the system. As long as it is implemented as documented, the quality system will continue through any perturbations the company may encounter.

5.5.2 Structure of a quality manual

There is no specified structure for a quality manual in the ISO 9000 standards; however, the need for an organized and useable manual is certainly implied. In the apparent absence of any other quality system documentation, some companies have elected to develop their manual as their first step toward establishing a quality system that will meet the ISO 9000 standard. They plan to develop an acceptable manual defining a quality system specification for the company. The company then intends to use the manual as the guide for developing a documented ISO 9000-based quality system.

Most companies, however, have some type of quality system in existence. Candidate companies typically use as much of their existing quality system and its related documentation as possible. As such, the existing system documentation serves as a guide in developing the manual. As noted, at least some basic content or concepts for the manual can be derived from such documentation.

Frequently, quality manuals are developed or modified so as to follow the same order of element presentation as in the selected quality system standard. Although this parallel structure is not required by the ISO 9000 family, it does provide an excellent means of assuring both a recognizable structure and a subject matter correlation to the standard. Such a format has proven beneficial to both internal and external manual users. Since the workforce is familiar with its use, however, the candidate company with an existing documented quality system would likely maintain its current quality manual structure. The ISO 9000 standards only require coverage of the specified system elements, and most manual formats can accommodate such content.

The quality manual can also be developed as a compilation of the company's existing key quality system procedures. This can be based on the governing procedures that address each quality system element. In other companies, it may mean a single procedure for each system element with supportive procedures and work instructions. In still other companies, the decision might be to pull up all of the primary and supportive procedures for each element into the quality manual. Only the work instructions would then be elsewhere in the documentation hierarchy. In small companies, it may even be convenient and reasonable to put all documentation into one comprehensive quality manual. Nothing prohibits how a company does this, except the resultant manual must be logical, useable, and understandable. Use of existing documentation should always be to the extent possible, because of user familiarity and the fact that much learning is captured in existing procedures.

The structure of the company documentation, including the quality manual, should tend to reflect the structure of the company. If there is a corporate quality manual that forms the core of the subordinate company's guidance, then it is often incorporated into the subordinate company's quality system responsibilities and documentation. Another acceptable approach is to include individual company facilities, or even functional specifics, in subsets or appendices of a basic quality system manual.

Whatever makes sound business sense and meets the ISO 9000 standards should be considered in determining the structure of the quality manual. Thus, ISO 10013 indicates that a manual may

- Be a direct compilation of documented quality system procedures.
- Be a grouping or section of the documented quality system procedures.
- Be a series of documented procedures for specific facilities or applications.
- Be more than one document or level.
- Have a common core with tailored appendices.
- Stand alone or have reference structure.
- Have other numerous derivations based on organizations.

Some quality manuals are actually a collection of quality manuals, one for each major function or process, which in total form the company quality manual. When used in this manner, the company must assure the structural elements of the standard are addressed in such a way as to assure cross-functional accomplishment. Full coordination and review of all system documentation being released, by all affected functions, is an essential aspect of this type of quality manual approach.

Stand-alone quality manuals are also used, with each element of the standard addressed in its own section or procedure. The system element must be covered from the applicable policy to its implementation and acceptance. Although acceptable to the standards, such an approach is ordinarily suitable only for small companies. More often the necessary deployment and structure is through the linked documentation concept, and is achieved through referencing supportive procedures in the manual. The documentation linkage methods presented earlier for quality system documentation also apply to quality manuals.

The primary upward linkage for the quality manual is to the quality policy and the selected standard. Although the company's quality policy may be documented for use apart from the manual, the ISO guideline standard expects the policy to also be presented in the manual, preferably in the front of the document. By placing the policy directly in the manual, the necessary document linkage is assured.

Some customers and third party auditors regard the procedures referenced directly in the quality manual as part of it. As such, when forwarding the company quality system manual to a third party for review and demonstration of its adequacy to meet the standard, such procedures are often requested as well. This situation may actually work to the company's advantage since it may provide better coverage of the element; however, it also causes the prudent company to assure it limits the references in the quality manual to only the primary or governing procedures for each system element.

5.5.3 Contents of a typical quality manual

The exact contents of a quality manual is clearly up to the company and how it can best meet the standard. This focus precludes any cookbook approach to the wording of each system element. The ISO 9000 approach forces the company to decide what content is most reasonable for its operations. The manual developed through this process specifically suits the company, but this does require some work.

Although the exact text of the manual is open, certain basic considerations do exist. Aspects of quality policy deployment, descriptions of how the company intends to meet the standard, and the setting of quality system requirements are all mandatory for acceptable operations and ISO compliance. The latter requirements for defining, developing, implementing, documenting, controlling, and maintaining the quality system are all generalized contents of an acceptable quality manual. As reflected in ISO 10013, a quality manual normally contains the following:

- Title, scope, and field of application
- Table of contents
- Introductory pages about the organization concerned or the manual itself
- The organization's quality policy and objectives
- Description of the organizational structure, responsibilities, and authorities
- Description or elements of the quality system
- References to documented quality system procedures, if appropriate
- Definitions section, if appropriate
- Guide to the quality manual, if appropriate
- Appendix for supportive data, if appropriate

Note that the order of content is optional.

The quality manual's title should describe its intended use. If it is limited, the title should reflect the limitations (for example, quality manual for engineering development, or for plant #6). A statement of the manual's scope should expand the planned utilization noted by the title. The scope presents a definitive description of what overall aspects are covered. The field of application provides information as to what area, company, organization, or process the manual has been designed to address. Sometimes the field of application is regarded as the focus of the manual.

As noted, the company's quality policy should be considered an essential item in the quality manual. Usually the policy is placed near the beginning, and is signed by the person who has ultimate responsibility for its implementation. Any policies in subordinate sections may also be signed by those directly responsible (for example, the manager of purchasing for approval of the purchasing section).

The company's quality objectives are either stated as a subset of the policy section or placed alone. In this section, the company's primary quality objectives are defined, explained, deployed, implemented, as well as how success in this endeavor is judged.

Many companies have some introductory pages that convey general information, such as the nature of the company's business or history. Also, included here is manual-specific information. Subjects include current issue and effectivity; a description of how the manual is revised and maintained; who is authorized to input or approve changes; how procedural revision status is determined; how distribution is handled; whether proprietary information is included; and other data determined by the company.

The quality manual should have a table of contents that lists the titles of all its sections and their accompanying pages. Any unique numbering or code system should also be explained, such as might be used for addressing referenced text, diagrams, and figures.

A quality manual usually has a description of the company organizational structure, including the management responsibilities and authorities in relation to the quality system. The organizational description is high level and can often be satisfied by an organization chart with a legend to explain all functional and administrative responsibilities and authorities. Users must be able to determine the role of all organizational elements in relation to the quality system.

The description of the company's approach to all of the quality system elements is by far the major content of all quality manuals. It is in this section where the company quality policy on each element of the quality system is described in sufficient detail to assure system adequacy for meeting the selected standard. The section must address the directive and instructional content. This portion of the manual contains the definition, application, implementation, operation, and control of the company quality system. Such detail can only be developed by the affected company for its specific business operations.

To determine the most suitable approach to use in addressing each system element, consider such aspects as the nature of the requirement, the type of business, the most suitable approach for the company, workforce capability, company resources, and the planned documentation structure. The methods and means by which the company commits to accomplish the requirements, and assure its continuing compliance to the standard, must be clear to the quality manual users.

Several optional sections of a quality manual may be considered. These include a definitions section, a user guide, and any necessary appendices. A definitions section is appropriate if the company uses uncommon terms not found in dictionaries. These may include technical or industry-based words and expressions, unique combinations of words, and acronyms.

Some companies have a sufficiently detailed quality manual as to justify a user guide. This section addresses the question of, How do I find what I need in the manual? A subject index, a keyword reference listing, or some such aid for facilitating usage is often beneficial.

Finally, appendices for supportive material may be helpful. Such things as flowcharts, graphs, forms, and awards may be placed in this section. Whatever is located in this section, it must be directly supportive to the manual and its use. The appendices should not be used for window dressing.

5.5.4 Preparation and development of the quality manual

The steps to develop a quality manual depend on the extent of satisfactory existing quality system documentation. They may also depend on whether some type of manual already exists and is simply being focused to a new quality system standard. Notwithstanding these situations, there are some basic steps that must be considered regardless of the exact nature of a company's anticipated development process (see Figure 5.7).

The initial step is to organize personnel and resources for the task. Many of the development activities are likely at the management level, clearly with support as needed. These activities may involve a focused, centralized effort, or they may be a type of coordinated functional involvement. The basic considerations and actions required for the preparation and development of the quality manual will need to be defined and assigned. This may be accomplished either by means of a separate group effort or even through the shortfall analysis process.

1. Establish and list existing applicable quality system policies, objectives, and documented procedures, or develop plans for such.

2. Decide which quality system elements apply according to the quality system standard selected.

3. Obtain data about the existing quality system and practices by various means, such as questionnaires and interviews.

4. Request and obtain additional source documentation or references from operational units.

5. Determine the manual's structure and format.

6. Classify existing documents in accordance with the intended structure and format.

7. Use any other method suitable within the organization to complete the quality manual draft.

Figure 5.7 Plan for developing a quality manual (reference ISO 10013:1995).

If shortfall analysis is used, the next step is to include all of the detailed tasks and assignments required in the overall implementation plan. Manual development activities must be scheduled for early completion since all subsequent ISO 9000 implementation efforts are dependent on the manual for policy interpretation, direction, and guidance.

The company can use several ISO guidelines to aid quality manual development. They facilitate the implementation of the contractual directive, including the requirements for a quality manual. Of particular interest is ISO 10013, *Guidelines for developing quality manuals,* on which this discussion is based.

The company must select the best structure and format for its manual. The structural considerations presented earlier in this module for all quality system documentation also apply to the manual. Following normal flow, a draft table of contents is often the first section to take shape; then the layout and content sequence for the manual is developed. Next, the basic presentation and style of each section or procedure is determined. The nature of how the company wishes to address the individual procedure format, such as policy, purpose, scope, responsibilities, methods, documentation, references, records, and so on must all be carefully considered.

The next step in the manual development process is to obtain or develop the actual contents of the procedures or sections. This may be a matter of editing or focusing existing procedures, but often it is writing original material. This phase is usually the largest and longest activity in the development process.

It is essential that the flow down document linkage be established. Of course, as noted, the manual must acknowledge the company quality policy and selected ISO 9000 standard. Most companies also show any other source documents at the beginning of each quality manual section or procedure. The supportive or subordinate documents are then either referenced in the text of the procedures or listed at their end under a separate "referenced documents" heading.

Prior to its completion, the quality manual needs to undergo a thorough coordination. Due to its broad application and status, this review must involve both management and targeted workforce users. Hopefully, both will have been involved in the development process, and the final coordination will simply be a stamp of ownership. Acceptance by the intended users is absolutely essential, since the manual becomes the basis for the remaining quality system implementation activities.

5.5.5 Issue and control of the quality manuals

The issuance process for quality manuals must be defined and stated in the manual itself. As noted, the issuance process must have included a final review and coordination with the intended manual recipients. At this point, an applications review needs to occur with functional management. This is not for quality manual content but rather for functional application of the manual. The affected organizations and related management must agree with the extent of the planned manual usage. All functions must assure their roles are properly defined. Any reservations must be resolved, since the document must be implemented as stated by the company. Document release should be withheld until there is consensus and acceptance.

Definition of the quality manual release process must include the identification of what function, office, or individual can authorize and grant final release and issue approval. It is customary for the approval to be signed by the individual most responsible for the affected company organization or operations, such as the CEO or plant manager. It is advisable to reflect this level of approval by signature. This is frequently in conjunction with the same page or location as the quality policy approvals. Even in the case of manuals developed for electronic and code-released documentation systems, a signed original or assigned personal release code should be available for auditing purposes.

If desired, the company can require approval and release signatures by individual manual sections as well. For instance, the engineering section in the manual might be signed by the company's head of engineering. If this is done, an overall approval is still needed for the basic manual and/or the core section.

The manual should be distributed to a controlled list of recipients, assuring that the processing of changes will also be controlled. Distribution must include those individuals or departments that received the original or early version. The methods used to assure currency of the manuals are quite similar to those used in any document and data control system, but since it is a management-based, company-level document there are some variations. The methods may include

- Manuals assigned and distributed to approved individuals.
- Revisions physically placed in approved manuals by distribution agent.

- Revisions forwarded to the approved owner for manual update.
  - —A poor method is to use the honor system to assure update.
  - —A fair method is to forward a new table of contents with each new revision.
  - —A better method is to require receipt and/or return of obsolete documents.
  - —The best method is to use electronically based manuals that are always current.

Whatever method is used, it must provide absolute assurance that users will work to the latest appropriate revisions and that obsolete documents are removed from possible inadvertent use.

There should be some orientation accompanying the release of all documentation changes. Certainly the original release of the manual will require training, particularly as it relates to the affected users' areas of operations. The degree of the training depends on the extent of change from the previous method of operation.

Training or orientation needs to address what is different from previous versions or methods, and should afford users the opportunity to clarify any point not entirely understood. The worst thing a company can do is to put changes into the manual without alerting users as to the existence of the changes and their scope. This is true of manuals, as well as operating procedures and work instructions.

The documentation change control procedure for the company must also apply to the quality manual. This should not differ significantly from the basic system. Although the quality manual must be approved by the chief executive, the authorized person for release approval varies by document anyway. Everything else in the documentation and data control system should apply to the quality manual.

Conclusion

The development of the company's quality system documentation should be in accordance with the task definition and schedule that was established by the detailed implementation plan. The quality policy sets the company position on its planned approach in meeting quality requirements. The quality system manual initiates the deployment of the policy and demonstrates how the company intends to meet the requirements of the selected ISO quality system standard. The quality system procedures and work instructions complete the implementation and documentation of the company quality system.

The individuals selected to write the documentation must transmit focused and acceptable data. The company quality system documentation should be direct, clear, user-friendly, and practical. It should also assure that the implemented system is effective. The management representative and the documentation authors must be certain that all aspects of the ISO 9000-based writing process are addressed, including such things as document hierarchy, linkage, data transfer, and usability. Completed documents must be reviewed and released through the document and data control system.

The quality manual is usually used by customers and the third party registration bodies to determine whether the quality system, as described and implemented, is capable of meeting the ISO quality system standard. As such, the purposes, structure, contents, development, issue, and control of quality manuals need to be addressed in detail. The quality manual is often the key to successful ISO implementation and compliance.

Implementation actions required by this module

1. Determine hierarchial structure, format, and interrelationship of planned documentation.
2. Select authors and present the requirements and expectations for system documentation.
3. Be sure authors understand all basic roles and objectives of quality system documentation.
4. Be sure all authors understand where their documents fit into the document structure.
5. Assure that all applicable ISO 9000 company quality system operations are documented.
6. Utilize any appropriate ISO 9000 guidelines to aid in the writing process.
7. Assure the schedule for writing documents is understood and maintained.
8. Assure that all level one and two documentation is developed early in the writing schedule.

9. Be sure the planned document and data control system is in place for document release.

10. Do not permit authors to begin writing until they have spoken to potential users.

11. Make certain that all documents are useable, understandable, and acceptable to the target audience.

12. Have authors use flowcharts and other graphic methods to enhance communication.

13. Resolve all areas of conflict in the new documentation.

14. Make sure the quality manual addresses all applicable quality system elements in the ISO standard.

15. Train the workforce to use the new quality system documentation.

16. Assure revision levels using a controlled and positive document distribution system.

Step 6: Other Implementation Activities

6.1 ISO 9000 awareness for all personnel

6.1.1 Providing ISO 9000 background information

6.1.2 External company benefits

6.1.3 Employees need details on how ISO benefits them

6.1.4 Keeping employees current on implementation status

6.1.5 Taking the fear out of the registration process

6.2 Modifying company management style

6.2.1 Senior management commits to ISO 9000 standards

6.2.2 The company quality system as viewed by ISO 9000

6.2.3 Working success at the total company level

6.2.4 Deploying the company policies and strategies

6.2.5 The workforce plays a vital role in achieving success

6.3 Training on ISO requirements and documentation

6.3.1 Providing training for immediate application

6.3.2 Training on ISO standards or company documentation

6.3.3 Training required for the authors to get started

6.3.4 Employee training associated with new documentation

6.3.5 Training associated with preparation for audits

6.4 Transition activities as ISO comes on-line

6.4.1 Dealing with transitory dual quality systems

6.4.2 Benefits and problems with workforce involvement

6.4.3 Operations must continue during transition phase

6.4.4 New documents reflect new methods and techniques

6.4.5 Overlooking the need for training causes failure

6.5 Clarifying user responsibilities

6.5.1 Documentation is the optimal approach, so follow it

6.5.2 Quality policy deployed to all employees

6.5.3 Employees must use appropriate documentation content

6.5.4 Knowledgeable employees are the key to good records

6.5.5 Adhering to a planned training schedule

Conclusion

Questions answered in this module

1. Why is employee acceptance of ISO 9000 standards so important to implementation success?

2. Who or what should be the major source of ISO 9000 data for all employees?

3. Does awareness of ISO 9000 implementation status really aid process ownership?

4. Is it necessary to reaffirm company commitment to ISO and its attendant benefits?

5. Why is employee ownership linked to demonstrated management commitment?

6. What is meant by stating that management must remove its barriers to implementation?

7. Are employees the true operators of a company quality system?

8. Why is just-in-time training essential to having a capable workforce?

9. Should employees be trained on ISO standards or the resultant company documents?

10. What is the best type of training—on the job, classroom, self-study, computer-based, or outside the company?

11. How must the company deal with any transition period during incremental compliance?

12. What must been done to assure that users fully understand their responsibilities?

13. What is the best approach to prepare the workforce for the audit environment?

14. What are the mandatory areas of user responsibility during a compliance audit?

15. Why is it essential to include all user training and involvement in the implementation plan?

16. Must employees be capable of stating the company quality policy verbatim?

Step 6

Other Implementation Activities

In addition to the documentation activities described in Step 5, a number of other implementation actions are necessary to assure a smooth transition to an ISO 9000 quality system. The actions in this module relate to the general support efforts required for implementation. These need to be addressed by virtually all companies implementing ISO quality standards.

This module is unique in that it groups and summarizes, in one place, all support activities for ISO 9000 implementation. Some of the actions may have been accomplished during the initial implementation phases. Others may be associated with the identification and resolution of shortfalls, the release of new methods and/or new documentation, or the verification and audit program. These actions may need to be addressed throughout the implementation process, some at various points of time and others continuously. On the basis of not knowing the exact point of presentation or usage, they are summarized and presented in this module for convenience. The other modules may briefly discuss them at points of recommended presentation.

Tasks that may be only indirectly associated with ISO 9000 implementation are not covered in this module. These include such tasks as selective organizational changes, modification of plant layout due to differential product line registrations, and the development of post-registration advertising and marketing strategies. Such actions are clearly company-specific business decisions, which may only be the by-product of active ISO 9000 implementation. Some companies may elect to closely link such activities to their implementation plan and schedule. Whatever the approach, employees should be generally aware of these actions.

6.1 Initial ISO 9000 awareness for all personnel

Assisted by the ISO management representative, senior management should always provide the workforce with basic information on the ISO 9000 family of quality standards. These data may be presented in general, functional, or group sessions. Presentation may be in concentrated meetings or spread out over time. The company must decide what approach is most suitable to its organization and operations.

6.1.1 Providing ISO 9000 background information

Employees must know (1) why the ISO 9000 family is attaining worldwide acceptance; (2) how and where ISO originated; and (3) why it has been adopted by the United States and other countries as their national quality standard.

The senior manager must present the planned ISO implementation as a logical move for the company and its workforce, one providing enormous benefits for the company itself, employees, customers, suppliers, and shareholders. The future ISO 9000-compliant company will have a basic quality system that has the means of increasing company efficiency and effectiveness while meeting worldwide standards of system acceptance. The ISO 9000-based quality system must also be shown to involve every employee in the process of achieving customer satisfaction (see Figure 6.1).

6.1.2 External company benefits

In addition to the internal benefits derived from implementing the ISO quality system, the senior manager must present the business advantages to the company in the competitive marketplace. The marketplace disadvantages to those companies not implementing the ISO 9000 family should also be discussed. Employees should readily conclude that the earlier the company implements ISO 9000 and starts reaping the internal and external benefits, the faster and more effectively it can achieve an improved market position.

The senior manager needs to convey the fact that ISO 9000 is changing the nature of the quality movement and, as such, the environment in which the company has been operating. Further, "our" company, which has been successful in the business environment of the past, will be

- Improvement is likely in all company operations.
- The company is recognized as complying with the accepted international standard.
- The company's competitive position in the global marketplace is improved.
- The effect of ISO implementation is felt by all of the company's stakeholders, even suppliers.
- Employee involvement brings increased process ownership.
- ISO 9000 standards produce sound, repetitive, stable processes within the company.
- Greater market share and improved efficiency yield stability.

Figure 6.1 Conveying the benefits of ISO 9000 implementation.

quite capable of successfully competing in the new quality environment once the ISO 9000 family of quality system standards is installed.

6.1.3 Employees need details on how ISO benefits them

As employees listen to the description of the ISO 9000 family, and its advantage to the company, they will be wondering about any direct benefit to them. They will have heard that a revised ISO 9000-based quality system will be more efficient, and they will likely be concerned about any resultant downsizing. The senior manager must clearly state the primary intention of the company is to gain increased market share! If downsizing were the planned goal, ISO 9000 implementation would not be a necessary prerequisite. The senior manager should indicate ISO 9000 implementation will require company resources and commitment, but that management views ISO implementation as an investment in the future of the enterprise.

It should sincerely be management's goal to separate, in reality and in the minds of employees, the implementation of ISO 9000 from near-term workforce reductions. Hopefully, personnel reductions in the long term will be avoided by the anticipated increase in market share and the required increase in operational output. Employees will share in the added security that comes with increased company market share. In addition, management will be encouraging more direct employee contribution to business operations.

6.1.4 Keeping employees current on implementation status

The awareness sessions should update employees on where the company stands in relation to its planned ISO 9000 implementation. This factual information should be periodically updated throughout the implementation process. Convincing employees that ISO 9000 implementation is the key to the company's future, and then not keeping them posted as to what is occurring, holds the potential for some fears to develop within the workforce.

The periodic update can be through the company newsletter, group meetings, bulletin boards, or flyers at the facility exits (see Figure 6.2). One of the best summaries is a posted time line of the implementation schedule with a where-we-are versus where-we-planned-to-be comparison. As a supplement to these displays, be sure to give credit to participants and/or areas that provide outstanding contributions to the implementation process. Some companies use a volunteer system for

- Meetings—General workforce, group, individuals
- Printed and distributed materials—Newsletters, flyers at exits, handouts in group
- Printed and posted materials—Area bulletin boards, facility entry points
- Electronic data—Electronic mail, networks, start-up screen notes
- Interactive means—Group discussion, locally posted progress charts
- Involvement—Shortfall analysis input, documentation review, and so on

Figure 6.2 Methods used to convey ISO 9000 data.

selection and assignment of the ISO 9000 implementation personnel, even having incentive bonuses for excellent performance. If so, the volunteers' names and their contributions can be part of the periodic status report. Most companies do not have such a generalized resource base and have miserly selected their implementation personnel based on participant knowledge and performance. Whatever the means of selection, participants deserve recognition for their work.

6.1.5 Taking the fear out of the registration process

If quality system registration is planned as the culminating action to ISO 9000 implementation, then the final subject that should be addressed in the general employee awareness sessions is the nature of the registration process. Everyone should be familiar with the concept of independent auditors. Employees should be able to see how such a review, and the approval of the company's performance and compliance to the ISO quality standards, are of interest to present and future customers. Employees need to hear the company has chosen an appropriate registrar, or will do so soon, as well as when the planned registration audit will take place.

No fear of the registration process should be conveyed. The focus must be on how the company will address its ISO 9000 implementation through a well-planned and success-oriented process. The company's own auditing activities will help prepare everyone for the actual methods used by the registrar. The registration audit should be presented as an opportunity for the company and its employees to demonstrate their success in the process of ISO 9000 quality system implementation.

6.2 Modifying company management style

Not necessarily in the initial ISO awareness sessions, but within a reasonable period of time, several other subjects must be presented to middle management and the general workforce. Many of these subjects may convey a change in management style (see Figure 6.3). Depending on the existing management approach, these topics may be new or they may just reaffirm current practices. These subjects need to be presented by senior management either in person or in some type of officially

- Reaffirming commitment to ISO 9000 implementation
- Visibly involving management leadership in the implementation process
- Judging management performance by ISO 9000 involvement
- Using the total company quality system as operating basis
- Deploying quality policy and strategies to the entire workforce
- Communicating with the workforce on quality system changes
- Exchanging data between management and the workforce
- Acknowledging employee involvement as a key to success

Figure 6.3   Changes in management style.

sanctioned transmittal. An acceptable method might be a president's column in the company newsletter, a memo from the chairperson posted to bulletin boards, or a periodic flyer reporting the president's state of the company. In many respects, the topics presented are simply an expansion of the original awareness session information. However, by individuals hearing or seeing it again, positive reinforcement is achieved.

6.2.1 Senior management commits to ISO 9000 standards

A restatement of senior management's commitment to the ISO 9000 implementation process should be addressed first. This can be accomplished by a brief review of the internal benefits to the company and the marketing potential of being registered or certified to the ISO 9000 family. Senior management should also discuss any other proactive approaches taken to assure a successful future. If the company has planned or implemented any organizational or structural changes to facilitate the implementation process, this is a good time to announce them.

Certainly, if the management representative has not been appointed or if the person's identity has not been announced, this would be an appropriate time for sharing that information with the workforce.

Finally in separate sessions, it must be made absolutely clear to all middle managers that a significant measure of their performance will be based on ISO 9000 activity. This evaluation includes their personal involvement and the success of their unit during the implementation process. It should also be clear that the company will supply the necessary training resources for middle managers, as well as their employees.

6.2.2 The company quality system as viewed by ISO 9000

Perhaps a week or two after the first discussions on management style, the anticipated changes to any existing quality system should be conveyed to the workforce. Depending on the company, compliance changes may vary from the creation of a basic company ISO 9000 quality system to making only minor procedural changes to the existing quality system. For the company to fully understand what ISO 9000 requires, management should discuss the necessary involvement of additional functional organizations in the company's quality system. If senior management does not present this, members of certain functional organizations may have difficulty comprehending their role in the ISO quality system concept. Management must continue to reinforce the necessity for expected, expanded functional involvement.

The concept of the quality system as the primary means of operating the company will be foreign to much of the workforce (and many managers). They can, however, readily visualize a quality system, after seeing documented detail on how specific activities will be accomplished, as a primary means of operating the company. The presentation should be designed to eliminate many employees' ingrained belief that quality is the responsibility of the quality assurance function. They also need to be reminded that a quality system is far more expansive than a quality *assurance* system. Although complete employee acceptance of the quality system concept should be an immediate goal, it may take a while for the idea to be fully accepted. Obviously, management's changing role will be closely observed by the workforce to see if this new approach is actually being practiced.

6.2.3 Working success at the total company level

The next change in management approach to be presented should be the expected, increased information exchange within the company's structure. Improved flow of company data is based on recognition, by ISO standards, that both functional and structural quality system elements are addressed. This improved exchange of system and process data includes the operational interrelationship of all organizations contributing to quality. Functional interfaces must become increasingly transparent to the development and movement of both data and product.

Organizations must not be allowed to optimize their functional activities at the expense of the company. Management must assure that process optimization will only be acceptable when achieved at the company level. Many individuals and units may have endured incomplete or inaccurate product and/or data because of functional suboptimization. Employees will understand the need to assure the internal supplier/customer concept is elevated to a functional management responsibility. Only by viewing process optimization at the total company level will the entire company benefit.

6.2.4 Deploying the company policies and strategies

Another consideration in the area of improved communication is management's involvement in the development and deployment of the company quality policy. The nature of the policy, and the commitment it represents, must be shared with all company organizations and levels. Employees also need to know the basic content of the attendant quality objectives and strategies used to guide the company.

One way to have an entire workforce with a focused constancy of purpose is to have management recognize that shared strategies yield a dividend in understanding, support, and ownership. Employees need to know that management recognizes their prior efforts as only an indication of the potential contribution they can make to future company success. The workforce should know that management is committed to removing communication barriers. Having a company constancy of purpose permits all decisions at all levels to be biased toward achieving the quality policy and objectives. Senior-level recognition and acceptance of the need to modify management style are imperative.

6.2.5 The workforce plays a vital role in achieving success

A final modification of management style should be presented as an acknowledgment that the company not only wants but needs input from all employees (see Figure 6.4). This situation is particularly valid when it comes to employee assistance during ISO implementation. Employee input must include the identification and location of potential improvement of any methods or documentation needed to facilitate or achieve ISO 9000 compliance. Involvement and input create ownership in a process.

The workforce operates the company quality system. Management must acknowledge it now recognizes that each employee knows more about his or her job than either the company's technical base or management staff. It is in the company's best interest for all employees to fully support and contribute to the ISO 9000 implementation process (see Figure 6.5). The company's success in achieving workforce commitment to the ISO 9000 implementation process will initially depend on management's reputation. Acceptance will certainly be enhanced over time as the sincerity of management's statements is validated through recognized leadership actions.

Figure 6.4 Process of achieving employee input and ownership.

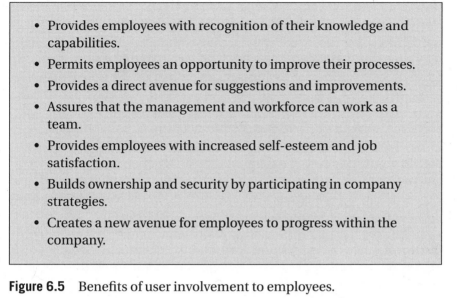

- Provides employees with recognition of their knowledge and capabilities.
- Permits employees an opportunity to improve their processes.
- Provides a direct avenue for suggestions and improvements.
- Assures that the management and workforce can work as a team.
- Provides employees with increased self-esteem and job satisfaction.
- Builds ownership and security by participating in company strategies.
- Creates a new avenue for employees to progress within the company.

Figure 6.5   Benefits of user involvement to employees.

6.3 Training on ISO requirements and documentation

Considering the potential benefits from all employees being familiar with the ISO family, a general exposure to the contents of the selected ISO 9000 directive standard is appropriate. This orientation is a logical precursor for understanding the details of the company documentation upon which employee training will be based. With these brief considerations as to the nature of application, the following specific training examples are discussed.

6.3.1 Providing training for immediate application

Employees' ISO 9000-related training should be presented just prior to the anticipated point of its application. Not having the opportunity to apply the training causes employees to forget its content. Such a situation normally involves delays or even retraining when the company actually wants its people to apply what they have learned.

Training of personnel on the specific subject needed for near-term application ensures that the training is definitive and of the appropriate amount. This just-in-time concept causes classes to be short, frequent, small, and focused on immediate needs. Even so, the total number of class hours or on-the-job (OJT) hours may be low. Training in this manner is often keyed to when ISO 9000 implementation activity peaks move from one area to the next. The possibility of additional classes is quickly offset by the advantage of having recently trained and focused employees.

6.3.2 Training on ISO standards or company documentation

Should employees be trained on the actual ISO directive standard or on the resultant company documentation based on the standard? The answer appears to be predicated on whether employees will be part of the actual documentation activity or not. That is, they may be assigned to utilize the ISO directive standards as the source of requirements and/or as guidance for writing corresponding company documents. If such is the case, there is an obvious need for training on the ISO 9000 documents. If, however, the employees will simply be exposed to the resultant company documentation, then it may be best to train them on the company documentation they will be using.

Training on the nature of the planned document and data control system will be necessary for all employees. The training should be early in the implementation process if employees have been assigned as authors; it should be later if they are potential system users (see Figure 6.6).

- Total workforce needs general awareness training on the standards.
- Training on company documentation remains primary for the workforce.
- Employees involved in level one documentation need standards training.
- Authors and auditors often use ISO 9000 standards directly.
- Employees involved in a registration visit will need a standards update.
- Training should always be timed for immediate use.

Figure 6.6   Training on company documents or ISO standards.

6.3.3 Training required for the authors to get started

For those involved in writing documents, training on the selected ISO quality system standard (such as ISO 9001) should always be presented in conjunction with the basic guideline documents (such as ISO 9000-1 and ISO 9004-1). Prior to writing, the authors must be exposed to basic ISO quality system concepts. Once these are understood, the authors move into detailed training on the requirements and contents of the selected ISO 9000 standard or assigned system element. Depending on the nature of the company business, it may be appropriate to examine other applicable support documents, such as ISO 9004-3 for processed materials; ISO 9000-3 for software; or ISO 9004-2 for services. As the authors get further into the ISO directive and begin to work on specific compliance-based writing assignments, additional guideline documents may need to be consulted (see Appendix B).

Using documentation within the existing quality system that might be suitable to meet all or part of ISO 9000 standard's requirements should also be discussed. Hopefully these considerations provide the potential document authors with an existing reference base for dealing with their tasks.

Some knowledge of the potential impact the anticipated document and data control system will have on their writing activity is essential. Authors should know (1) whether the document and data control activity will be centralized or functionally based; (2) the nature of the quality system documentation hierarchy used by the company; (3) the identification and assignment of the planned documents; and (4) the individual document layout and format. The planned variations within the document control system, such as specifications versus procedures versus work instructions, also require some training or discussion as applicable to the authors' assignment.

One can now see why the development and writing of the specific document and data control procedures must occur quite early in the implementation and documentation process.

6.3.4 Employee training associated with new documentation

Training on the new ISO 9000 quality system documentation may take several approaches, depending on the degree of involvement and responsibility the affected employees have in the subject phase of the process. If employees have no direct responsibility for the subject, the training should be directed toward the primary differences between the existing documented quality system and the new ISO 9000-compliant documented system. If employees have direct responsibility or involvement in a given subject or task, the training must be focused on understanding and performing what is required by the documentation (see Figure 6.7).

Many employees will likely need both an overview for general awareness of the basic system changes, and a detailed level of instruction on those new or revised documents that govern the specific tasks for which they are responsible. Such diverse requirements will likely challenge even the best training program scheduler, but the end results will benefit the whole company.

Even when the training task is to expose employees to documents that govern their assigned tasks, the successful instructor will always

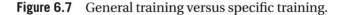

General
- Awareness of new processes
- Knowledge of new document control
- Expected employee involvement
- Role of an auditee
- Methods of process control
- How registration is accomplished
- Structure of new company documentation

Specific
- New approach to assigned tasks
- Measuring process parameters
- Proof testing documentation
- Completing required forms and charts
- Auditing of assigned process
- New work instructions
- Location of job-related data and resources
- How assigned activity achieves quality policy

Figure 6.7 General training versus specific training.

start by reviewing the policy statements in the appropriate sections of the quality manual. Starting at this level assures that employees understand the source of the requirements upon which their company's quality system is based. Once the company policies are understood, the instructor can cover the governing quality system procedures, the supportive work instructions, specifications, forms, tags, and so on. In this manner, the instructor demonstrates the hierarchial structure of quality system documentation.

Employees must understand how the company quality system documentation is structured. They must be comfortable as to where their operating documents fit into the overall documentation scheme. Once this is accomplished, the mandatory, detailed, line-by-line review of those directive or governing documents will be meaningful. The methods described may result in a different course content for each element or subject area, but the basic approach to the training process should remain constant.

An excellent test of employees' understanding is whether they can restate the contents of the instructional material. This level of understanding is an essential objective for any company that is training its supervisors to perform on-the-job instruction at the point in the process where implementation is intended.

6.3.5 Training associated with preparation for audits

Another area where specific training is required is the preparation for the customer or registrar compliance audit. The affected employees may be very anxious as this visit approaches. Their concerns can be relieved if employees are aware of what the company and the registrar specifically expect of them. This auditee training provides potential auditees with an understanding of the roles of the company and the customer in the auditing process.

Although the basics of the auditing process can be presented in the classroom, the prospective auditees will learn much more about the process by actually taking part in some on-the-job practice audits as auditors or auditees. The auditees experience an actual audit environment through exposure to the company's compliance verification and registration preparation audits. These audits should be conducted by the company's internal quality audit function in the same manner and method as would the registrar. The company audits not only identify areas where improvement is still necessary, but they also serve to further train and coach the auditees in how to deal with auditors. Removing mystery from the audit process also tends to remove the employees' fear of being audited.

6.4 Transition activities as ISO comes on-line

Although a small company may be capable of a point-in-time conversion to a new ISO quality system, most companies will find themselves undergoing the transition over some extended period. Experience shows it is in the company's best interest to keep this transition period as short as possible. Assuming some activities will be impacted by the transition period, no matter what the length, the company must provide guidance as to how to handle activities during transition. This includes the following:

- Scheduling transition activities in the implementation plan
- Dealing with temporary problem of having dual quality systems
- Handling ISO user involvement during ongoing production
- Proofing new methods and documentation during ongoing production
- Working heavy training load around ongoing production
- Budgeting implementation versus production resources during the transition

6.4.1 Dealing with transitory dual quality systems

The first area of concern relates to how the company will deal with the possibility of operating in a dual quality system environment. This situation reinforces the need for a detailed schedule of implementation tasks. Proper identification and scheduling of tasks can keep the existing quality system versus ISO quality system overlap as short as possible. Occasionally, activating the new ISO system may be a direct, item-for-item replacement of the existing documentation. This may permit a simple switch over in given functional areas. The likelihood all of the attendant support documentation also being capable of a simple exchange is very remote. By choosing areas and prioritizing aspects of the writing process, however, most of the essential elements in a given area can be suitably scheduled and successfully brought on-line at the same time.

No matter what the efforts are to avoid it, there will still be a dual quality system conflict that can not be alleviated by the scheduling process. The company must instruct employees as to what they are expected to do on a task-by-task basis during the transition period. Experience reveals companies that overlook or underestimate the problems of a dual system environment will face a significant level of implementation chaos. Without the necessary guidance, management will be amazed at how quickly resourceful employees can develop a multitude of varying and uncontrolled approaches.

6.4.2 Benefits and problems with workforce involvement

During the quality system transition phase, the user workforce will be supporting the authors' document development and writing processes. Much of this support is likely to be informal, involving such methods as discussions, interviews, and observations. While these contacts are in progress, it is quite certain the authors will be interfering with the affected employees' full productivity. Since it is imperative for the workforce to be involved in the documentation process, some scheduled time for this activity should be included in the implementation plan. Involving the workforce benefits the company in the following ways. The workforce

- Provides firsthand knowledge of the process and any problems.
- Is a source of methodology when no directive documentation exists.
- Increases the usability of the documentation through user review.
- Introduces practical user-friendly solutions to problems.
- Facilitates audits by being aware of, and providing the rationale for, changes.
- Increases company process ownership.
- Helps to optimize company operations.

Many companies simply provide a nonproductive or overhead budget for these situations. It is more convenient for cognizant supervision, however, if budget allocations are matched with a visitor schedule, phased to production needs. The authors may have to meet with the potential document users by supervisor arrangement, perhaps on a scheduled day or period. The benefits of user input to the documentation development and review process more than offset the burden of the schedule. In fact, in those companies where shortfall review has found the absence of a documented quality system, user input may be the only practical way to capture and document the process in procedures.

6.4.3 Operations must continue during transition phase

The same scheduling and budgeting problems continue as operations are impacted by the transition to the ISO 9000 system. In this case, the production interference difficulties are compounded by workforce users being directly involved in the proof testing of the new documentation. This testing can take different forms: (1) It may involve the use of draft documents where the users attempt to follow the drafts and offer their critiques; or (2) It may involve final acceptance and use of the document as monitored by authors, supervisors, and other users. Whatever the reason for user involvement, the company will have to provide some guidance as to how the user input and production process are performed. The company must also decide what constitutes a satisfactory acceptance test result.

6.4.4 New documents reflect new methods and techniques

The need for training on the company's new ISO 9000-based documentation has been addressed. There must also be provisions for awareness training on the new methods and techniques that the company has introduced in association with the new documentation. In some companies the new support techniques may be as simple as the use of new logbooks, tags, and forms. In other companies, it may be the new ISO quality system has been largely computerized and employees will be required to use a terminal to make data entries, locate governing procedures, obtain reports, and so on. If the use of computers by the general workforce has not been included in the company's previous standard methods of operation, then an overall gap in computer literacy will need to be remedied.

Employees are affected by the following changes.

- New quality system documentation
- Possible new functions with which to deal
- New methods and processes within job assignment

- New or modified documentation directing processes
- Expected involvement in the process improvement
- Expanded training activities for redefined tasks
- Possible exposure to new technologies, such as computer input
- Management recognition of contributions

Clearly, the need for training on the use and benefits of these new techniques, methods, and devices is mandatory for proper use.

Step 5 determined that one aspect of communicating data was the use of various facilitating techniques such as flowcharts, matrices, and so on. While data would appear to be easily conveyed using these techniques, such is only true if users understand the methods. Training needs to include information on how to use and interpret all of the new data transmission techniques in the company documentation. Experience shows most employees have a general understanding of such methods, however, the training must assure that user interpretation is accurate and universal. Once employees understand these techniques, they will be encouraged by the workforce and increasingly used.

6.4.5 Overlooking the need for training causes failure

While many of the points discussed in section 6.4 may appear to be quite obvious, it is surprising how many companies do not provide for them in their planning process. If necessary actions are not in the plan, then the likelihood of their accomplishment is remote. Unfortunately, they are often addressed only after the implementation process has broken down. At that point, after-the-fact remedial action must be rushed into place to minimize the impact on the implementation plan. An earlier admonition noted that the prudent company assures that the implementation plan covers every necessary remedial action. The complete admonition is that the remedial action must be identified, defined, scheduled, assigned, and the resources allocated.

6.5 Clarifying user responsibilities

In addition to the necessary employee training associated with the newly developed ISO quality system, the company must assure that all employees understand the specific actions for which they have been assigned accountability. Information on user responsibility may be integrated into the training activities or presented to the employees in separate one-on-one sessions. However accomplished, knowing the basis upon which job performance is measured is of vital importance to all employees (see Figure 6.8).

6.5.1 Documentation is the optimal approach, so follow it

Hopefully, the system documentation authors have successfully completed their assignments. If so, the primary tasks assigned to individual user employees can be accomplished by simply following the new company-developed ISO 9000 directive documentation. Actual compliance to the ISO standard, deployment of the company quality policy and objectives, and adherence to the new company quality system can all be achieved by strict commitment to this principle. An important corollary to this principle is any variation existing between what is stated as a requirement and what is actually being done—for whatever reason—means the company is in noncompliance with the ISO standards.

Each employee has the responsibility to immediately identify such situations to management as being noncompliance variations in need of

---

- Mandatory adherence to ISO 9000-based system documentation
- Knowledge of document location and basic content
- Immediate identification of compliance variation problems
- Support and focused implementation of the quality policy
- Working to the latest or most appropriate revision of documents
- Knowing what is being done, why it is done, and why it is acceptable
- Preparing and retaining accurate and complete records
- Identifying subjects where training needs to be reinforced

Figure 6.8 User responsibilities.

resolution. Further, if what is required by the quality system documentation no longer appears logical to the situation, it should also be escalated for examination as a potential variance. The company policy must require adherence to the documentation or, if appropriate, to take steps to have the documentation reviewed for reaffirmation or revision.

6.5.2 Quality policy deployed to all employees

Another key responsibility assigned to the workforce is assisting in quality policy implementation. As discussed, most of the implementation is derived from employees adhering to the ISO 9000-based documentation. Employees, however, must have a basic understanding of the policy itself, how it applies to them, and how their particular activities support the policy. The employees do not have to know or express the policy verbatim but they should be able to explain its basic points. Employees must know how they or their unit are specifically supporting the company with regard to the policy and its objectives. Some companies have printed the company quality policy on small wallet-sized cards as memory boosters, while others have simply posted the policy throughout the facility.

The key point to convey in any discussion with employees on quality policy deployment and implementation, is how the specific functional users can assist in the policy's achievement. Although the basic policy does not change, the methods of its implementation vary for each organization and function. For a given unit, the means of supporting the policy may be reducing cycle time, reducing scrap, or improving first-pass acceptance. For another unit, the specific policy implementation may be achieved by a six-sigma accuracy in processing insurance claims forms. By tying their actions to the company quality policy, employees can see how they are directly supporting company goals. This type of training is best achieved by group sessions or personal discussions. Such activities should be led by the cognizant supervisor, with or without direct involvement from the management representative.

6.5.3 Employees must use appropriate documentation content

Employees must be aware of the contents of the documentation that affects them. Constant reference to the documentation may very well be needed during the first series of usage. On the other hand, it is unlikely employees will continuously refer to the specific procedure or work instruction each time a task is performed. As presented in Step 5, the new document and data control procedure provides the most recent revision of each document to the site or repository most suitable for access by the affected employees. If properly designed, the document and data control system has been developed with a means for notifying the supervisor or employees of each document change.

Thus, experienced employees may not need to examine the governing procedure on a daily basis. The extent to which employees may need to refer to the documented procedure can vary greatly. The reference may be virtually continuous for a detailed lab analysis instruction, but for simple tasks it may only be required when a document change is processed. In either situation, it must be emphatically established that it is always the employee's responsibility to work to the latest or most appropriate document revision.

It is common for an auditor to ask employees what document they are following and then to find that the document is not at hand. Disturbingly, it is also common for employees, when asked to obtain the governing document, are unable to do so. Even worse, some employees may not even know where the documents are located. Some employees may find the document but then are unable to demonstrate familiarity with it. They may not be able to locate the paragraph or section that governs their assigned task.

These situations are completely unacceptable to customers, registrars, and the company itself. These situations are totally unacceptable in any quality system, but particularly in the new ISO 9000 environment. They clearly demonstrate many employees simply do not use the directive documentation supplied to them. The document knowledge and availability test is one of the system compliance tests that both company and registrar auditors will likely use. It is imperative that supervisors assist employees in developing capability for discharging this responsibility.

As the time approaches for the actual company auditing activity to begin, auditors will often ask employees about the nature of the specific task they are performing. Auditors want to know what the employees are doing, why are they doing it, and how do they know that what they are doing is correct or acceptable. While it may appear everyone ought to be able to answer these three simple questions, it is surprising how many people are unable to address all three points. Of course, the answers are all in the documents to which the questioned employees are supposedly working. The auditor is simply performing a knowledge check.

Frequently, employees are aware of the information necessary to answer the auditor's question; however, many have not thought the questions and answers over ahead of time and have trouble providing satisfactory responses. The cognizant supervisor must train all employees to perform each job assignment with these three basic questions in mind. Prudent supervisors will periodically challenge employees to correctly respond to these three questions. Everyone should be able to answer: What am I doing? Why am I doing it? How do I know it is correct? The answers to these questions are obvious responsibilities of assigned employees. This training exercise will yield a significant payback during the actual customer or registration audit, both in employee ease of mind and the appropriateness of the responses.

6.5.4 Knowledgeable employees are the key to good records

A final workforce responsibility relates to the process of developing accurate records of satisfactory company performance. The ISO 9000 standards have significant requirements for records in almost all system elements. The records are used as objective evidence that the product or service has been processed in accordance with all related specifications and procedures. Normally, user employees prepare the records as a part of their assigned tasks. These same employees must be completely aware of the significance of complete and accurate records.

Employees must also be aware of the fact they are solely responsible for the preparation of task-related records. Whatever the end result of their record preparation, it will often stand as the company's sole evidence of acceptable performance. Records may not be amended, except in very unusual circumstances, and then usually they can only be augmented. It is imperative that employees do not take a casual approach to this assigned task. Supervisors must assure that employees understand the significance of records in achieving ISO 9000 compliance. Since employees hold the key to satisfactory records, it is well for supervisors to create an environment where a question on records is likely to be asked before the fact. Management must assure that all employees have accepted the concept that the task is not complete until accurate records are available.

6.5.5 Adhering to a planned training schedule

All of the points on user responsibilities presented in this section are real-world situations that must be covered as part of employee training. Since many of these factors have a new ISO 9000-based requirement, it is likely employees will not have had any such training until exposed to the company's implementation efforts. By accomplishing orientation and training tasks in conjunction with the ISO 9000 implementation process, the company assures its employees are knowledgeable and committed to compliance in all areas of responsibility. Including these activities in the detailed implementation plan provides a guide for assuring that all tasks discussed in this module are accomplished.

Conclusion

Although most companies assume their biggest ISO 9000 compliance shortfall will be in the area of documentation, there is usually an equal amount of effort in other ISO 9000 support areas. These areas include (1) provision of general ISO awareness for the workforce; (2) modification of company's management style to the new ISO environment; (3) specific training on new methods of ISO 9000 compliance and documentation; (4) handling the transition period between the current quality system and implementation of the ISO quality system; and (5) clear establishment and understanding of user responsibilities in the ISO environment.

Company employees must completely understand and accept the need for ISO implementation. They must be fully aware that benefits exist for both the company and its employees. The various methods of developing and maintaining employee ownership are dependent on enhanced communications from management. The improved communications should include straightforward information on the total implementation process, the verification activities of the company, and the registration concept.

The existence and nature of the ISO-based operating environment are typically dependent on a change in the way management relates to the workforce. The change in management style involves not only increased communication, but also greater employee participation in operating the ISO quality system. Encouraging and accepting employee contributions can take many forms, but a management approach which recognizes that employees have the ability to make meaningful contributions is most successful.

As the company undergoes implementation of the operational and documentation changes associated with ISO compliance, training specific to those process or document changes is necessary. Employees must accept the fact that their complete adherence to the requirements of the new documentation is the best assurance for achieving ISO 9000 compliance. They must be alert to any variances from the stated requirements.

Management must be certain that the nature of company operations during the transition period to the ISO-based quality system is well defined. The company should try to keep the transition period as short as possible. Management must guide employees on how the company plans to operate in a potential dual quality system situation.

All employees will want to aid the company in complying to the new ISO quality system. The nature of what is required of each employee should be thoroughly understood by the affected individuals. In preparation for the audit environment, employee confidence can be elevated by knowledge of the audit process and by practicing actions and answers in real auditee situations.

Implementation actions required by this module

1. Develop a plan that informs the workforce of the reasons for ISO 9000 implementation.
2. Assure that the workforce understands and accepts the benefits to both the company and its employees.
3. Establish an ongoing method for providing implementation status to the entire workforce.
4. Assure that employees accept their role in achieving customer or registration approval.
5. Functional management must accept their new role in the ISO 9000-based quality system.
6. Assure that the quality policy has been deployed to all employee levels.
7. Provide visible evidence of management involvement and support for the ISO 9000 process.

8. Determine ISO 9000-related training needs and assure their full and timely accomplishment.

9. Decide how each training requirement will be satisfied, that is, through OJT training, classroom instruction, and so on.

10. Assure selected authors understand what is expected and where documents fit into the ISO scheme.

11. Prepare employees for an audit by exposing them to the company's audit environment.

12. Utilize the implementation plan to guide the transition period to the ISO system.

13. Assure that employees understand specific responsibilities assigned to them.

14. Implement a method to assure that the workforce is using the appropriate versions of documents.

15. Assure employees understand that their greatest contribution is achieved by following documentation.

Step 7: Validating Company Compliance to ISO

7.1 Has ISO 9000 implementation been achieved?

7.2 Evaluating the company's overall compliance

7.3 Establishing the internal quality audit program

7.4 Management responsibilities in assuring compliance

7.4.4 Management commitments to employees must be maintained

7.4.5 Management must assure total ISO 9000 compliance

7.5 Preparing for the customer/registration audit

7.5.1 Concern for the effective compliance requirement

7.5.2 Continuous improvement of the quality system

7.5.3 Do not overlook mandatory training requirements

7.5.4 Considering an independent preassessment

7.5.5 Company decision on need for registration

Conclusion

Questions answered in this module

1. Under what conditions may the implementation plan be modified or rescheduled?
2. Why is determining complete and effective ISO 9000 compliance difficult?
3. What is the difference between determining quality system adequacy and compliance?
4. What are the best means of obtaining valid user input to ISO 9000 implementation?
5. What company function provides the best internal quality auditor candidates?
6. Must company auditors be certified by outside agencies?
7. How should auditing procedures be developed if no prior audit program exists?
8. At what point should the company begin its internal quality audit program?
9. Must audits always cover the company's entire quality system?
10. How do auditors know when they have met the requirement for objective evidence?
11. Are self-governance audits valid evaluations of compliance or are they a conflict of interest?

12. Is evidence of having audited all system elements required before the compliance audit?

13. Up to what point prior to the compliance audit can system changes still be processed?

14. Is it necessary to have an independent preassessment prior to the compliance audit?

15. Without previous training records must auditors be retrained on their current job?

16. Why does management confidence in the ISO 9000 system seem to keep gaining strength?

17. How does a company determine if its quality manual is ready for the adequacy audit?

18. Who has final say as to whether a company's ISO 9000 system is satisfactory?

Step 7

Validating Company Compliance to ISO

The company is now approaching the point where its ISO 9000 quality system implementation process is nearing completion. The plan has served as a guide throughout the process, and, if it has been adequately followed, has assured all aspects of the implementation effort have been addressed. At this point, the company should examine the effectiveness of its resultant documented quality system. In most companies, some activities are still in the process of being completed. Even so, the company can now start to verify its compliance in all completed areas. Although the system is based on the selected ISO 9000 quality standard, most of the compliance evaluation will be based on the company's quality system documentation.

7.1 Has ISO 9000 implementation been achieved?

The company's ISO 9000 implementation plan was developed using all of the information available at the time of its origin. Each action was defined and scheduled for the anticipated point-in-time completion. It is, however, a very rare plan that does not involve some midcourse corrections or additions. The management representative is responsible for any adjustments to the plan as implementation is in progress.

7.1.1 Individual delays in schedule compliance impact all

Schedule adjustments are normally related to synchronizing output of various areas. When task areas miss the planned schedule, managing the implementation process becomes more difficult. This fact holds true whether the real problem is with actual task/area performance or with the schedule. As a result of possible missed connections, management will likely adjust some tasks and the schedule. This is especially true as the implementation end point or compliance due date approaches. If properly managed, there is little likelihood of any activity being too far behind the planned schedule.

7.1.2 Minimizing the span of implementation completion

The result of these completions, delays, and adjustments, is that full implementation is not achieved at a single point in time, but rather incrementally over some period of time. The success of the management representative (or the implementation plan coordinator), is judged by how narrow he or she can control this time band. Even with the probable need for some schedule adjustments, however, the plan is still serving its purpose by providing the total universe of activities that must be achieved. Everyone knows when all actions are eventually discharged, full implementation will have been accomplished.

7.1.3 The concepts of existence, adequacy, and compliance

Three distinct processes have occurred during the implementation activities. The first process relates to the creation or existence of quality system documentation that covers all elements of the selected ISO 9000 standard. The second process is assuring the company quality system, as documented and directed by the newly written or revised documentation, is adequate for meeting the ISO quality standard. The third process is accomplishing quality system implementation and assuring that its full and effective compliance has been achieved by management and the workforce.

The first and second processes are matters of assuring the company's documented quality system, as created, is capable of addressing all requirements in each system element of the selected ISO quality standard. The primary term used for this part of the implementation activity is *achieving adequacy*. This means the company's documented quality system, if fully implemented, appears adequate to meet the requirements of the ISO quality standard. Achieving adequacy is the direct responsibility of the management representative and his or her assigned authors. Adequacy is essential for ISO 9000 compliance and must precede the next implementation phase.

This latter phase involves the company's actual performance or compliance to its documented ISO 9000-based quality system. The activity is termed *demonstrating compliance*. Demonstrating the company has achieved compliance to the company's documented quality system is the second consideration in how the company is judged successful. In summary, the three steps to achieving ISO 9000 compliance are (1) *establishing existence* of a documented system; (2) *achieving adequacy* by developing a quality system capable of meeting the standard; and (3) *demonstrating compliance* that the company does, in fact, meet the documented system.

The documentation's existence and adequacy are determined by a paper-to-paper comparison between the selected ISO standard and the company's quality system documents. The evaluation of compliance must be determined by an on-site, paper-to-performance comparison audit. This is done by examining the degree of compliance attained by employees as they follow the governing procedures and work instructions.

7.1.4 Once implemented, monitoring compliance is essential

Eventually, in accordance with the implementation plan, all documents will have been completed, accepted, and released to the affected employees for system implementation. Also by this time, employees will have had the necessary training suited to their needs and experience. Employees will now be attempting to work to the stated requirements in the documents. Full implementation may appear to be in place. At this point, functional management, *and all employees*, must continually evaluate compliance levels. Any variation to the requirements must be corrected by either changing the prescribed performance or the appropriate document.

7.1.5 Preparing for the verification process

As the documents are utilized over a relatively brief period, compliance in some of the more subtle operational aspects (that is, functional interface relationships), should be proven. With these successes, the cognizant functional management usually determines that full compliance has been achieved. Once this internal or functional management view on compliance is declared, the next step is to utilize one or more independent means of corroborating this sometimes biased position.

7.2 Evaluating the company's overall compliance

The company is now ready to formally evaluate its compliance with the newly developed ISO 9000 quality system. The approach uses the approved documented quality system procedures as the primary basis for evaluating compliance. The company has the ability to perform the evaluation at various levels of formality. The simplest is user review and feedback from the affected workforce; the most formal is using the company's internal quality audit program. Either approach attempts to determine whether there are any compliance variations between what has been documented as required performance and the actual demonstrated company performance (see Figure 7.1).

7.2.1 Gaining improvements through user suggestions

No matter how much time and effort are spent trying to resolve all documentation and implementation issues, there will still be problems or considerations that will not be identified until the new documentation has been used. Extended usage gives employees a chance to eventually identify any remaining variations between requirements and performance. These concerns must be transferred to the management representative, the implementation plan coordinator, functional management, or the affected documentation authors for resolution. User feedback is very important in determining the company's final version of the quality system documentation.

- Positive or negative feedback from the user workforce
- Self-governance audits performed by user functions
- Using document writers for evaluating compliance
- Auditor training activities informally examining compliance
- Functional and area management evaluating compliance
- Involving the formal internal quality audit function

Figure 7.1   Internal methods of evaluating overall compliance.

If management has created an interactive environment where employee participation and contribution are encouraged, then many recommendations will be received. Some of these suggestions will be suitable for inclusion as corrections and improvements; others may not be valid at all. Often employees are simply identifying an apparent variance for the management representative or affected writer to consider. Whether the input is used or not, the contributor should be acknowledged for attempting to personally help the implementation process. One measure of how receptive management is to employee inputs is the ratio of user suggestions to those actually accepted and implemented. User feedback is perhaps the primary means of upgrading the documents to the point of full acceptance. Of course, as noted, user involvement in the process also has the advantage of encouraging ownership.

7.2.2 Benefits from users examining their own compliance

Another proven method often used to evaluate compliance is the concept of self-governance audits. These are ordinarily simple single-point comparisons of what the documents require versus what the employees are actually doing. Self-governance audits are planned and scheduled by the cognizant functional management, using its personnel as the auditors. The company may or may not elect to have the provision for these audits included in the implementation plan. The local management may wish them to become an ongoing tool for assuring compliance. The reasons for self-governance audits include the following:

- Assigned employees are from the same general area.
- Employees are aware of activities within their area.
- Assignees have some degree of related experience.
- Employees can be assigned as time is available.
- Employees report to the management responsible for implementation.
- Corrective actions are the responsibility of local management.

The employees selected to perform these focused audits are not usually the individuals who are directly responsible for the tasks or areas being reviewed. Managers may use employees from the shop, lab, office, technical staff, supervision, and so on to achieve an independent approach for the evaluation. Whatever the method, the cognizant functional management is responsible for resolving these employee-identified problems. The success of this proactive activity is dependent on the area management's demonstrated concern for compliance.

7.2.3 Document writers as compliance auditors

Some companies use the documentation writers as auditors to specifically evaluate the level of employee understanding and compliance with the documentation. Since the authors have been involved in writing activities in the affected areas, their auditing assignments will need to be related to areas for which they did not have writing responsibility. Audits of this type are usually beneficial to auditor and auditee alike. Most companies schedule these reviews directly in the implementation plan. As such, the affected authors understand they have not completed their task until these auditing assignments are discharged.

7.2.4 Using the internal quality audit function

Fortunately, the ISO quality system standards also require a built-in mechanism for a semi-independent review of company compliance. As noted, ISO standards require that an internal quality audit function be created and implemented by the compliant company. The primary purpose of the audit function is to evaluate and report company performance to requirements. The process provides the company leadership with a means of collecting data for making well-considered decisions. Data collected by the internal quality audit function are independent of the normal functional management structure. When appropriate, the functional managers may use the quality audit function to either verify their position of compliance or to identify those areas that need improvement. The internal quality audit function can be a tremendous tool for both senior and middle management.

The internal quality audit program is perhaps the most suitable measure available to validate both the company's documentation and its compliance to that documentation. The audit program is not the only such tool available, but it is the most objective and beneficial to ongoing company operations. It is best utilized once the company has achieved most of the major changes in the implementation process. The internal quality audit function is examined further in section 7.3.

7.2.5 Auditing as part of auditor training

The early company evaluations ordinarily reveal a wide range of compliance. Some areas may still have variations that they are resolving. A formal internal quality audit at that point may be unnecessary—and even inappropriate. While the internal auditing function is certainly the most significant means of evaluating ongoing compliance to the ISO 9000 standards, it may not be the best approach to determine whether the company has achieved initial compliance levels. The quality audit function is traditionally more formal than what the company may need during the initial compliance phase.

The company may still use its candidate auditors to work with the management and workforce in the early verification environment. Most internal quality audits are basically quality system audits; however, a good audit function should also have the capability to perform other types of audits, such as the following:

Primary audits

- Functional quality system audits
- Incremental quality system audits
- Quality system audits for registration
- Complete quality system audits
- Supplier quality system audits
- Third-party quality system audits

Secondary audits

- Process verification audits
- Product or hardware audits
- Self-governance audits
- Third-party limited audits
- Spot or follow-up audits
- Audits on specific problems
- Joint contractor audits
- Customer satisfaction audits

Experience with various audit types, levels, and topics is beneficial to the audit function for future use.

7.3 Establishing the internal quality audit program

As noted, a fully operational internal quality audit function is required by the directive ISO quality system standards. A sound internal quality audit function is clearly beneficial to the company's operation. The audit program is a means of providing management with independently derived data on the company's performance. The system element requirements used in the internal quality audit may be taken directly from the selected ISO quality standard or from the company's quality system documentation.

One of the ISO 9000 requirements for management is to assure that the company quality system is effective for the purpose intended. Evaluating system effectiveness may take many forms but the method that offers the greatest opportunity for unbiased independent data is the internal audit. The audit function provides the following:

- Independently derived data for management review
- Assurance that the company quality system meets ISO 9000
- Data basis for company operational and process improvements
- Basis for quality system corrective actions discovered in audits
- Evaluation of the effectiveness of the existing quality system
- An avenue for investigation of special concerns

Reprinted from the Center for International Standards & Quality "ISO 9000 Internal Quality Auditing" with permission from Georgia Tech Research Corporation 1995.

If the audit function is established as a tool for management to identify areas for proactive measures, then it can be greatly beneficial as the company moves toward world-class status.

7.3.1 Developing a successful company audit program

The audit program should be designed to periodically evaluate compliance with all quality system elements. This review can be performed incrementally on specific system elements or on the total quality system in one comprehensive audit. Either way, all quality system elements should be examined at least annually. Beyond evaluating whether requirements and goals are being achieved, another purpose of the audits is to determine whether there are any areas or elements needing improvements. The identified improvement opportunities will not be limited to quality system methods and documentation, but may also apply to virtually all aspects of company business. Since the quality system is one of the primary means of operating the company, auditors will likely be involved in many functional areas.

The internal quality audit function should use a set of performance criteria that stress professionalism and protocol. There are ISO 9000 family guidelines for internal quality auditing best practices. The set of three ISO 10011 audit program guidelines include best practice information on the function's management, operation, staffing, and training. The titles are ISO 1001-1, *Guidelines for auditing quality systems, Part 1—auditing;* ISO 10011-2, *Guidelines for auditing quality systems, Part 2—Qualification criteria for auditors;* and ISO 10011-3, *Guidelines for auditing quality systems, Part 3—Managing audit programmes.*

7.3.2 The need for internal quality audit procedures

Not only do these documents provide sound guidance for the audit function but they also describe the audit protocol and methodology used by third party auditors. The ISO 10011 approach is the same one used during the ISO 9000-based customer or registration audit. It benefits the company to use an internal audit program paralleling the auditing methodology of customers and registrars.

Experience indicates the internal quality audit function is the most likely ISO quality system element to be absent from a typical candidate company's existing system. Companies implementing ISO 9000 must often develop documentation to cover the internal auditing function. Developing documentation on a process which does not currently exist causes the assigned authors to seek information on the best practices for the function. Using ISO 10011 guidelines tends to result in acceptable and beneficial audit programs. These guidelines have standardized the basic internal quality auditing approach taken by many companies.

The compliant company must have fully operative procedural coverage for its quality auditing function. The company can take advantage of the proof testing phase of the documentation process by utilizing its audit function to evaluate the documented quality system. This will yield at least three advantages: (1) evaluation of company performance to system documentation; (2) acceptance of the internal quality auditing procedures; and (3) initiating the development and collection of quality audit records.

The internal quality audit procedures must provide direction for such activities as

- Developing, managing, and operating the internal quality audit program
- Establishing and maintaining acceptable audit protocol
- Training and assigning auditors
- Documenting and reporting results to management and auditees

These subjects are in keeping with the guidelines in the ISO 10011 standard, as well as being generally acceptable to most non–ISO 9000 quality system auditing standards. Internal quality audit (IQA) procedures must include the following:

- Determining audit subjects
- Scheduling audits
- Providing notification of audits
- Developing audit plans
- Performing audits
- Assigning auditors
- Providing audit inbriefing and outbriefing
- Developing audit final reports
- Reviewing corrective actions
- Closing audits

7.3.3 Building internal quality auditor resources

Performing these audit process activities requires auditor and auditee training such as that described in Step 6. Auditor trainees gain a great deal of experience and on-the-job training during the initial efforts used to validate documentation. The company also benefits from its expanded auditing force during its initial quality system evaluation phase. A larger examiner base likely results in better and quicker system element coverage. The expanded auditor base also produces a number of individuals who, although not planned as permanent auditors, become excellent auditees and audit support personnel. Another advantage is that any major problems will probably be identified early in the process. Thus, prompt remedial actions can be taken.

Many companies select candidate auditors from all functions. Then the company or audit manager can tailor each audit team by matching individual backgrounds from the auditor reservoir to specific subjects. Consequently, everyone benefits. Auditor trainees learn their responsibilities, and they learn how to perform an audit; how to deal with auditees; and how to create a productive audit environment. They learn the audit activities and auditees' responsibilities in an actual audit environment.

The auditors experience the problems of planning and conducting an audit (see Figure 7.2). They have a chance to manage the auditor/auditee interface. This experience will be advantageous when the eventual customer or registrar audits take place, because a greater number of individuals will understand the auditing process.

Auditors must always make their decisions based on objective evidence—which is their acquired, firsthand, factual knowledge. This mandatory pursuit of objective evidence can be achieved by observation, interview, records, and process results. As auditors and auditees examine company compliance with each aspect of the governing documentation, they begin to appreciate the benefits of the auditing process. The examination also results in a firm reinforcement of the need for a fully documented quality system. Even though evaluation of implementation success can be performed using outside agencies, the prudent company utilizes its internal quality audit function as the primary means of assuring such reinforcement.

7.3.4 Should the company use special outside auditor training?

The question often arises as to whether the company should send candidate auditors to outside training programs that specialize in ISO 9000 auditor training. The ISO 9000 family does require the compliant company to use trained and experienced auditors in its program. The methods and means of achieving competent auditors is at the company's discretion (see Figure 7.3).

Advertisements would lead one to assume no that satisfactory company auditing of ISO 9000 quality systems can be performed without outside auditor training. There is no ISO 9000 requirement for such independent instruction. The only requirement for training in this manner is for individuals interested in becoming auditors in the employ of a

Stalling and diversions by auditee	Audit solutions
• Prolonged in briefing by auditee	• Preschedule inbriefing
• Tour too extended or unrelated	• Preset tour/schedule
• Excessive questioning/discussions	• Offer to meet again
• Input materials not provided	• "No show" phone number
• Arguments on noncompliance	• Deal only in facts
• Different faces on same problem	• Insist on counterpart
• Meetings/visits not scheduled	• Lead auditor intervention
• Counterpart unavailable	• "No show" phone number
• Auditee scheduling lunches/dinners	• Such refused at inbriefing
• Intentional obstruction of audit	• Lead auditor intervention

Adhering to auditee rules and regulations	
• Safety and smoking practices	• Follow auditee rules
• Lunch and break periods	• Follow auditee schedules
• Use of phones, clerical, copiers	• Use only to facilitate audit
• Control of proprietary data	• Auditee approval and rules
• Parking of automobiles	• As auditee provides
• Odd-shift auditing	• Prearranged with auditee
• Unproductive time periods	• Lead auditor assistance
• Company/union discussions	• No direct involvement
• Classified/secured areas	• Follow auditee rules
• Unsolicited negative information	• Provide to counterpart

Reprinted from the Center for International Standards & Quality "ISO 9000 Internal Quality Auditing" with permission from Georgia Tech Research Corporation 1995.

Figure 7.2 Problems for audit team to overcome or avoid.

registration company. Training programs with this goal are approved by the national board established for such purposes, such as the Registrar Accreditation Board in the United States. Grandfathering of experienced auditors with suitable credentials has also been used to satisfy the requirement.

	Lead Auditor	*Auditor*
Education:	Degree in related field or equivalent experience	Degree in related field or equivalent experience
Experience:	10+ quality system audits 2+ audits as a lead auditor assistant	4–10 quality system audits 2+ audits beyond trainee level
Special:	Suitable management experience; articulate; good presentation skills; personable, objective, and poised; possesses excellent writing and organizing skills	Management experienced desired; articulate, personable, and objective; possesses excellent writing and interview skills

Reprinted from the Center for International Standards & Quality "ISO 9000 Internal Quality Auditing" with permission from Georgia Tech Research Corporation 1995.

Figure 7.3   Recommended auditor training/experience.

Since, however, most companies are interested in eventually becoming registered, knowledge of what is taught to potential registrar personnel is of obvious interest. It is not unusual for the interested company to send one or more individuals to outside lead auditor or internal quality auditor training. These employees will likely receive sound training, as well as a good understanding of how the registrars actually operate when auditing a company for ISO 9000 compliance. Management must always remember, although auditor knowledge of the process is important, it is essential to have it coupled with as much experience as possible. Experience is really the only way one learns the auditing profession.

7.3.5 Audit program must fit company culture

As the audit environment develops, a wealth of performance data is collected for management consideration. As the process unfolds, the environment begins to reveal the nature of acceptable audit protocol and methodology for the specific company culture. Although the nature of how company auditors apply the protocol and procedural methodology varies, the requirements may not vary at all.

The ISO 9000 standards require the company to have some type of training appropriate to the auditor assignment. The training can be developed and presented using several acceptable methods. The company may use capabilities, (1) within the ISO implementing company; (2) offered by the parent corporation; (3) supplied by third party consultants on-site; or (4) offered by a training firm. Companies often save money by bringing the training activity to their facility. They can then train many employees for the same price as sending several people off-site for training. If the latter is done, it ought to be with the plan of having employees return to perform subsequent in-company auditor or auditee training.

7.4 Management responsibilities in assuring compliance

By this point in the process, the company has invested a significant amount of time and money. Even if the initial reason for the company's ISO 9000 implementation was to secure registration, the realization of many additional gains will have become fact. By now, the organization and documentation of the company's operational methods should have enlisted significant management support. Management usually acknowledges that the advantages of a well-structured company quality system have easily justified the resources required for implementation. Of course, this gain is true whether implementation was performed for ISO registration or not.

7.4.1 Senior management is clearly responsible for compliance

It is always the responsibility of prudent management to operate the company in the most efficient and effective way possible. As such, it is not surprising to find the management of the ISO 9000-compliant company to be completely satisfied with the newfound quality system capabilities. In addition, management now has a means of determining whether the company is working to its ISO 9000-based system of requirements. The installed documentation has been used by the company to capture what it has determined to be its optimal approach for successful operation. As noted, a documented, efficient, repetitive process covering each aspect of company operations will benefit every company. All stakeholders will support such a management position.

As the company moves down the final stretch toward full implementation, management must maintain its support and encouragement for the completion of all remaining tasks in the plan. Since senior management originally approved placing all of the implementation tasks in the plan, it indicated full ISO 9000 implementation would only be achieved after all compliance evaluations have been successfully closed. With such a mandate in hand, the management representative will likely have been able to maintain the company momentum through to this point of verifying quality system compliance.

Unfortunately, once the verification process is completed, senior management often takes the position that any corrective actions are the responsibility of the managers and employees who were unable to demonstrate their compliance. The source of this management failing apparently relates to overlooking its own requirement that the implementation process is not complete until all actions necessary for compliance are closed. If such is the case, the management representative must take prompt action to maintain senior management's involvement in these final phases. As the final compliance evaluations are completed and any corrective actions are identified, the management representative assures that each scheduled action is given directly to the responsible member of functional management. The period for corrective action resolution should be scheduled to minimize the impact of the problem.

7.4.2 Management review for quality is an excellent tool

Another significant management obligation is its ongoing review of the basic quality system. These senior-level reviews are not only required for compliance with the ISO 9000 standards, but can also be instrumental to the company's success. The directive standards state that "the supplier's management with executive responsibility shall review the quality system at defined intervals sufficient to ensure its continuing suitability and effectiveness."

As the company gets closer to completing its ISO 9000 implementation, the next senior management status review will likely concentrate on resolving any open actions. Functional managers with any delinquent corrective actions will be very motivated for near-term closure.

While management involvement early in the implementation process was primarily one of commitment and resources, now it shifts to assuring that any open actions are successfully closed, whether unfinished actions or corrective activities. This is the obvious route to the conclusion of the company's implementation process.

Although the management review requirement must be satisfied in order to comply with the ISO 9000 standards, it is prudent for any company to have a periodic senior-level review of quality system performance. This means the company has placed the quality system at the highest level of attention and concern. This review must be performed and documented on a regular basis. The stated purpose of the review is to examine the continuing suitability and effectiveness of the quality system. The records of the management review must address the means by which the suitability and effectiveness was determined. Companies which direct such a degree of attention to the quality system will find themselves operating at a more efficient and effective level than prior to the reviews. Reviews permit management to accomplish its responsibilities (see Figure 7.4).

7.4.3 Internal quality audits aid management review process

As noted, one of the best ways to collect current quality system data to use in the management review and decision process is through the company's internal quality audit function. The company's audit data relates well to the requirement for determining the continued suitability and effectiveness of the quality system. The audit data will either provide assurance the company is still in compliance with system requirements,

- Operating company using ISO 9000 quality system baseline
- Achieving ISO 9000 compliance
- Using management reviews for monitoring and assurance
- Maintaining commitments made to employees at process initiation
- Maintaining and assuming ongoing ISO 9000 compliance
- Achieving ISO 9000 registration, if desired

Figure 7.4 Fulfilling management closure responsibilities.

Management must provide the following:
- A company quality policy to meet ISO standards
- Senior approval of the quality system/documentation
- Creation and assignment of a company audit function
- Appropriate resources for operation of audit function
- Assignment of auditing leadership and support staff
- Approval of company audit program and plan
- Management review and use of selected audit data
- Assurance that corrective actions will be achieved
- Adjudication of any audit related disputes

Reprinted from the Center for International Standards & Quality "ISO 9000 Internal Quality Auditing" with permission from Georgia Tech Research Corporation 1995.

Figure 7.5 Management commitment to the audit function.

or will identify those areas needing improvements. Improvements may mean restoration of compliance or finding new areas where improvements have been identified. Either of these help the management staff to comply with its defined managerial obligations.

The audit function has the responsibility to serve as a management tool for collecting data independent of the normal reporting channels. Reciprocally, there exists a required management responsibility and commitment to the operation and integrity of the internal quality audit function (see Figure 7.5). These management responsibilities include such aspects as assuring continued independence of the audit function reporting chain; providing adequate resources and staff to support the management-approved audit functions; and reviewing and assigning corrective action to the affected auditee management.

7.4.4 Management commitments to employees must be maintained

As noted, employees' roles in an ISO-compliant quality system are expanded to permit more involvement in the quality system process.

Employees at all levels should be involved in ISO implementation. This involvement may range from simply understanding the quality policy and quality objectives to becoming significant contributors in achieving a compliant system. The success of this change in employee role is primarily based on management's acceptance of the concept.

It is imperative that the nature of the employee role in the implementation process does not vary from the original management commitment. This is especially true as the company moves toward completion of the ISO 9000 implementation process. Continued employee contribution benefits the company in its new ISO 9000-compliant environment. Management is solely responsible for creating and maintaining an environment in which employee participation can flourish. This must continue through the system validation phase and beyond. Much of the fine-tuning needed for full compliance will come from involved employees. The workforce also observes and reacts to management's support of this important aspect of achieving ISO 9000 compliance.

7.4.5 Management must assure total ISO 9000 compliance

Management's final task in assuring full ISO 9000 implementation is to aggressively maintain the new quality system as a primary means of operating the company. Any variation of management's commitments regarding the sanctity of the quality policy, and the resultant new quality system, will cause the system to fail. Confidence in the continuity of the quality system is reinforced each time management acts to support it. This is another situation where management both controls and reflects the company attitude in relation to the necessity for compliance. Positive management attitudes must be present during ISO 9000 implementation, validation and beyond.

7.5 Preparing for the customer/registration audit

The company preparing for an audit by either a customer or a registrar will eventually reach a point where all of the actions and tasks identified in the ISO implementation plan have been accomplished and verified. Invariably, the concern then shifts to how well each of these tasks has been implemented. Is the new quality system truly effective?

7.5.1 Concern for the effective compliance requirement

Company concern for system effectiveness often escalates to a level where some tasks are reexamined with the belief they might be further improved. Experienced management will quickly see the company is entering into a situation where it may never judge itself completely ready for the anticipated compliance audit.

Based on having completed and verified the implementation plan, prudent senior managers should simply acknowledge everything the company has developed in preparation for ISO 9000 has now been judged in compliance with the standard. The results can and will be improved once the new system has been operating for a while. In fact, since methods of dealing with system change are an integral part of the ISO 9000-based system, future process and documentation changes are expected. Such changes may even be acceptable during the customer or registration audits because they are part of normal system operation. Experience shows the professional auditors will not have a problem with in-process improvements during their audit, assuming the existing method complies with the requirements. Although the visiting auditors have no problem with these changes, employees are likely to be quite anxious.

7.5.2 Continuous improvement of the quality system

Once the company is truly compliant, improvement or upgrade changes are appropriate but constant system reevaluation is *not* recommended. The company does need to know, however, the strengths and weaknesses in its quality system. It must identify these before the external auditors' visit. The company must have plans in place to address any weaknesses in the near term.

A system weakness should not be misconstrued as a noncompliant activity! It is an activity within the quality system that management would like to improve once time and money are available. It may be related to poor efficiency or high costs within a given process or task. A system weakness is usually one that is compliant when it is performed in a best effort manner, when sufficient time and resources are available. Achieving an optimal quality system, in total, on the first pass is highly unlikely. While such is always the goal, the system actually evolves and matures over time. In order to be ready for outside auditors, the company must manage its weaknesses and declare itself sufficiently prepared to undergo the independent examination. It must be acknowledged that even the best companies have strengths and weaknesses in their quality system.

There exists a possibility that some corrective actions may still be in progress during the outside audit. A closure plan is absolutely required for any aspect of open corrective actions. An auditor can only judge the company in compliance when some method of temporary compliance is in place, pending the closure of any final corrective action. To be successful, companies must assure they have completed all open actions that are possible in the near term. These are *not* corrective actions requiring long-term scheduling, such as may be associated with equipment delivery and installation.

The company should never attempt to undergo an audit without having documented procedures addressing the compliance methods for each ISO 9000 quality system element. Of course, the method of achieving compliance must be effective. It may not necessarily be the optimal approach at the point of audit, but it should be capable of effectively achieving the desired results.

7.5.3 Do not overlook mandatory training requirements

A sometimes overlooked corrective action that may affect the company's preparedness for an outside audit is the completion of all training necessary for successful ISO 9000 implementation. Except for newly assigned employees, with any training-related restrictions, the company should have training documentation and records available for every employee. Even those training classes and OJT activities that relate to auditor/auditee interfaces need to be completed and documented. The pertinent documentation and associated records also include satisfying the internal auditor qualifications that the company has deemed necessary.

7.5.4 Considering an independent preassessment

Although compliance to ISO 9000 and the resultant company quality system may have been completely verified internally, many companies still prefer having an independent audit for insurance. Management may feel uncomfortable entering into the critical customer or registration audit without an independent review. Consequently, some companies elect to

> • Preassessment is not required for implementation and/or registration.
>
> • Preassessment is an independent look at the company's compliance.
>
> • Some companies use it; some do not.
>
> • Decisions tend to be based on the current confidence level.
>
> • Possible external preassessment auditors are corporate or corporate-based audit teams; third party or consultant audit teams; and those supplied by a registrar.

Figure 7.6 Considerations for choosing a preassessment by external sources.

utilize outside auditors to perform a confidential preaudit. Such an audit independently verifies the adequacy, documentation, and performance compliance of the company's new quality system (see Figure 7.6).

Verification by corporate audit function. This is the most frequently used approach in companies that are part of a large corporate structure. This type of audit may include beneficial recommendations based on the visiting auditors' prior experiences and observations. It is also an excellent way for company auditors to gain experience, which can later be passed on to resident company auditors and auditees.

Verification by independent consultants. The benefit of this audit is that it is confidential, provides recommendations if desired, and does not have the normally protective corporate umbrella. Audits by third party companies often come as part of a package arrangement that also provides training on ISO awareness, ISO documentation, and internal quality auditing. This latter type of training often includes the opportunity to actually perform auditing.

As with all consultants, such third party companies should be used only to augment company capabilities or fill company knowledge gaps. The outside consultants should not be placed in charge of any aspect of company ISO 9000 implementation because they do not have the necessary awareness of company operations, resources, limitations, and so on. In addition to performing audits, outside consultants are excellent sources of ideas and information for management and ISO 9000 implementation teams.

Verification by registrar preassessment. The final method of obtaining an unofficial outside review comes very close to being a conflict of interest. The method utilizes a registration company to perform a preassessment. This is usually done by the same registrar the company has selected for the official registration audit. The preaudit can take two forms: (1) a detailed review of the company's quality system manual and any direct or referenced supportive documentation developed for ISO 9000 compliance; and (2) what is done in the first preaudit approach but with the addition of an on-site compliance audit. The detail level of the on-site audits tends to vary greatly by registrar.

The first type of registrar preassessment judges documentation adequacy and where it needs upgrading. The second type of preaudit provides the same but also includes a set of compliance audit findings that require resolution. Clearly, if the preaudit company is also the registrar, evidence of having resolved these findings must be presented prior to the registrar returning for the formal registration audit.

Since this latter type of registrar preaudit simulates the actual registration audit, the assumption is usually made that when the findings are addressed, the company will be capable of passing its registration audit. While such is often the case, the registrar maintains a caveat that is based on the following:

- Sampling nature of audits
- Time between the two audits
- Potential for system compliance degradation
- Opportunity for a detailed examination

The registrar can not promise or even imply any preapproval as the result of a preassessment or its firm could lose its accreditation. In reality, the registrar also gains from such a preassessment. After a preaudit, the registrar is in a much better position to develop a tailored audit plan for the company.

7.5.5 Company decision on need for registration

Only management can decide on the preaudit method. Management may also decide to use its own auditors or those of the corporation.

Going outside the corporate confines, it may determine a third party consultant or registrar is most suitable for company needs. Weighing in this decision is the consideration whether the company is planning to undergo registration or not. Registration is not a compliance requirement of the ISO 9000 standards. The primary purpose of the company's ISO 9000 implementation program was to develop an effective quality system that complies with the international quality standards. As noted, the registration has come about through other channels. The registration process is simply a means of demonstrating the company has obtained independent third party concurrence of its compliance to the selected company ISO quality system standard.

Note: The primary compliance concurrence for the company to obtain must always be regarded as customer approval. If the customer does not agree the company is in compliance with the selected ISO 9000 standard, it matters little if the company, the corporation, or the registrar have said otherwise. The customer may use the company's registration for consideration in its supplier approval and control process (see Figure 7.7).

ISO 9000 registration
- Provides customers with added ISO 9000 compliance assurance.
- Is essentially quality system based, not product oriented.
- Is available for customers to plan the extent of supplier oversight.
- May be used as total oversight in noncritical purchases.
- May be used as partial oversight in critical purchases.
- May not be required or used at all (even though benefit is derived).

In summary, the customer uses registration to the extent desired!

Figure 7.7   Customer use of registration.

Conclusion

The company eventually arrives at a point of considering its planned ISO 9000 implementation complete and ready for final evaluation. The problems encountered during the implementation process have been resolved. Adequacy of company documentation to describe the quality system is coupled with the company's compliance to the documented system. As such, the affected managers determine the functions, areas, and processes in total compliance with the ISO 9000 standard.

The company now wants to evaluate compliance by means that are independent of the cognizant managers. The initial evaluation of the company's documented quality system is by the user workforce. This is one of the best evaluations the company can use. It can also utilize independent teams to review the degree of compliance. These teams may be implementation team participants or formal teams of auditors from the internal quality audit function.

ISO standards require that the company establish an internal quality audit function to act on its behalf to independently examine compliance to its ISO 9000-based quality system. This objectivity permits management to make improvement judgments without the bias that sometimes clouds the decision process. Since company audits are performed to the same guidelines used by the registrar, the company audits give an advanced look at how registration audits will be performed.

As the company moves into the compliance evaluation phases, the evidence of management commitment must shift from supplying process resources and guidance to assuring that all identified final corrective actions are fully resolved; that compliance is verified; and that preparations are made for the customer or registrar visit. Management should readily accept and implement the ISO requirement for the periodic review of the quality system. Management must maintain its commitment to have the company workforce included in the compliance and improvement process. This commitment must always be readily apparent to employees.

Many companies still elect to utilize an outside agency to provide a final independent evaluation of the company's compliance. This type of audit can be performed by the company's parent corporation, an independent consultant, or by an accredited registrar. Using registrars provides some basic understanding as to how they will operate in an actual registration audit.

Registration is not a requirement of the ISO 9000 standards. It is used as an independent judgment of compliance, but the final judge of company compliance is the customer.

Implementation actions required by this module

1. Establish a system of both formal and informal, ongoing ISO 9000 compliance audits.

2. Utilize formal internal quality auditing as the primary means of determining compliance.

3. Assure that the audit function's reporting chain demonstrates an ability for independent judgment.

4. Assure all aspects of the company ISO 9000 quality system are functioning effectively.

5. Perform ISO 9000 compliance verification audits to include the goal of auditee training.

6. Assure continuing compliance is accepted as local management responsibility.

7. Assure that the workforce has accepted its role and ownership in the ISO 9000 methods and procedures.

8. Create an environment that encourages workforce participation in problem identification.

9. Develop and use selection qualifications for company internal quality auditors.

10. Utilize ISO 10011 as a guide for developing basic internal quality audit procedures.

11. Implement a sound corrective and preventive action system for any problems identified.

12. Determine the customer and/or registrar to perform the compliance audit.

Step 8: The Customer/Registration Audit

8.1 Selecting a suitable registrar

8.2 Preparing for the registrar's arrival

8.3 Registrar personnel at the company's site

8.4 Completing the registration audit

8.5 Achieving final audit closure and registration

Conclusion

Questions answered in this module

1. What factors should be considered when selecting an ISO 9000 registrar?

2. For best market position, should the company select a foreign or domestic registrar?

3. Does a company still need to be registered if it does not plan to sell to the European Union?

4. Considering no cost, why would any customer fail to invoke a registration requirement?

5. Why do the ISO 9000 standards not require some form of registration process?

6. What is the difference between accreditation, registration, and certification?

7. Must registrars be under contract before they will answer questions?

8. What must be done before the registrar's audit team arrives at the company's site?

9. How much position selling can be done to convince a registrar that a company is in compliance?

10. What benefit is derived from using company audit facilitators during the registration audit?

11. Will the registrar reveal the intended audit plan before the actual audit?

12. What does the company need to do to prepare for the registrar's inbriefing?

13. Are most registrars looking for things that tend to fail the company?

14. Will the registrar keep the company advised of any findings?

15. Can registrars truly question any employee about the quality system?

16. What is done if the registrar and the company disagree on ISO 9000 compliance?

17. Does the registrar ever examine or use the company's quality system audit data?

18. How many quality system audit findings are allowed before a company fails its audit?

19. Does the registrar ever provide the compliance audit results to company customers?

20. What determines when registrars need to return for follow-up on corrective actions?

21. How often does the registrar visit a company to maintain its registration?

22. What is the difference between corrective action verification and validation?

23. How long does the company have to resolve negative findings from a compliance audit?

24. What is the company's responsibility between registrar's surveillance visits?

25. How will the company be notified of satisfactorily completing the registration process?

The Customer/Registration Audit

The company has finally arrived at the point of having to deal with the official ISO 9000 compliance approval audit. Depending on the situation, the audit may be performed by either a customer or a registrar. A great amount of preparation has gone into getting the company ready for this day. If preparatory activities have been performed as described in this text, the company should be fully capable of passing any compliance audit.

If the customer does not require ISO registration, the customer may elect to perform the compliance audit directly, using its own auditors. Note, however, that customers who choose registration over their own audit are becoming increasingly prevalent. The independence and validity of the registration process give the customer confidence in the registered company's quality system.

Cost considerations play a significant role in the decision to register. Registration requires the auditee company to bear the cost of the entire process. Most customers are beginning to regard supplier registration as both a quality and an economic plus. Many have even started to require official ISO 9000 quality system registration as a primary requirement for doing business with them.

8.1 Selecting a suitable registrar

For the purposes of this review, it is assumed an official registration of the company is required. Whether performed by the customer or the registrar, the nature of any official compliance audit is essentially based on the same audit criteria and methods. In many respects, the auditee company should notice no difference between the customer and the registrar's audit. The following ISO 9000 registration discussion applies to all companies entering the official compliance approval stage.

8.1.1 Successful independent evaluation offers benefits

As indicated in Step 1, the registration requirement only becomes a foregone conclusion when the company plans to do business with the European Community (EC). Even then, registration is only required when the company is involved in the manufacture or sale of regulated products, as defined by the EC. The registration concept, however, has spread beyond the original EC approach, and increasing international marketing pressures have resulted in virtually a universal acceptance of the ISO registration concept and process.

As the result, a number of companies have recently achieved accreditation and are now operating as registrars. In theory all are equally capable, but, in fact, some are more highly regarded than others. It is generally the sole responsibility of the candidate company's management to select the registrar it believes will be best suited to the company. Since the registrars are operating a market-based business, there is always room for some degree of negotiation as to costs. There is never, however, negotiation on the nature of the registration process. It is controlled to rigid standards, and any improper variation could lead to the loss of the registrar's accreditation.

8.1.2 Early contact with registrars

Most companies select and establish contact with their registrar while the company is undergoing ISO 9000 implementation. In-process conversations on various issues are often beneficial in obtaining the registrar's point of view. The company's position can not be presold through telephone conversations, because this is an unethical, unacceptable approach. The registrar's evaluation is always based on objective evidence, that is, acquired firsthand knowledge on the part of the auditors. The astute candidate company, however, can gain enough knowledge through these contacts to reasonably know what to expect.

As noted, the registration process is a fairly standardized and confidential contractual activity between the company and the registrar. It begins with the company's management representative contacting the registrar and discussing various aspects of the company's business base, facilities, and product lines; ISO 9000 implementation and plans for registration; and the proposed schedule for the registration visit (see Figure 8.1). The registrar then provides information on its approval for auditing the candidate company; a proposed audit team and audit costs; and the available audit dates (see Figure 8.2).

Once all of the details are worked out between the two parties, the company indicates when it will be ready to send its quality manual and related procedures for review. Prior to this review, the registrar may want an initial monetary commitment. Once the company's quality system manual has been deemed satisfactory, with or without some required changes, the on-site audit may be arranged. Most registrars require all quality manual changes to be completed and returned to them before the on-site audit takes place. The size of the audit team and duration of the visit will depend on the size of the company, since that factor normally governs the amount of time required for the audit.

8.1.3 Significant influences on registrar selection

The company initiating its own ISO 9000 implementation activity always has the choice of selecting whatever registrar its management deems

---

- Nature and structure of the company
- Location and size of the company
- Business and product/service lines
- ISO 9000 directive standard selected
- Intended audit scope, estimated time frame, and schedule
- Company and audit principals involved
- Nature of company quality system documentation
- Availability of company quality manual

Figure 8.1   What registrars will want to know.

- Basis of approvals for auditing the company and its product line
- Nature of contracts, commitments, and costs
- Date(s) available for potential registration audit
- Documentation required before the on-site visit
- Registrar's position on the need and/or nature of preassessment
- The nature and composition of registrar's audit team
- Referrals from within the company's industry

Figure 8.2　What companies should ask candidate registrars.

most suitable (see Figure 8.3). There are, however, times when a customer either directs or strongly influences the company's registrar selection. The customer's motive for stipulating which registrar to use may be based on direction from its prime customers or its strategic commitment to a target marketplace. This situation is particularly true of some customers who are trying to standardize their usage of third-party oversight functions to gain increased supplier control and confidence.

- Is there any evidence of customer preference, stated or unstated?
- Do certain registrars show up repeatedly in the company's industry?
- Are the company's competitors tending to use a single registrar?
- Does the corporation have plans for a blanket contract?
- Would using a foreign or domestic registrar be most beneficial?
- Does the company have any networking data on registrars?
- If there are no other influences, should a local registrar be used to control costs?

Figure 8.3　What to consider when choosing a registrar.

When the ISO 9000 candidate company is trying to expand its market base by entering into a potential customer's supplier base, it is entirely appropriate to inquire if registration is a requirement. Further, a candidate should ask what registrar the potential customer prefers. Occasionally, a specific registrar is named. Often no direct recommendation is given. If the latter is the case, then it is prudent to ask what registrars are used by the customer's current suppliers. This inquiry may reveal an unstated customer preference that may be influencing supplier selection.

Some companies find it beneficial to utilize registrars that operate within a certain business or industrial base, such as the steel or chemical industries. Registrars usually start their operations in certain industries because of the original background and experience of their management and auditors. As such, they tend to receive their original accreditation in those industries. Registrars may later add capabilities and get approved for more business groups or commodities, but often they retain the original bent that generated their early success.

The ISO candidate company may be in an industry that tends to use only one or two registrars. If such is the case, experience shows it is usually wise to obtain the registration through one of the same registrars used by the competition. This method of selection is particularly valid if potential customers might wonder why the company has varied from the pattern set by either the company's competitors or the related industry.

Some corporations find it beneficial to establish a business relationship with a given registrar for the eventual registration of all facilities within its corporate structure. This increasingly common approach is often used for its economic benefits and convenience. The corporation can bring its various facilities to the point of audit as it sees fit, and can vary selection of the ISO standard focus at the various units in accordance with the corporation's best interests. This arrangement is suitable when the company is part of a corporation that has centralized functions. These may be related to the candidate company, but located in sister facilities. Conversely, the centralized functions may be at the candidate company but not reporting to it. Examples of centralized functions include corporate procurement, product development, or corporate marketing.

8.1.4 Consider using a foreign registrar

Should a foreign or domestic registrar be used? Logically, the answer is based on which one is most advantageous to the company. If the primary purpose of registration is for access to a foreign marketplace, it is advisable to use a registrar that has acceptance in the target countries. The same consideration would be true if the company's basic industry is tending toward foreign registrar use. Many foreign registrars now have offices in the United States. Some foreign registrars also have working arrangements with domestic firms, which may essentially result in a foreign registration.

If the company does not have any requirement for using a foreign registrar, then using a domestic firm approved by the U.S. Registrar Accreditation Board is probably satisfactory. At least in theory, there should be little difference in the standards and capabilities of accredited registrars worldwide; however, some registrars have gained more regional acceptance than others. Although the U.S. registrar accreditation process was late getting started and approved, it has emerged as a program having general acceptance within the U.S. industrial base.

8.1.5 Various networking approaches yield registrar data

Since the company approvals resulting from the registration process are well documented, information about which company has been working with which registrar is readily available. As such, any company considering a specific registrar can contact other companies that have used the firm. This networking process is perhaps the best way to gather current information to help management make the best selection.

In addition, many localities have formed business-supported ISO 9000 user groups through the local ASQC section, university, or business association. The whole purpose of a user group network is to share information about ISO implementation, compliance practices, use of registrars, and so on. The interest generated within the local business community is quite surprising. One such group, which was started recently in a major U.S. city, had over 100 businesses represented at the very first meeting and has continued to grow ever since.

8.2 Preparing for the registrar's arrival

All tasks established in the ISO 9000 implementation plan must be completed before the registrar's audit team arrives. Completion involves all implementation activities, including company compliance verification efforts, employee training, and so on (see Figure 8.4).

- Complete all actions in the implementation plan.
- Complete all verification and validation activities.
- Complete all open company audit corrective actions.
- Identify the company's position on marginal compliances.
- Use company ISO implementers as audit facilitators.
- Set up a system of monitoring audit results in progress.
- Prepare facilities for use by registration auditors.
- Organize audit contact scheduling and prepare for inbriefing.

Figure 8.4 Preparing for the registrar's arrival.

8.2.1 Addressing corrective actions and marginal compliance

Coupled with completion of the planned tasks, is the need to complete any remaining corrective actions that may have been identified during the company's compliance review and verification efforts. The visiting auditors should find all company-determined corrective actions satisfactorily discharged. Company preparations for the registration audit often involve continued verification of its quality system effectiveness, sometimes up to the point of registrar audit team's arrival. Any last-minute, minor problems must have a remedial plan available, and must be in the process of resolution when the registrar arrives.

If the company's preparations for the audit have been sound and thorough, it will have likely identified all potential compliance issues. These are situations where the company has determined the level of its compliance is only marginally acceptable. Such situations are common, and virtually every company will have some with which to contend. These borderline situations are often based on cost disbursement considerations that are deemed inappropriate for the time period in which the audit will take place (for example, investing in a new computerized system). The borderline situations may also relate to an equipment or software implementation or scheduling problem that conflicts with the customer-designated compliance due date.

Management must determine if the current marginal method is still capable of meeting the standard. Sometimes the marginal acceptance is based on all company participants having to maintain an exceptional degree of process discipline. If compliance can be demonstrated, it will likely be satisfactory. In these situations, the company should establish a management-approved position on how company personnel will respond to policy questions when the auditors are examining the subject area or process (see Figure 8.5).

The company personnel must never intentionally mislead the registrar auditors. On the other hand, it is completely acceptable to assure uniform presentation of the company's policy position on why an area or process has been deemed compliant. If all company facilitators respond with the same general position, most auditors will determine the company has thoroughly evaluated the situation and has it in hand. Many auditors tend to look for variation in responses or uncertainty on the part of the individuals being interviewed. Identifying the few remaining potential issues and establishing a company position on each is not subterfuge by any means. It is only assuring everyone is capable of relating the company position on that particular aspect of compliance.

- Any areas of marginal acceptance must currently be ISO compliant.
- Remaining open corrective actions must have some closure plan.
- Equipment or software purchases and/or installations need completion dates.
- A control plan must be presented if compliance depends on exceptional process discipline.
- Company facilitators and area managers must know company position.
- All company representatives should present the same position.
- There should be no subterfuge with auditors. Discussions should be open and honest.

Figure 8.5   Establishing positions on marginal acceptance.

8.2.2 Putting the best foot forward during the audit

The company should never attempt to sell its compliance in any area or process where it simply does not meet the ISO quality standard. The same is true when the company fails to adhere to its own quality system documentation. A previously undetected significant area of noncompliance may be discovered by the company just prior to the registrar's arrival. If there is time, it should be corrected. When the resolution can not be achieved in time, the company must develop and implement a corrective action plan. It should be presented to the registrar at the audit inbriefing. It may result in a finding by the registrar, but it will be recorded as being company discovered and in process before the visiting audit team arrived.

8.2.3 Maintaining continuity of implementation expertise

During the development and discharge of the implementation plan, the participating personnel were heavily involved in assuring all tasks were completed as planned. In most companies, certain individuals probably revealed a talent for the process. As such, they likely were selected to play an increased role as the company moved toward implementation completion. On the basis of their performance, these people are prime candidates for the roles of company internal quality auditors and/or company registration audit facilitators. The functional background of these employees is usually not a factor. Thus, company facilitators should possess the following qualifications.

- Awareness of company operations
- ISO 9000 implementation involvement
- Objective and deliberate approach
- Even temperament and disposition
- Communication skills
- Interpersonal skills
- Management experience
- Knowledge of company procedures

Clearly the company's audit facilitators must have some degree of audit orientation, and some additional training. Facilitators must be schooled in the methodology of how the company plans to interface with the visiting auditors. Audit aspects need to be handled in the same way by all facilitators. The company must standardize its approach to such activities as auditor/auditee/facilitator interface; monitoring, verifying, and collecting data; facilitating the audit process; and initiating and monitoring corrective measures. The role of company facilitators includes

- Documenting registrar findings and providing feedback
- Validating registrar findings and assuring facts
- Collecting audit flow data and forwarding it to management
- Coordinating the auditor/auditee interface and escorting the auditor
- Initiating corrective actions prior to audit completion
- Handling disagreements and establishing common, factual ground
- Assuring the auditor has all necessary data and visits all areas
- Coordinating scheduled visits to planned areas and personnel

This type of advanced training for company facilitators assures that the company approaches the registration audit professionally.

Management may view the most important ongoing aspect of the registration audit to be the real-time collection of data on the nature of auditor findings. The prudent company wants to develop any necessary remedial actions as soon as possible. All participants should be advised on which aspects the visiting auditors are concentrating, at specific times in the audit process. Many companies arrange for input to an "audit central" terminal or location that builds a systematic database. This approach permits management and the workforce to have a readily accessible scorecard on audit progress. It also prevents delays every time management wants an update. The nature of this feedback system should have been initiated and refined during the internal quality system verification audits. If the devised feedback system is working, there should be no surprises at the daily company briefings conducted by the registrar's lead auditor. Such a feedback system is for company communication and awareness, not subterfuge.

8.2.4 Registration auditors need a base of operations

Visiting auditors need a quiet location to plan or discuss the company's audit. The area should be private and equipped with desks and telephones, as well as a set of quality system documentation. By the company setting up such an area before the registration auditors arrive, the audit process is facilitated and the activity will move along easily.

In fact, the company should do anything it believes will facilitate the audit. There is no problem with having an audit area coffee pot or soft drinks available. Such a move keeps visiting auditors and company facilitators working, and out of company canteen areas at inappropriate times. Anything that facilitates the audit likely also reduces its duration. Remember the company is paying for the entire process one way or the other, so economies of audit time mean company money saved. The company should not plan activities that do not contribute directly to the audit (for example, social activities, such as evening dinners).

8.2.5 Effectively organizing registration audit schedules

The visiting audit team will devise a tentative plan. The lead auditor should always provide advanced plan information to the company's management representative or audit coordinator prior to the visit. At the very least, the plan must be presented to the company at the registrar's inbriefing. This advanced notice is for the company's planning purposes, such as to assure its key individuals are available for interview. In this example, the alternative of having key company people on standby during the audit is simply not in the best interest of the company or the registrar. Although the schedule may require a daily update or reconfirmation, the accepted schedules should be regarded as at least a solid plan for the next audit day.

As the visiting auditors get into areas or processes where problems appear to exist, the audit plan and schedule may be modified by the lead auditor. Resources will be reduced in those areas or processes where no major concerns have been identified, and the resources applied to the apparent problem areas. There is an advantage to presenting a sound and compliant "first face" to the auditors.

8.3 Registrar personnel at the company's site

The visiting auditors perform their assignment according to the guidance provided in ISO 10011, *Quality auditing*. As recommended, the company has also used this ISO 9000 document to guide it through its own verification audits. Thus, employees should have acquired a general familiarity with the nature of the upcoming registration audit process.

8.3.1 The detailed registration audit plan

The proposed audit plan (see Figure 8.6) contains (1) the scope of the audit; (2) the areas or topics for examination; (3) the identification of the auditors and their assignments; (4) the approximate duration by audit category; and (5) any company documentation required by the visiting auditors. Hopefully, the company audit coordinator has had the opportunity to review and approve the plan ahead of the audit team arriving, and has forwarded any requested documentation.

The audit plan must be acceptable to both parties, so there is advantage to its early review. In case there is some area of concern (for example, the proposed audit team has a former company employee on it), the company has the option of requesting a change. Once the plan is approved, however, the registrar's audit team begins its preparations. These involve examining the submitted company quality system documentation, preparing the inbriefing, developing checklists, and so on.

8.3.2 Inbriefing provides an opportunity for liaison

At the registrar's inbriefing, the prudent company sends its senior management, other key management personnel, and its audit facilitation team. After the usual introductory formalities, the lead auditor reviews, in detail, the final plan for the audit, revealing any last-minute changes. He or she then advises how the visiting team will conduct the audit. Any questions or comments from the company are encouraged before adjournment. A typical inbriefing agenda is shown in Figure 8.7.

The company introduces its audit facilitators and indicates their assigned registrar auditor partner. The company senior manager, or management representative, addresses any areas in need of clarification and then accepts the final audit plan. The visiting auditors may then be presented with a company operational overview. This activity should be a brief orientation. It may or may not involve a short walk-through tour. The sum of these introductory company activities should not exceed 30–60 minutes, depending on the company size. Remember the company is paying for the visitors' time, and it is advantageous to get the audit started.

Audit ID _____ Audit type _____	Start date _____
Auditee_____	Contact _____
Address _____	Phone_____

Audit requested by_____	Title _____
Representing_____	Phone_____
Address _____	Client/customer/auditee _____

Audit organization_____	Lead auditor _____
Address _____	Auditors_____
Phone _____	

Audit purpose/objectives_____ Audit scope _____

Audit dates _____ Arrival time _____ Duration _____

Organizations affected _____

Quality standard/references/requirements _____

The following documents should be provided prior to the audit:

_____

The following documents should be provided upon arrival:

_____

A _____ minute inbriefing with senior members of auditee management is requested upon arrival. The auditee may provide_____ minute appropriate orientation to the auditor team.

The audit is scheduled by the following elements:

Element _____ Duration _____ Auditor _____

Element _____ Duration _____ Auditor _____

Element _____ Duration _____ Auditor _____

Support requirements requested of auditee are: _____

The lead auditor will hold status meetings at ____ P.M. daily. The audit outbriefing is tentatively scheduled for _____ . A final report will be forward _____ weeks after audit closure.

Signature_____ Date _____

Lead Auditor

Reprinted from the Center for International Standards & Quality "ISO 9000 Internal Quality Auditing" with permission from Georgia Tech Research Corporation 1995.

Figure 8.6   Audit plan outline form.

1. General introductions
2. Acknowledge preliminary assistance in liaison and scheduling
3. Reason for audit (internal/customer/third party, etc.)
4. Review of audit plan
   a. Purpose/objective of the audit
   b. Type/scope/subject of the audit
   c. Duration of the audit
   d. Audit elements for assessment
   e. Auditor(s) by elements
   f. Duration by element
   g. Audit methodology
   h. Types of documentation used by auditors
   i. Documentation required from auditee
   j. Anticipated schedule for outbriefing
5. Anticipated assistance or scheduling needs
6. Intention to follow company rules and/or hours
7. Absolute confidentiality to be maintained
8. Thank attendees: two groups of professionals with same goal—to successfully complete the audit

Reprinted from the Center for International Standards & Quality "ISO 9000 Internal Quality Auditing" with permission from Georgia Tech Research Corporation 1995.

Figure 8.7 Agenda for inbriefing, conducted by lead auditor.

If the plan does not include a daily status briefing for the company's management representative or audit coordinator, this should be arranged before closing the inbriefing. The end result of the inbriefing should be a mutual understanding of what is to take place, how it will be conducted, and by whom. The attitude both parties must convey is, there exists two groups of respected professionals with the same goal—to complete a successful and beneficial audit.

Should the company reveal proprietary data to the registration auditors? This is left to the affected company, however, it should be remembered that the registration audit is the result of a mutually signed definitive consulting contract. It is not likely the registrar company is going to jeopardize its reputation by mishandling such privileged data.

The company's concern for the security of its proprietary data is probably related to the fact that registrar auditors concentrate in areas of expertise gained by previous employment, in places that may have been considered competitors. To ease company fears, experience shows no violation of proprietary data by registrars ever being noted. The registration auditors attempt to avoid the use of proprietary data whenever possible; however, the nature of some companies is such that virtually all operational documents are proprietary. All such data used in the course of the visit is selected only on the basis of what is specifically required to conduct the audit. The visiting audit team does not make copies of such data, and all data are returned prior to the audit team's departure. Also, no audit final report ever reflects any indication or content of such privileged information.

8.3.3 The company is exposed to a thorough audit

As noted, the audit is conducted according to the guidelines presented in ISO 10011-1. As such, the auditors attempt to collect sufficient objective evidence to permit them to judge the client company to be satisfactory. We noted that registrars operate in a competitive environment and do not wish to develop a reputation for failing companies. They would clearly like to pass each candidate company. They must also, however, maintain the acceptable ISO 9000 compliance level upon which their accreditation is based. The company seeking to be registered will experience a comprehensive, professional, and unbiased audit of its entire quality system.

The registration audit results are based on objective evidence that demonstrates the degree of company compliance to the governing documentation. As noted, objective evidence is acquired, firsthand, factual knowledge, and it may be derived by observation, interview, records, or process results. The visiting auditors ask questions of enough personnel and observe enough situations to determine whether compliance exists. The same questions may be asked of many people, while many different questions may be asked of certain individuals. Thus, there are many observations but only one decision.

- The more observations, the more valid the decision.
- Observations must be based on factual objective evidence.
- Observations may be recorded as both positive and negative.
- Observations must be in all affected areas and functions.
- Same question to many people, many questions to one person.
- More than one auditor may be involved in reviewing a subject.
- Observation results tallied and decision is proposed by the lead auditor.
- Lead auditor establishes the registrar's official position.

The auditors collect and record an enormous number of observations, often giving the company cause for concern. As they relate to company compliance, however, these observations may be recorded as either positive or negative. Each auditor makes many notes and records much data (Figure 8.8). The volume of each auditor's recorded observations and findings tends to create considerable company anxiety, particularly with those auditees who appear to be the basis of the writing activity. The auditors may even move quickly from area to another area as they seem to eagerly pursue a given topic or concern. They may even supply another member of their team with data for examination in his or her assigned area. Finally, with the frustrated company facilitators absent, the auditors will caucus periodically to assure they are developing sufficient data to arrive at valid conclusions. In summary, by the time these professional auditors have finished, they will have questioned, observed, and examined virtually all of the company's affected personnel, operations, documentation, and records in pursuit of a valid position on the company's compliance (Figure 8.9).

8.3.4 Company facilitators are mandatory for process

Assuming the company has also used the same ISO 10011-based approach in its verification process, its facilitators can greatly help the registration audit process. They can even guide the auditors toward those factors that are best suited for deriving the evidence required. In a short period of time, the working relationship between the facilitator and the auditor can aid the audit flow and provide mutual confidence in the process and participants. By maintaining this close liaison with the visiting auditor, the company facilitator can observe where apparent problems are developing. Perhaps the facilitator can even have data presented that will dispel the concern.

Auditee/site _____ Auditor_____

Element being assessed _____

Requirements/reference _____

Date/Contact/Location/Time	Observations made	Remarks +/−
1.		
2.		
3.		
4.		
5.		
6.		
7.		
8.		

Reprinted from the Center for International Standards & Quality "ISO 9000 Internal Quality Auditing" with permission from Georgia Tech Research Corporation 1995.

Figure 8.8   Typical auditor observations/data collection form.

Audit ID _____	Finding #_____	Date _____
Auditee/site _____	Auditor _____	

Requirement: _____

_____

_____

Deficiency: _____

_____

C/A assigned to: _____ Signature _____ Date _____

Root cause of deficiency: _____

_____

_____

Root cause action taken: _____

_____

_____

Effectivity:_____

Action to resolve specific finding:_____

_____

Auditor follow-up: _____

_____

Name_____ Date _____ Accept/Reject

Comments: _____

Reprinted from the Center for International Standards & Quality "ISO 9000 Internal Quality Auditing" with permission from Georgia Tech Research Corporation 1995.

Figure 8.9   Typical negative finding/corrective action form.

If unable to resolve the concern, the company facilitator can initiate corrective actions, which may be to a point of resolution before the audit team departs. If such is the case, the registrar's final report will reflect the acceptable closure of the item.

8.3.5 Mutual respect is mandatory for audit success

Mutually accepting each other's assignment is sometimes severely tested by disagreement between the visiting auditor and the company facilitator. In order to resolve issues to a point where some agreement can be achieved, the auditor normally attempts to reduce the apparent problem to the basic facts. This is so important for audit success that, if this approach is not attempted by the auditor, the company member should initiate reduction of issues to factual agreement.

Individuals can ordinarily agree on the basic facts, even though they may not agree on the interpretation or implication of those facts. Thus, auditors or auditees should

- Know that disagreements and issues of interpretation will arise.
- Attempt to be as objective as possible.
- Reduce the issues to basic simple facts.
- Find points of agreement, no matter how minor.
- Build on agreements until there is a fact list.
- Sign list of facts that are in agreement. Remember, facts may be based on process, paper, or people!
- Do not attempt to agree on interpretation of facts.

Therefore, a single expired blueprint on a desk does not implicate the entire document and data control system. The factual finding should indicate a single, expired document found in a work area. On the other hand, a number of such cases may indict the company's overall compliance to its own document and data control system, or even the adequacy of the system itself. As noted, auditors must always make many observations before interpreting the data. The registrar's lead auditor will insist his or her auditors adhere to standard audit policy and protocol. There will be no shortage of data upon which the lead auditor will base his or her decisions.

Since they accompany the visiting auditor and view the ongoing activities, the final evaluation of audit data can be reasonably judged by the company's facilitators. They observe any repeated problems in a given topic or area, and know if they will likely add up to a negative finding. The facilitators can keep the company leadership aware of the nature and status of any success-determining factors. The facilitators must always assure there are no surprises for company management, during the audit or at the audit team outbriefing. Frequently, the facilitators may decide to initiate remedial actions before the auditor has arrived at the point of considering the situation merits a negative finding.

8.4 Completing the registration audit activity

Companies that benefit the most from the registration audit are those that regard the audit process as more than just an independent performance review. Progressive management views the audit as an opportunity to identify and resolve any areas of ISO 9000 noncompliance, which were not discovered by their internal verification activities. Prudent company management should be trying to achieve optimal operational processes. As presently determined, these processes are represented in the company's new documented ISO 9000 quality system. An independent review that results in a successful audit provides a high level of process confidence for the company. Based on successful registration audit results, management can determine if the company is approaching its goal as planned. Of course, the audits may have identified some problems for resolution, but the external assistance permits the company to continue moving in the direction of its optimal performance goals.

8.4.1 Root cause and comprehensive corrective action

An error many companies make in preparing for the registrar is that they have not considered the total aspects or ramifications of identified problems (see Figure 8.10). Whether they are from the company or the registrar, auditors generally do not try to expose the entire scope of an identified problem. The audit process is designed to detect any problems of compliance at the key points of examination. These are usually points in the process where the auditor believes compliance risk is high. This sampling nature of internal quality audits virtually assures auditors will not be able to expend sufficient time to expose every aspect of an

- Take corrective action to the root cause.
- Avoid a quick-fix approach to corrective action.
- Be certain all possible occurrences are addressed.
- Be certain all possible applications are examined.
- Verify and validate corrective action implementation.
- Assure employees are trained in the new approach.
- Document changes in the quality system documentation.

Figure 8.10   Corrective actions must be complete.

apparent noncompliance. The auditors are simply in the position of noting an unacceptable finding has been detected and documented for company corrective action. Frequently the company has previously identified the same problem found by the registrar's auditor, but has failed to expand its corrective actions to cover all occurrences.

8.4.2 Last-minute procedural corrective actions are high risk

Corrective actions that are associated with the need for procedural changes are high-finding risk areas for most companies. The problem is that procedural changes appear to be such an easy solution. The company, however, must be certain the corrective action selected and the resultant procedural changes are not just a quick fix. Corrective action must be a well-considered process. The quick fix typically occurs when the company does not examine the total effect of the proposed remedial changes on all possible applications.

The registration auditors usually examine basic procedural revisions, particularly those made just prior to their arrival. The auditors want to see whether all other affected or referenced documents were addressed. The prudent company must always assure correcting a procedure to reflect a new approach is never judged acceptable until all of the referenced and/or related procedures are compared for compliance to the planned change. Obviously, it makes no sense to correct one procedure and have a number of others become invalid in the process. It is surprising how many companies have done just that. Examples of such oversights are not well received by the company senior management when the lead auditor points them out during the outbriefing.

8.4.3 There are usually some negative findings

Registration auditors examine compliance from a slightly different perspective than the company. As such, it is common to reveal some negative findings at even the best-prepared companies. A preassessment may have reduced such variations. If the company is well prepared, any corrective actions identified by the registrar are probably simple to accomplish. Company management should not be surprised or upset by some level of recorded findings. Its primary consideration should be whether the findings are of major consequence. A company that must only forward evidence copies of its closed corrective actions to the registrar, should regard its entire ISO 9000 implementation process as successful.

As mentioned in Section 8.3, prior to the outbriefing, senior company management must review the overall audit results. The company facilitators will have collected data upon which this preliminary review can take place. The facilitators should review the results with management, using the same perspective that they believe the registrar's lead auditor will use. Company management should not be surprised at the outbriefing on any major issue or significant finding. The company position on what will be required to resolve any anticipated problems must be a conscious decision based on resources. Commitments must not be spontaneously created by the responsible company manager during the outbriefing.

8.4.4 The audit results are presented in an outbriefing

The outbriefing is conducted by the lead auditor or, in a small company, by the sole registrar auditor assigned. The normal routine is to remind attendees of the audit process and the areas that were examined (Figure 8.11). The lead auditor then reviews each area from the aspect of audit results. The lead auditor provides an overall rating as to "satisfactory," "satisfactory, pending corrective action," or "unsatisfactory." For those companies that have undergone the ISO 9000 implementation process described in this text, it is very unlikely the overall rating or even the rating on individual aspects will be judged unsatisfactory. Company

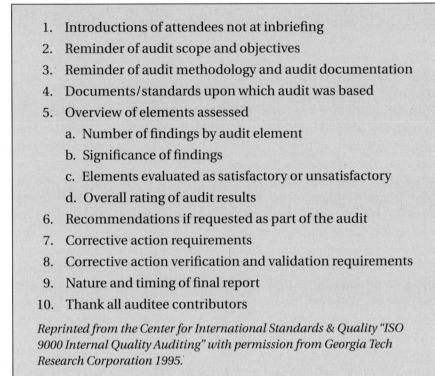

1. Introductions of attendees not at inbriefing
2. Reminder of audit scope and objectives
3. Reminder of audit methodology and audit documentation
4. Documents/standards upon which audit was based
5. Overview of elements assessed
    a. Number of findings by audit element
    b. Significance of findings
    c. Elements evaluated as satisfactory or unsatisfactory
    d. Overall rating of audit results
6. Recommendations if requested as part of the audit
7. Corrective action requirements
8. Corrective action verification and validation requirements
9. Nature and timing of final report
10. Thank all auditee contributors

Reprinted from the Center for International Standards & Quality "ISO 9000 Internal Quality Auditing" with permission from Georgia Tech Research Corporation 1995.

Figure 8.11   Agenda for outbriefing, conducted by lead auditor.

management needs to know that a rating of "satisfactory, pending corrective action," is very common and quite respectable. Unless compliance has completely broken down just prior to the registration audit, the corrective action should not amount to extensive remedial activity. A satisfactory rating in all, or even many, elements should be cause for congratulations.

The lead auditor is available to discuss or explain any practice and method used during the registration audit. He or she will not be amenable to arguments about the findings and overall results. Disagreement on the interpretation of audit results should be minimal due to the objective evidence in the auditors' hands. The participants agreed on the facts as the audit progressed. The management representative will have had the opportunity for discussions during the daily briefing. If possible, major issues should have been identified and resolved in the daily briefings. The discussions should always try to either reach a point of common position or a defined and mutually understood point of disagreement.

Disagreements can be appealed. Since the audit process is meticulous in documenting the nature and extent of each finding, the company is ordinarily at a disadvantage. Usually copies of the detailed findings are provided to the company at the outbriefing. The findings should have been given to the management representative daily. Sometimes the findings are provided to the respective company facilitators when they are recorded. Regardless of method, the company must have a set of the findings prior to the audit team's departure. Since the company's relationship with the registrar is likely to be a long one, it is in the best interest of both the company and the registrar to maintain good will. This is true regardless of the audit results.

When closing the outbriefing, the registrar explains the process of audit closure. He or she identifies those corrective action requirements that must be resolved before the final report is issued. The lead auditor also advises if the registrar's team needs to return to the company. The purpose of such a visit would be to verify and validate the company's corrective actions. As noted, the registrar has three options for follow-up.

1. The registrar can accept the company's corrective actions based on its statements and verifications, or based on a review of submitted document revisions.

2. The registrar can tentatively accept the company's corrective actions, and

   a. Acceptance can be deferred until the next surveillance visit, but

   b. The recommendation can still go to the registration council.

3. The registrar can elect to perform an on-site verification audit.

8.4.5 Will the registration auditors need to return?

Frequently the audit team will not need to return. The lead auditor will only require documentation of corrective action closures to be forwarded for approval. As noted, the registrar has the option of performing the corrective action approval during the next surveillance audit. Frequently, however, the registrar schedules an interim visit especially for the purpose of corrective action verification. If the submitted corrective action documentation does not appear to be positive enough to resolve the identified problems, the registrar can refuse its acceptance or may even return to investigate.

In the majority of cases where corrective actions require significant quality system improvement, the lead auditor advises the company management of a two-step approval process. The first step involves the registrar receiving, reviewing, and accepting the company's written documentation on its corrective action closure. The second step involves an on-site visit by a member(s) of the audit team to perform a verification and validation audit on the corrective actions. Verification assures action was taken, and validation determines if the action was effective.

The lead auditor may advise that the follow-up audit is needed to provide the registrar with increased confidence of satisfactory closure. Closure indicates that the company fully complies with both the ISO 9000 standard and the company's quality system documentation. The registrar must be completely confident of closure before recommending the company's registration to the accreditation board. A registrar's approval means eventually awarding use of its certification logo to the candidate company.

8.5 Achieving final audit closure and registration

Once the registrar's audit team departs, the company must address the findings and make sure it investigates each problem to the point of defining its root cause. Most registrars keep the audit open until all issues are acceptably resolved. Some registrars publish an interim report, showing in-process company corrective actions as pending, with a final report or revision completed at final closure.

8.5.1 Responding to any audit findings

As noted, most companies are advised at the outbriefing about the findings and whether the registrar will return and approve the corrective actions on-site. The auditee company must always undergo its own verification and validation process to assure its actions are suitable, effective, of full scope, and fully implemented. The company must never be so overconfident as to rely on the registrar's auditors as the first to evaluate its corrective actions.

Management's primary concern must be that corrective actions are taken to resolve the root cause of the problem. The company must absolutely avoid addressing only the symptoms of a problem. By definition, valid root cause resolution eliminates the possibility of the same problem recurring. The company must assure it has determined the actual base or root cause of the problem and has corrected or eliminated it. Further, it is management's responsibility to assure thorough examination of all situations or areas where the same problem might exist. If these areas are likewise affected, the appropriate corrective action must be extended to eliminate the entire condition.

For instance, a problem with inadequate records control found in one unit must not be regarded as the only place where the problem might exist. The company should investigate records control throughout all units where there is any requirement for such control. If a company only addresses the registrar-identified problems in specific areas, it is open to the returning auditors quickly exposing additional company failures.

The company decides on the time period required to implement and confirm the effectiveness of corrective actions. It is in the company's best interests to make the period as short as practical. The company should avoid committing to an impractical schedule. When it does, it is usually the result of management not having thought through the entire remedial task, scope, and duration.

On occasion, the company will find itself having to institute corrective actions that require some extended time period. The registrar will normally request a detailed plan and schedule for any prolonged remedial activity. The company is wise to forward its plan to the registrar early in the remedial process. Management must be certain that the registrar agrees that the plan appears to be suitable to resolve the concerns. The company should leave enough time in the plan to have the effectiveness of the corrective actions evaluated by its internal quality audit function. The management representative should not try to have all corrective actions closed at the same time. Items should be closed as soon as practical within the structured plan framework. Incremental closure of compliance actions permits effectiveness evaluations to be appropriately scheduled.

All corrective actions taken as the result of a registration audit must be in effect for sufficient time to permit the reviewer to judge whether they are truly working as planned. This period may be as short as the first time through (or the next time), for a software-based change. A change in the company's training program, however, may take several months to completely validate. The registrar's auditors expect the company to show the following:

- The cause of the problem has been completely defined.
- Appropriate root cause corrective action has been developed.
- Corrective actions have been implemented in all affected areas and/or functions.
- Corrective actions have been effective in eliminating the problem.

This serial relationship in the corrective action process is either termed its *verification and validation* or *effectivity and effectiveness.*

8.5.2 All findings have been addressed and resolved

The company will eventually arrive at a point where it has documented all of the completed corrective actions and considers them effective for the purposes intended. It forwards copies of the documentation to the registrar. The registrar's lead auditor then reviews the results to determine their acceptability. Hopefully, the company's actions are considered valid. The approval and registration process proceeds as follows:

1. Company assures all required corrective actions are closed.
2. Company forwards evidence of corrective action and schedules a visit by the registrar's audit team.
3. All corrective actions are verified by the registrar.
4. On-site visit by the registrar may or may not be required.
5. Corrective action effectiveness is validated by the registrar.
6. Registrar's recommendation is forwarded to the registration council.
7. The registration council notifies the company of its success.

Of course, if the results are unacceptable, the company has more to do. Such an awkward situation tends to indicate that the management representative or the audit coordinator did not maintain sufficient liaison with the registrar to anticipate the lead auditor's concerns. Companies must be absolutely certain of what it takes to satisfy the registrar prior to forwarding corrective actions. If the problems found were more extensive than the company anticipated, then ongoing liaison permits the company to be certain of the acceptability of the expanded corrective action plan.

The management representative must maintain liaison with the lead auditor on any questions or concerns during the internal process of identifying, implementing, and verifying corrective actions. When this is accomplished, it is highly probable any documentation submitted to the registrar will be judged satisfactory. Assuming the registrar has accepted the company's corrective action evidence, then management can schedule another visit by the registrar. In fact, most companies schedule the revisit just prior to the remedial process being fully completed. Management must remember to always leave enough time to demonstrate that the corrective actions are effective.

8.5.3 Assuming the registrar needs to revisit

Management personnel often become very concerned when they know the registrar auditors are returning. Managers worry that the registrar will perform a total re-audit of the quality system. This is not the case. The auditor will ordinarily be from the original audit team. The focus of his or her attention is the company's corrections of the original findings. Of course, to establish the adequacy of company actions, the auditor is required to examine some aspects of each problem beyond the area of first discovery.

On occasion, the auditor will encounter an additional compliance problem that is unrelated to any found during the original audit. In such a situation, the registrar's normal approach is to identify the problem; ask that corrective action evidence be sent to the registrar's office; and indicate that the registrar will check the situation at the next surveillance visit. The visiting auditors ordinarily do not add new findings to the original audit report. Such a move implies the original audit was not entirely satisfactory. Further, an additive approach does not permit timely closure of any audit.

Seldom would the auditor find a major system breakdown during a corrective action audit. If he or she did detect a problem of such magnitude, it could jeopardize the candidate company's near-term success.

Compliance to the requirements of the documented quality system precludes such concerns.

Note: If the auditor finds a problem that causes major concern for employee safety or other company liability, he or she may well ask for evidence of immediate correction to assure a no-fault position.

8.5.4 Achieving closure on the registration audit

Once all remedial actions are resolved and accepted by the registrar, the final report is published and sent to the company. It is also sent, with the registrar's recommendation as to the company's registration, to the registration council. Audit protocol assures that the final report never contains any surprises in either audit substance or interpretation. Generally the final report reflects the outbriefing, as amended by any subsequent company remedial efforts (see Figure 8.12).

When the registrar notifies the registration council of its recommendation for company registration, the council customarily reviews and accepts it. In theory the council can reject the recommendation but it would be an indictment of the accreditation approval program. Such an action is unlikely to occur. The registration council is the agency that authorizes placement of ISO 9000-approved companies on the register.

The registration process has a means for candidate companies to file formal appeals or complaints about the registration process. The appeal may be in respect to the process, the registrar's performance and conduct, or the audit results. If used at all, the appeal process should only be considered when other approaches have failed. The company should always address its concerns to the management of the registration firm before considering an official appeal.

8.5.5 Involvement with a registrar is long term

The surveillance visits mentioned are customarily one-person, one-day, on-site reviews to ensure the company has not departed from the operational base upon which it was registered. The surveillance audits are conducted approximately every six months. They are usually unannounced, although the advanced conversations on personnel availability tend to provide sufficient notice. Between visits, the registrar expects the company to forward documentation noting any major changes in

1. The auditee name, address, cognizant management, and telephone number
2. The date and duration of the audit
3. For whom the audit was performed
4. The audit scope and objectives
5. The audit methodology and method of documentation
6. The type of audit and the standards/documentation used
7. The audit function, auditors, and assignments
8. All elements examined, with results
   a. Findings in each element
   b. Significance of findings by element
   c. Evaluation of results in total
   d. Conclusion of auditors
   e. Corrective action requirements
   f. Verification and validation of corrective actions
9. Recommendations of audit function, if requested
10. Audit report distribution and/or routing

Reprinted from the Center of International Standards & Quality "ISO 9000 Internal Quality Auditing" with permission from Georgia Tech Research Corporation 1995.

Figure 8.12 Outline for final report.

the conditions upon which the prior audit was based or approved. The registrar usually retains these interim transmittals for examination at the next review. Also during this visit, any previously identified areas of marginal acceptance and any unverified corrective actions are examined.

Every three to five years, the registrar conducts another full-scale registration audit, similar to the original one. If the company and the registrar have been maintaining proper communication, exchanging procedural revisions and approvals, and assuring satisfactory surveillance audits, the next major audit should not be difficult. Since the registration process allows the company to use the registrar's logo to indicate the company has been ISO audited and approved, periodic system reviews are quite appropriate. The registrar's reputation is at risk if the marketplace finds the company has failed to meet its ISO 9000-based quality system commitments.

In response to a final question that is frequently asked, the contractual relationship with the selected registrar is designed to be long. Thus, the initial selection needs to be well considered. Although there is nothing that prohibits a company from changing registrars once the original contract expires, such a step should not be taken lightly. The ramifications of such a change could be significant.

A new registrar would have to reestablish that the company's documented quality system is capable of meeting the ISO 9000 standard, and that the company's performance is in compliance with the quality system documentation. This requires repeating the same steps taken by the original registrar. The company is at risk in this situation, since the new registrar may consciously or otherwise feel obligated to show it is "better" than the previous one. Of course, the associated auditor time and costs are at least equivalent to those previously expended. Finally, the company also has to prepare for a visit by the new registrar. The effort associated with such an exercise depends on the company's confidence in its state of preparedness.

Conclusion

The company must be certain that the results of its registrar selection process are in its best interest. Also important are the preferences of the customer, the industry, and the targeted market. The selection process may include information from industry contacts, trade associations, professional societies, and other forms of ISO 9000-based networking.

The contractual arrangement between the company and the selected registrar will be long term. The company assures it meets the ISO quality system standard, while the registrar performs quality system audits to verify the company's compliance to the standard. If the results of the audit are satisfactory, the registrar will authorize the company to use the registrar's certification logo in the marketplace.

The company's primary preparation for the registrar's visit is to assure all of the tasks in its implementation plan have been completed and verified as effective. The company also needs to make provisions for (1) the visiting auditors' quarters and services, (2) an audit status feedback system, (3) a company position on marginal issues, (4) approval of the registrar's proposed audit plan, and (5) scheduling availability of key company personnel.

The registration audit team provides an inbriefing upon its arrival. It follows the basic auditing process of ISO 10011. The auditors collect objective evidence, by means of many observations, to ascertain the actual degree of company compliance to the selected ISO 9000 standard.

The registrar's lead auditor provides company management with results of the registration audit. They either verify company compliance or identify areas where compliance can be improved. The lead auditor determines the need to return to verify any company corrective actions.

The company must investigate any corrective actions to determine their root cause. Necessary actions must be taken to prevent recurrence. Once all validations of correction have occurred, company management can request closure.

If another onsite visit is required, the registration auditor will examine the company's corrective actions on the findings from the previous audit. The auditor will not add new findings to the basic audit report. Since the registrar will conduct surveillance visits about every six months, some verifications may be deferred until that point. The registration process calls for a complete re-audit every three to five years.

Implementation actions required by this module

1. Identify various influencing factors that must be considered in registrar selection.

2. Utilize inputs from customer, marketing, and so on to select two or three suitable registrars.

3. Use networking and direct contact with the registrars to make a final selection.

4. Establish liaison with the registrar and begin planning for the compliance audit.

5. Assure all actions in the implementation plan and all open corrective actions are complete and effective.

6. Establish a company audit facilitation and response plan to use with the registrar.

7. Select and equip the company's facilities that will be used by the registration auditors.

8. Select and train company employees to act as facilitators during the compliance audit.

9. Obtain the registrar's tentative audit plan for awareness and company approval.

10. Develop the company's agenda and attendance for the in-briefing with the registrar.

11. Implement a company program for audit status and corrective action initiation.

12. Assure that the company has a plan for addressing all corrective actions identified in the outbriefing.

13. Implement corrective actions to the root cause(s) and possible application to the entire company.

14. Develop a plan and schedule a follow-up visit from the registrar, if such is required.

15. Establish the company liaison and surveillance requirements with the registrar.

Appendix A

Quality System Elements from ISO 9000 Standards

System element	Paragraph number	ISO 9001	ISO 9002	ISO 9003	ISO 9004-1 equivalent
Management responsibility	4.1	•	•	◊	4.1,4.2,4.3
Quality system	4.2	•	•	◊	5.0
Contract review	4.3	•	•	•	—
Design control	4.4	•	x	x	8.0
Document and data control	4.5	•	•	•	5.3,11.5
Purchasing	4.6	•	•	x	9.0
Customer-supplied product	4.7	•	•	•	—
Product identification and traceability	4.8	•	•	◊	11.2
Process control	4.9	•	•	x	10.0,11.0
Inspection and testing	4.10	•	•	◊	12.0
Control of inspection, measuring, and test equipment	4.11	•	•	•	13.0
Inspection and test status	4.12	•	•	•	11.7,11.8

System element	*Paragraph number*	*ISO 9001*	*ISO 9002*	*ISO 9003*	*ISO 9004-1 equivalent*
Control of noncon-forming product	4.13	•	•	◊	14.0
Corrective and preventive action	4.14	•	•	◊	15.0
Handling, storage, packaging, preservation, and delivery	4.15	•	•	•	10.4,16.1, 16.4
Control of quality records	4.16	•	•	◊	5.3,17.2,17.3
Internal quality audits	4.17	•	•	◊	5.4
Training	4.18	•	•	◊	18.1
Servicing	4.19	•	•	x	16.4
Statistical techniques	4.20	•	•	◊	20.0

Legend:
• = Comprehensive requirement stated
◊ = Requirement stated, but not comprehensive
x = No requirement stated for element

Appendix B

Status of the Current ISO 9000 Family of Standards as of August 1, 1995

Standards	Status	Title
ISO 9000-1 (was 9000)	Published	*Quality management and quality assuance standards—Part 1: Guidelines for selection and use*
ISO 9001	Published	*Quality systems—Model for quality assurance in design/development, production, installation, and servicing*
ISO 9002	Published	*Quality systems—Model for quality assurance in production, installation and servicing*
ISO 9003	Published	*Quality systems—Model for quality assurance in final inspection and test*
ISO 9004-1 (was 9004)	Published	*Quality management and quality system elements—Part 1: Guidelines*
ISO 9000-2	Published (in revision)	*Quality management and quality assurance standards—Part 2: Generic guidelines for the application of ISO 9001, ISO 9002 and ISO 9003*

Standards	Status	Title
ISO 9000-3	Published (in revision)	*Quality management and quality assurance standards—Part 3: Guidelines for the application of ISO 9001 to the development, supply and maintenance of software*
ISO 9000-4	Published	*Quality management and quality assurance standards—Part 4: Guidelines for the application of dependability management in quality assurance*
ISO 9004-2	Published	*Quality management and quality system elements—Part 2: Guidelines for services*
ISO 9004-3	Published	*Quality management and quality system elements—Part 3: Guidelines for processed materials*
ISO 9004-4	Published	*Quality management and quality system elements—Part 4: Guidelines for quality improvement*
ISO 10005 (was 9004-5)	In publication cycle	*Guidelines for developing quality plans*
ISO 10006 (was 9004-6)	At CD stage	*Guidelines for quality in project management*
ISO 10007 (was 9004-7)	In publication cycle	*Quality system requirements for configuration management*
ISO 9004-8	At CD stage	*Guidelines on quality principles*
ISO 10011-1	Published (in revision)	*Guidelines for auditing quality systems, Part 1—Auditing*
ISO 10011-2	Published	*Guidelines for auditing quality systems, Part 2—Qualification criteria for auditors*
ISO 10011-3	Published	*Guidelines for auditing quality systems, Part 3—Managing audit programmes*

Standards	Status	Title
ISO 10012-1	Published	*Quality assurance requirements for measuring equipment, Part 1 — Management of measuring equipment*
ISO 10012-2	At DIS stage	*Quality assurance requirements for measuring equipment, Part 2— Measurement assurance*
ISO 10013	Published	*Guidelines for developing quality manuals*
ISO 10014	At CD stage	*Economic effects of the management of quality*
ISO 10015	At WD stage	*Guidelines for continuing education and training*
ISO 10016	At WD stage	*Inspection and test records— Presentation of results*
ISO 8402	Published (in revision)	*Quality management and quality assurance—Vocabulary*

Note: The working groups for many of the standards are in the process of developing design specifications for the next revisions of their affected standard. The five standards in the ISO 9000 series are included in this process. A TC 176-approved document design specification will assure that the end product meets customer requirements for documents that are more applicable, useful, and understandable than the current ones.

Appendix C

Special Considerations for Small Businesses

According to a recent ISO TC 176 study, over 80 percent of the businesses in the world are small or medium-sized businesses. The definition of small and medium-sized businesses is based on employment levels. The size definitions, however, vary by country. In some countries, the definition of small may be those businesses with fewer than 10 employees while in another country, it may be fewer than 100 employees. The more business development in the country, the greater the employee numbers. The study resulted in the TC's 1994 decision to develop an official handbook on the subject. Its purpose will be to provide ISO 9000 guidance for small and medium-sized businesses. Unfortunately, this handbook will probably not be available until 1996.

It has been stated that the ISO 9000 documents have been written by large businesses for large businesses. While it is true that travel costs have resulted in most ISO 9000 international activities being performed by national representatives from large businesses, the ISO 9000 documents were not intentionally developed for large businesses. Even so, the documents do tend to reflect the operations and resources of large firms. The standards are generic, however, and are designed to be appropriately applied by the affected candidate business, regardless of its size. The business must use its own frame of reference in its application of the selected ISO 9000 standard. The resultant quality system should be based on the nature of the implementing company's business activity, customers, resources, facilities, workforce, and so on. As such, the quality standards should be equally applicable to both large and small businesses.

The problems seem to arise when the customers (or registrars) of small businesses expect them to have a quality system with all the capability of large businesses. Even when the small businesses try to tailor their quality systems to what they actually need, general acceptance of their position may be difficult. The ISO 9000 standards state a business only needs to have a quality system that *is suitable and effective for its operations.*

Small businesses encounter all the same implementation problems as large businesses, but usually have fewer resources to apply to the process. In addition, small businesses tend to have less experience, particularly when it comes to quality system concepts, tools, and terminology than large businesses. Many small businesses must resort to using consultants in order to understand the ISO 9000 quality system concepts, and to determine the most effective way to implement ISO 9000 directives. Most of the small businesses do not proactively attempt to implement ISO 9000, but tend to wait until a major customer directs that implementation and/or registration be accomplished. Compliance often becomes a condition for further business. Small businesses usually do not have confidence that ISO 9000 compliance will bring additional market share or even the possibility of increased efficiency within its operations. Compliance by small companies is often reluctantly achieved to satisfy others, not themselves. They look at the ISO 9000 family as a burden and not a benefit. In fact, they frequently see no benefit to their company at all. (*Note:* Experience shows the small businesses gain benefits proportional to their input.)

Small businesses normally have less formality and structure than their larger counterparts. Employees often have more than one area of responsibility, even performing assignments in a number of functional and structural system elements. Although there are generally fewer resources, small businesses can quickly respond to internal needs and emergencies. They are generally reactive rather than proactive. Small businesses address process output efficiency rather than process stability and repetitiveness. The use of system procedures of any type is minimal, particularly in the quality system area. Work instructions are often the procedures of choice. The concept of supplier control is not ordinarily practiced. Purchasing is based on ordering what the business needs. If the results are satisfactory, the relationship continues; if unsatisfactory, it does not.

Small businesses must apply ISO 9000 in a manner that benefits their operations. These businesses must scale down and simplify the extent of their quality system if they are going to be able to benefit from ISO 9000 implementation. The concept of having a quality system that is only extensive enough to effectively serve their needs is mandatory. The industry customers must accept the concept as fact; anything else that is forced on small businesses is overkill. For instance, because of the limited technology base or work scope, small business employees are often the expert in their particular assignment, so extensive training and documentation is often redundant to performance. It is also quite possible that a company ISO 9000-based quality manual may be all the quality system documentation needed to operate effectively.

The implementation of ISO 9000 by small businesses must be pursued on the basis of the businesses themselves knowing more about their operations than anyone else. Application of the ISO quality standard must be focused on what the businesses can logically do to comply with the requirement. Whatever is done to achieve compliance must make sense to the management and employees. For instance, the shortfall analysis may be performed by several individuals who have extensive company experience. They may well know of effective ways to gain compliance without overkill. The key to judging an ISO 9000 quality system is whether it is effective in operating and controlling its related quality activities and process output. Does the company's management, workforce, and quality system create the effectiveness required for achieving customer satisfaction?

The small business ISO 9000 implementation plan can be quite simple. Still it must be designed to achieve compliance with all applicable elements of the ISO 9000 standard. One person in management can provide the primary guidance role. Actions can be planned using individuals instead of teams. If teams are used, they can be few in number and/or lightly populated. (Note: Even with small businesses, the amount of applied resources will affect the rate of implementation.) Supervisors or employees can gather any available documentation, perform the shortfall analysis tasks in their own area first, and then coordinate results in other areas to assure a thorough review.

Shortfalls may be identified and assigned to area management for developing and performing the remedial actions. The business must show that what it is currently doing is capable of meeting the standard—as it affects the business. If a process or task needs to be originated or modified, the business should accomplish it in a logical and simple manner. If documentation needs to be developed or modified, the business should write only what is needed for the activity to meet the corresponding system element. Documentation writing can be performed by one individual, using his or her own experience or through an employee interview process.

.   Documentation requirements for elements such as design control and document/data control may all be satisfied by one controlled document, binder, or notebook. Governing procedures can be topical flowcharts with accompanying explanatory legends. Records can be as formal as a computerized system or as simple as a well-managed logbook and backup legible handwritten records. Auditing can be performed by one trained individual or by cross-functional independent auditors. Awareness, orientation, and training on new methods and documentation may be performed by means of group meetings or periodic management instruction. Management review can be performed and documented by on-line discussion with audit principals.

Calibration, testing, installation, and servicing may be performed by approved outside companies. Productive materials suppliers can be selected and used based upon ongoing performance, or third party, joint customer, industry, or corporate approvals. In short, if the innovative methods used for compliance by the small business can be shown to effectively meet the requirements of the ISO quality standards, the customer and the registrar should be satisfied. Compliance and effectiveness must be established as based on the performance of the user company, not the preference of the visiting auditors.

The eight-step ISO 9000 implementation process presented in this book can be used as guidance for all businesses, regardless of size. The requirements of the ISO 9000 standards and the validity of the eight-step approach to their implementation remains constant. Depending on the size of the business, the approaches in the text should be scaled to the appropriate level. ISO quality system standards are written in a generic format so the candidate business can decide the most suitable application of the standard for its situation. The candidate ISO 9000 business must establish its own compliance position and documented quality system! Failure to do so permits others to interpret what is best for another's business. Outside interpretation will almost always result in a quality system that is more extensive than the company needs for compliance. The company, regardless of size, must have thoroughly applied the ISO 9000 requirements to its operations, and be capable of presenting and identifying how it complies with the quality standard.

Appendix D

Contacting Governmental and Private Agencies

American National Standards Institute
phone 212-642-4900
fax 212-302-1286

American Society for Quality Control
phone 800-248-1946
phone 414-272-8575
fax 414-272-1734

Department of Commerce
phone 202-377-5276
fax 202-377-2155

European Community/Union
Public Affairs/Information
phone 202-862-9500

Government Printing Office
phone 202-783-3238
fax 202-512-2250

International Standards Organization
IOS Geneva
phone 41-22-749-0111
fax 41-22-733-3430

National Institute of Standards and Technology
Standards and Certification Information
phone 301-975-4040
fax 301-926-1559

Registrar Accreditation Board
phone 414-272-8575

Unipub EC Document Distribution
phone 301-459-7666
fax 301-459-0056

U.S. Chamber of Commerce
phone 202-463-5487

Recommended Reading

ASQC Chemical and Process Industries Division. 1992. *ANSI/ASQC Q90/ISO 9000 Guidelines for Use by the Chemical and Process Industries.* Milwaukee: ASQC Quality Press.

Bureau of Business Practice. 1992. *ISO 9000: Handbook of Quality Standards and Compliance.* Waterford, Conn.: Bureau of Business Practice.

Keeney, Kent A. 1995. *The ISO 9000 Auditor's Companion* and *The Audit Kit.* Milwaukee: ASQC Quality Press.

Lamprecht, James L. 1993. *Implementing the ISO 9000 Series.* New York: Marcel Dekker.

———. 1994. *ISO 9000 and the Service Sector.* Milwaukee: ASQC Quality Press.

MacLean, Gary E. 1993. *Documenting Quality for ISO 9000 and Other Industry Standards.* Milwaukee: ASQC Quality Press.

Peach, Robert W., ed. 1994. *The ISO 9000 Handbook.* 2d ed. Fairfax, Va.: CEEM Information Services.

Sayle, Allen J. 1991. *Meeting ISO 9000 in a TQM World.* London: Allen J. Sayle Ltd.

Schmauch, Charles H. 1994. *ISO 9000 for Software Developers.* Rev. ed. Milwaukee: ASQC Quality Press.

Wilson, Lawrence A., and LearnerFirst. 1994. *LearnerFirst™ How to Implement ISO 9000* (software). Birmingham, Ala.: LearnerFirst.

Index